MEMORY AND TESTIMONY IN THE CHILD WITNESS

MARIA S. ZARAGOZA
JOHN R. GRAHAM
GORDON C. N. HALL
RICHARD HIRSCHMAN
YOSSEF S. BEN-PORATH

EDITORS

APPLIED PSYCHOLOGY: VOLUME 1
INDIVIDUAL, SOCIAL, AND COMMUNITY ISSUES

SAGE Publications
International Educational and Professional Publisher
Thousand Oaks   London   New Delhi

For information address:

SAGE Publications, Inc.
2455 Teller Road
Thousand Oaks, California 91320

SAGE Publications Ltd.
6 Bonhill Street
London EC2A 4PU
United Kingdom

SAGE Publications India Pvt. Ltd.
M-32 Market
Greater Kailash I
New Delhi 110 048 India

Printed in the United States of America

Library of Congress Cataloging-in-Publication Data

Main entry under title:

Memory and testimony in the child witness / edited by Maria S.
  Zaragoza . . . [et al.].
    p.   cm.—(Applied psychology: Individual, social, and community issues; 1)
  Includes bibliographical references and index.
  ISBN 0-8039-5554-5 (cloth).—ISBN 0-8039-5555-3 (pbk.)
    1. Children as witnesses. 2. Memory in children. 3. Recollection
  (Psychology) I. Zaragoza, Maria S. II. Series.
  K2271.5.Z9M46 1995
  347'.066'083—dc20
  [342.766083]   94-32593

95 96 97 98 99 10 9 8 7 6 5 4 3 2 1

Sage Production Editor: Yvonne Könneker

Coventry University

Contents

Preface

On April 20, 1993, 13 of the leading researchers on children's eyewitness memory gathered for 3 days in the picturesque Amish country of north-central Ohio to participate in the Fifth Annual Kent Psychology Forum. This volume is the result of that meeting. The Kent Forum series is an international think tank dedicated to advancing areas of social concern in psychology. This is the second of three volumes on forensic psychology. The goal of this volume is to provide a highly readable and comprehensive overview of current research on assessing and enhancing the quality of children's eyewitness testimony that will be of use to researchers, clinicians, and policymakers.

We were very fortunate to have four prominent psychologist practitioners from the northeast Ohio community participate in the forum: Georgette Constantino and Suzanne LeSure, both of the Department of Pediatric Psychology at Children's Hospital in Akron; Steve Neuhaus of the Cuyahoga Juvenile Court, Cleveland; and Sue White of the Department of Psychiatry at the Metro Health Medical Center, Cleveland. We owe them a debt of gratitude for imparting their knowledge, broadening our perspective, and challenging us to conduct research that is more responsive to the needs and concerns of the mental health and legal professionals who work with actual child victims and child witnesses. Their ideas and perspectives are reflected in many of the contributions to this volume.

A conference and book cannot happen without the help of many people. I would like to thank Stevan Hobfoll and the Applied Psychology Center for organizing the Kent Forum series and for providing the resources that made the conference possible. Special thanks and acknowledgment go to Judy Jerkich for providing invaluable logistical and clerical support before, during, and after the conference. My students at Kent State—in particular, Jennifer Ackil, Missy Carris, Karen Chambers, Sean Lane, and Karen Mitchell—helped in ways too numerous to mention. I would also like to extend my personal thanks to the contributors to this volume for their enthusiasm and support for this project and for engaging in the constructive and stimulating dialogue that is recorded in this volume. Finally, I would like to thank Stephen B. Fountain for his unwavering encouragement and support.

Preparation of this book was facilitated by National Institute of Mental Health grant MH47858.

MARIA S. ZARAGOZA

Introduction

Shortly after joining the faculty of the Department of Psychology at Kent State University in fall 1984, one of my colleagues—a clinical child psychologist—stopped me in the hall and mentioned that she had read a recent newspaper article about a court case involving alleged child abuse. The article claimed that children's susceptibility to suggestion and lack of reliability as witnesses had been amply documented by psychologists, and my skeptical colleague asked me whether this was true. Although I had just completed a dissertation on the suggestibility of adults' eyewitness memory, I was unable to answer the question posed to me by my colleague. I could not think of a single eyewitness memory study involving children as subjects. Thus began my interest in children's testimony, an interest that eventually led to the creation of this book.

I soon learned that there were but a handful of laboratory studies of children's testimony and suggestibility, several of which had just appeared in a 1984 special issue of the *Journal of Social Issues* edited by Gail Goodman. Since then there has been a veritable explosion of research on children's capabilities as witnesses. Mounting pressures to prosecute cases of child sexual and physical abuse have increased the courtroom appearances of child witnesses and raised questions about the accuracy and reliability of their reports. This concern has been heightened by the media attention surrounding the increasing number of unsubstantiated, and sometimes bizarre, charges of ritualistic child sexual abuse allegedly committed by relatives, friends, or day care workers. As evidenced by the contributions to this volume, research psychologists have responded to this concern by conducting studies aimed at both assessing and improving the quality of children's eyewitness reports.

One of the most noteworthy recent trends in the study of children's testimony is the increase in the use of highly ecologically valid research paradigms (see, for example, chapters by Fivush & Shukat; Baker-Ward et al.; Poole & White; Saywitz; Fisher & McCauley; Davies & Westcott; Tobey et al.). Although there are volumes of laboratory research on children's ability to remember lists of pictures and words, only recently have researchers begun to examine children's ability to remember complex and personally relevant autobiographical events over long retention intervals (see Chapter 1 by Fivush & Shukat). There is increasing evidence that children have better memory for events that are significant to them and that their memory is better for events in which they have participated than for those they have simply observed (see, for example, Goodman, Rudy, Bottoms, & Aman, 1990). The work of Fivush and colleagues has shown that even very young preschoolers are capable of remarkably accurate long-term recall of naturally occurring but meaningful events, thus supporting the idea that laboratory studies with artificial stimuli may well underestimate children's memory abilities in real-world testimony situations.

Children's memory performance also depends heavily on the social, emotional, and linguistic context in which they are tested (see Chapter 6, Saywitz, for an excellent elaboration of this point), and for this reason it is important to assess children's memory abilities in contexts that are similar to those in which they will have to testify. In this volume, studies of the effects of question repetition on children's recall (Chapter 2, Poole & White; Chapter 3, Warren & Lane), of the effects of suggestive questioning (Chapter 5, Lindsay et al.; Chapter 3, Warren & Lane), and the use of anatomical dolls and other props as cues (Chapter 8, DeLoache) all contribute to this aim. In particular, they highlight the circumstances under which young children's memories might be disproportionately susceptible to error and distortion.

Several contributions to this volume also demonstrate the critically important role that basic research and theory play in our understanding of children's testimony. For, example, the chapters by Fisher and McCauley (Chapter 7), Saywitz (Chapter 6), and Bull (Chapter 9) provide excellent examples of the application of basic memory principles in the development of tools for improving children's performance. The chapter by DeLoache (Chapter 8) provides another demonstration that basic knowledge about children's cognitive abilities can have important practical implications. In this case, DeLoache examines the implications of her research on the early development of symbolization for the practice of using anatomically correct dolls when interviewing very young children who are suspected victims of abuse. In her research, DeLoache has extensively examined children's ability to understand the relationships between models (e.g., dolls) and what they represent. This research has consistently revealed that children $2\frac{1}{2}$ years of age and younger do not understand the correspondence between models and what they represent, apparently because very young children have difficulty with the notion of *dual representation* (e.g., the notion that a doll both can be an interesting object in its own right and can represent something else). The clear implication of DeLoache's work is that dolls should be ineffective and perhaps even a hindrance to young children's recall, a prediction that has received some empirical support. Thus DeLoache's research provides a clear and compelling example of the necessity and utility of theoretically grounded approaches to the study of children's testimony.

Finally, as revealed by many of the contributions to this volume, efforts to develop improved procedures for interviewing child witnesses and to validate these techniques are on the rise (see Chapter 6, Saywitz; Chapter 7, Fisher & McCauley; Chapter 9, Bull). A related trend is the small but growing number of studies aimed at evaluating reforms for accommodating child witnesses in the legal system, such as allowing children to testify via closed-circuit television (see Chapter 10, Davies & Westcott; Chapter 11, Tobey et al.). These are important and encouraging developments. Given that the testimony of child witnesses can be pivotal in the adjudication of court cases, especially those involving sexual and physical abuse, it is imperative that researchers continue to develop techniques that will maximize the accuracy and amount of information children provide.

The chapters in this volume provide an overview of the newest directions in research on children's testimony. The chapters in the first part of this book address fundamental questions about children's ability to remember and accurately recount experienced events. The second part elaborates on this theme, by reviewing very recent advances in the development of techniques for maximizing the quality of children's testimony. Finally, the chapters in Part III provide examples of psychological research designed to guide legal reforms for accommodating child witnesses in the legal system. Taken together, the chapters that constitute this volume do not provide a clear answer to the question of whether children are especially unreliable witnesses. Nevertheless, they provide a wealth of information about the variables that influence the quality and quantity of the information children can report.

MARIA S. ZARAGOZA

PART I

Approaches to Understanding Children's Eyewitness Memory

The chapters in Part I are particularly good examples of the breadth of research that is currently being undertaken concerning children's ability to accurately convey the events they have experienced. At least two dimensions characterize the studies in this part. One such dimension is the type of event children are asked to remember. Some of the studies employ more traditional laboratory analogues of the eyewitness situation (Chapter 5 by Lindsay, Gonzales, & Eso; Chapter 2, Poole & White; Chapter 3, Warren & Lane), while others study children's autobiographical memory for naturally occurring events in their lives (Chapter 1, Fivush & Shukat; Chapter 4, Baker-Ward, Ornstein, Gordon, Follmer, & Clubb). A second dimension is the central issue that the various studies are designed to address. Several studies focus on the issue of how well children remember events they've experienced (Chapter 1, Fivush & Shukat; Chapter 4, Baker-Ward et al.), and others are concerned with the issue of whether suggestive or nonsuggestive questioning affects children's memory for events (Chapter 5, Lindsay et al.; Chapter 2, Poole & White; Chapter 3, Warren & Lane).

Many studies of eyewitness memory have used situations in which subjects observe rather than participate in the target event. In addition, the event subjects view is rarely personally relevant. These circumstances have prompted some researchers to call for research that uses events that are more likely to occur in "real life." Two chapters in this part are examples of how the field has responded. Fivush and Shukat (Chapter 1) explore very young (3 to 6 years old) children's memory for autobiographical events. Of primary interest in their study is whether the reports of young children change over time in terms of either content or the way the reports are conveyed. Baker-Ward et al. (Chapter 4) use a potentially stressful, personally experienced event (i.e., a well-child physical examination) as the situation to be remembered. Their chapter considers the implications of the criteria researchers adopt when deciding whether a child's response demonstrates memory for an event.

Traditionally, children's memory for events has been assessed over relatively short time periods, often on the order of several minutes to several days. Because child witnesses are called upon to testify many months or even years after the event(s) in question, researchers have begun to look at the stability of children's memory over time. Perhaps no study comes closer to approximating the sorts of delays encountered by actual witnesses than that reported by Poole and White (Chapter 2), who examined children's memory for a staged event that occurred 2 years earlier. Still other examples of long delays before testing include the work of Fivush and Shukat (Chapter 1; up to 1 year after a previous interview) and Baker-Ward et al. (Chapter 4; up to 6 weeks). Their findings indicate that, although young children can remember accurate event information over long delays, they may be more susceptible to forgetting than older children and adults.

Much of the research on children's eyewitness testimony has focused on the issue of whether children's memories are more suggestible than those of adults (e.g., Ceci, Ross, & Toglia, 1987b; Zaragoza, 1987, 1991). Chapter 5, by Lindsay et al., examines children's suggestibility, but does so using a new approach. Specifically, Lindsay et al. introduce a novel experimental procedure for assessing some of the mnemonic factors underlying age differences in suggestibility. Of primary interest in their study is the issue of whether younger children are less likely to be aware that they are relying on postevent information when answering questions about an event than are older children and adults. This possibility has the implication that young children may be less likely to be able to ignore misleading information even if informed of the source of this misinformation at the time of the test.

Although the effects of misleading or suggestive questioning on the accuracy of eyewitness testimony have been much studied, most of the available research has examined the effects of a single exposure to misleading information. Given that real-world eyewitnesses are often subjected to repeated questioning over time, understanding the mnemonic consequences of repeated questioning is a critically important issue for research. The studies reported by Warren and Lane (Chapter 3) and Poole and White (Chapter 2) represent important steps toward filling this gap in the literature. Warren and Lane also look at the effect of suggestive and nonsuggestive questioning, but their distinctive contribution is that they examine the effect of the timing of repeated questioning. Their findings bear on such issues as whether repeated interviews, per se, are harmful to event memory, and whether children and adults are affected differently by the timing of interviews. Poole and White (Chapter 2) review a variety of research on the effects of repeated questioning, drawing a distinction between repeated questioning across sessions (multiple interviews) and repeated questioning within the same session. In doing so, they are able to offer insights into how young children and adults are likely to be differentially affected by repeated questioning.

The chapters that follow attest to the diversity of research approaches that are currently being employed to study children's eyewitness memory. While many questions about children's ability to accurately remember eyewitness events remain, the research reported in this part advances our understanding of children's capacities and limitations in new and important ways.

SEAN M. LANE

Content, Consistency, and Coherence
of Early Autobiographical Recall

ROBYN FIVUSH

JENNIFER R. SHUKAT

Preschool children are being called on in increasing numbers to testify in legal situations. Decisions about young children's ability to give credible testimony are often based on research aimed directly at determining children's ability to resist suggestible and misleading questions (Ceci, Toglia, & Ross, 1987; Doris, 1991). While this is certainly an important consideration, children's susceptibility to suggestion can only be interpreted within an understanding of basic memory abilities. Only by examining how and what young children recall, and how this process changes with development, can we assess children's memory abilities in more applied settings, such as the courtroom.

AUTHORS' NOTE: The data reported in this chapter are part of a larger longitudinal study of early memory and narrative development, which is funded by a Spencer Grant to the first author. Many people have been of invaluable help in data collection, transcription, coding, and analysis. We would especially like to thank Catherine Haden, Elaine Reese, Marcella Eppen, Laura Underwood, and Liza Dondonan.

5

Research over the last decade has amply demonstrated that even quite young children are able to recall personally experienced events accurately over extended periods of time (Fivush, Gray, & Fromhoff, 1987; Hudson, 1990a; Nelson, 1988; Sheingold & Tenney, 1982; Todd & Perlmutter, 1980). In fact, 4- and 5-year-old children are able to recall events that occurred 1 to 2 years in the past (Fivush & Hamond, 1990; Hamond & Fivush, 1990). But exactly what is it that young children recall about their experiences, and how might autobiographical recall change over time?

In this chapter, we present data from a longitudinal study of children's autobiographical memories across the preschool years. Three major issues are examined: the content, consistency, and coherence of children's recall. *Content* refers to the types of information that children are most likely to recall about events. For example, are older children more likely to recall the spatial and/or temporal location of an event than younger children? Or more of the participants? Do younger children focus on objects and older children focus on actions? *Consistency* refers to whether children recall the same information over time; that is, when children recall an event for the second time, do they recall the same information about that event as they did previously, or do they recall different information? Finally, *coherence* refers to the narrative structure of the recall. In the first section of this chapter, we present an overview of the data set and the theoretical framework of the study. In each of the next three sections, content, consistency, and coherence are discussed in detail. We then bring the data together to present an integrated account of the development of autobiographical recall during the preschool years. In the final section, we discuss implications for children's eyewitness testimony.

Overview and Theoretical Framework

The data to be discussed in this chapter are drawn from a larger longitudinal study of memory and narrative development across the preschool years. As part of this study, children were asked to recall personally experienced events at four time points: when they were 3 years 4 months, 3 years 10 months, 4 years 10 months, and 5 years 10 months old. In total, 19 children were interviewed at all time points. At each time point, the same female interviewer asked children to recall three specific one-time occurrences, such as an outing to the circus or a trip on an airplane. The events to ask each child about were determined immediately prior to the interview through discussion with the parent.

Of the three events asked about at the second, third, and fourth interviews, one event was one of the same events asked about at the previous interview. Thus children were asked about one event at the first interview and then again at the second interview (which were 6 months apart), one event at the second interview and then again at the third interview (which were 1 year apart), and one event at the third interview and again at the fourth interview (which were 1 year apart). Unfortunately, not all children could be asked about a previous event at a subsequent interview because similar events had occurred during the interim. For example, the child had been to another circus or had taken another airplane trip. In addition, several children did not focus on the event the interviewer was asking about but recalled a different, related event instead. For example, one child, when asked about going to Six Flags, an amusement park, recalled going to Raging Rivers, a water park. Finally, a few children simply refused to cooperate and would not answer any of the interviewer's questions. Of course, in these instances, we cannot know whether the child remembered the target event or not. Thus we focused only on those children who recalled some information, however minimal, about the event under discussion. Using this criterion, eight children recalled the same event at the first and the second interviews, seven recalled the same event at the second and third interviews, and nine recalled the same event at the third and fourth interviews. We will discuss several issues related to these limitations after the data have been presented.

Our theoretical focus in this study is on young children's spontaneous recall of personally experienced events. Although the interviewer opened discussion of the event with a general question (e.g., "Can you tell me about the time you went to Six Flags?"), no additional cues were used. The interviewer encouraged the child to continue responding by using open prompts (for example, "Tell me more." and "What else happened?"), expressing general interest (for example, "Wow, that sounds like fun."), or by repeating part of what the child said (for example, "Oh, so you saw a lion at the zoo. Tell me more."). In this way, we are able to examine what kind of information children choose to recall about an event, how this might change over time, and whether children are able to structure their recall into a coherent account of what occurred.

Several things need to be emphasized about the methodology. First, and most important, we are interested in children's *verbal recall*. Our focus is on what children tell us about their experiences. Of course, we do not assume that verbal recall is exhaustive—in fact, just the opposite. Research that has included both verbal and nonverbal measures of memory has consistently demonstrated that young children remember more about events than they recall verbally (e.g., Fivush, Kuebli, & Clubb, 1992; Price & Goodman, 1990; see Nelson, 1986, for a discussion and review). Rather, we assume that verbal recall is a process involving the retrieval and selection of a subset of the material that an individual remembers about an event.

Given this assumption, it follows that verbal recall may not necessarily be consistent across recall trials. Because verbal recall involves the selection of information to report, the individual may select different information on different recall occasions. For adults, this selection process may be a conscious decision based on various aspects of why and to whom one is reporting the events (e.g., Middleton & Edwards, 1990). But it may also be a function of what aspects of the memory become more or less salient over time (e.g., Robinson, 1992; Spence, 1988).

Research with children addressing this issue is quite sparse but what little exists suggests that children are sensitive to their conversational partner and will recall different information depending on such factors as familiarity and whether or not the conversational partner also participated in the event (Fivush, Hamond, Harsch, Singer, & Wolf, 1991). In this study, we focus more specifically on how saliency of information might change over the preschool years and thus affect the information reported. Virtually no data exist on this issue, although several theorists have postulated qualitative changes in the kind of information young children focus on and therefore are more likely to recall with increasing age (e.g., Hudson, 1986; Neisser, 1962; Nelson, 1988; Schactel, 1982). Notice that, in this study, we can examine both changes in how the same event is reported over time and how different events are reported as a function of age. In this way, we can begin to untangle whether children are actually encoding different information at different developmental periods or retrieving and selecting different information when recalling the same event at different ages.

Finally, it should be noted that our methodology allows us to examine not only what kind of information children spontaneously recall about events but how they organize that information. Several theorists have suggested that personal memories become more narratively coherent with development (Bruner, 1987; Fivush, 1988; Nelson, 1992). Although we know that children's narrative skills develop during the preschool years (Hudson & Shapiro, 1991; Peterson & McCabe, 1983), little is known about how the organization of the same event recalled over time may change.

In summary, this study focused on the content, consistency, and coherence of children's recall of personal experiences over the preschool years. Before turning to the data, however, several additional points need to be emphasized. First, both because there is a paucity of previous research addressing these issues and because we are relying on a small number of subjects, this study should be viewed as exploratory. Second, it should be borne in mind that we are focusing on spontaneous verbal recall; children are not provided with any cues or prompts. And, of course, children are not being given any misleading or suggestive information. Finally, the events that children are asked to recall are all special events that the children greatly enjoyed. Thus we are assessing children's spontaneous memories for distinctive, salient, and positively toned experiences.

Content of Autobiographical Recall

Our first question concerned the content of young children's autobiographical recall over time. What kinds of information are children most likely to report about their personal experiences and does this change with age? To answer this question, all information that children recalled about each event was identified and coded into one of the following six categories: (a) activities (such as "I *ran*" or "The car *spun* round and round"); (b) objects (such as "There were lots of *balloons*" or "I ate a *hot dog*"); (c) persons (such as "My *grandmother* was with me" or "My friend *Billy* came with us"); (d) locations (such as "It was *winter*" or "I was at my *Granddad's house*"); (e) descriptives, which included all adjectives, adverbs, and modifiers (such as "We went on a *really long* hike" or "We got *lots and lots* of candy"); and (f) internal states, which referred to thoughts, emotions, or beliefs (such as "I was really *scared*" or "Mom *didn't know* where Sea World was").

The mean amount of each type of information recalled at each interview time is shown in Figure 1.1. The top panel displays the type of information included about events recalled at the first and second interviews (when children were 3 years 4 months old and again when they were 3 years 10 months old), the middle panel displays information about events recalled at the second and third interviews (when children were 3 years 10 months old and 4 years 10 months old), and the bottom panel displays the type of information for events recalled at the third and fourth interviews (when children were 4 years 10 months old and 5 years 10 months old). As can be seen, at all four interviews, children recalled more information about activities and objects than about people or locations. They also embellish their recall

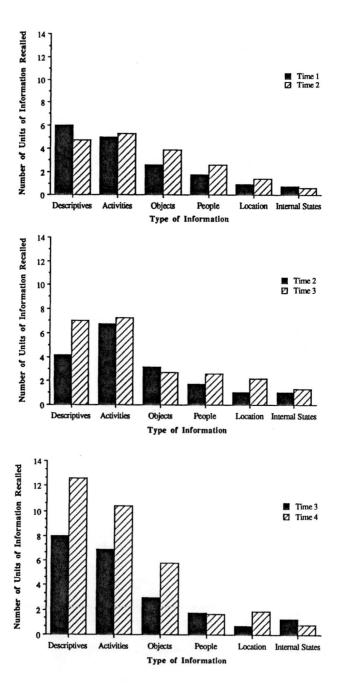

Figure 1.1. Mean amount and type of information recalled about events at each time point.

with many descriptives, indicating that their recall is richly detailed. Finally, children mention few internal states at any interview.

Most interesting, the types of information that children recall does not change over time, nor does the total amount of information recalled. This finding seems somewhat surprising. Previous research suggests that young preschool children recall less about events than do older preschool children (see Pillemer & White, 1989, for a review). In particular, younger children often need more cues and prompts than older children to recall as much information. Yet, in this study, there were no changes in the amount of spontaneously recalled information over time. Notice also that there is no decline in amount recalled for the same events over time. That is, when children were asked to recall the same event after a 6-month or 1-year delay, they recalled as much information, and the same type of information, as they had previously. It is particularly interesting that there is no decrease in descriptive information, suggesting that children's memories for highly salient events remain richly detailed.

Consistency of Recall

Given that children are recalling as much information over time, it becomes critically important to determine whether they are recalling the same information over time. That is, when recalling an event 6 months or 1 year later, do children recall the same aspects of the event or not?

Research with adults addressing this question has revealed somewhat contradictory findings. Several studies indicate that adults recall a high proportion of the same information across multiple recall occasions, ranging from 9 months (McCloskey, Wible, & Cohen, 1988), to several years (Neisser et al., 1994), to over 40 years (Wagenaar & Groeneweg, 1990). But there is also some indication that adults are extremely inconsistent in the information they report over a 3-year period (Harsch & Neisser, 1989). A critical factor in these studies seems to be whether the event being recalled was directly experienced or only heard about through the media, as in the majority of studies of so-called flashbulb memories (see Winograd & Neisser, 1992, for a review and discussion). For highly salient, emotionally laden events that are directly experienced, recall may remain consistent over long periods of time, but for less personally relevant and/or indirectly experienced events, recall may become more inconsistent as time since occurrence increases.

With school-aged children, again, some research has found high consistency of recall over the period from kindergarten through sixth grade (Hudson & Fivush, 1987). But when misleading or suggestive information is included in the retrieval questions, recall becomes substantially less consistent (Pipe, 1992; Poole, this volume), suggesting that consistency of school-aged children's recall may be jeopardized by the type of questions asked during recall.

With preschoolers, a very different pattern emerges. Even when no misleading or suggestive information is provided, preschoolers are remarkably inconsistent in the information they recall on multiple trials even after relatively short delays. Fivush et al. (1991) asked $2\frac{1}{2}$-year-old children to recall the same events 6 weeks apart. While the children were accurate in the information they recalled on both recall occasions, as determined by parents, they were extremely inconsistent in what they recalled. Only about 20% of the information recalled across the two interviews was the same. Similarly, Fivush and Hamond (1990) asked $2\frac{1}{2}$-year-old children to recall personal experiences and then asked them to recall these same experiences 14 months later. Again, less than 20% of the information recalled was consistent across interviews, although, again, about 90% of information recalled was accurate. Thus preschool children appear to recall different but still accurate information each time they recall an event.

In the present study, all the information that children recalled on each recall occasion was divided into three categories: information recalled only at the first recall of that event, information recalled only at the second recall of that event, or information recalled on both recall occasions. The mean proportion of information falling into each of these categories is shown in Figure 1.2. Clearly, children are extremely inconsistent in what they recall, and this is true at all three comparison points. Overall, less than 10% of information recalled is consistent across any two recall occasions. It should be noted that, although we did not ask parents to judge the accuracy of the child's recall for each and every event recounted, when accuracy was informally assessed by parents, it was extremely high, as has been found in previous studies using more controlled assessments (Fivush et al., 1987; Fivush et al., 1991; Hamond & Fivush, 1990).

Why might preschool children be so inconsistent in their recall? One possibility that has been suggested in the literature is that young children rely on adults' questions to guide their recall. Thus, if adults ask the same questions over time, young children will provide the same information, but if adults ask different questions over time, children's recall will seem inconsistent (Fivush et al., 1991). While it certainly may be the case that young children will answer the same question in the same way across recall trials, their inconsistent recall

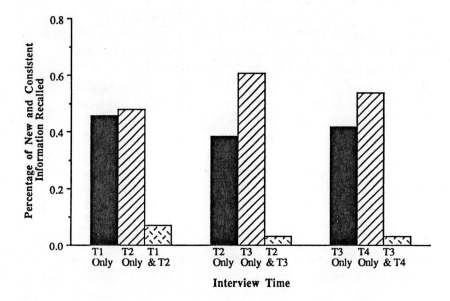

Figure 1.2. Consistency of information recalled about events across time.

cannot be completely attributed to inconsistent questions. In this study, children were inconsistent in their spontaneous recall of the same event on two different occasions.

Another possibility is that preschool children are inconsistent because their memories are not well organized. In particular, it has been argued that personal experiences are organized as canonical narratives (Bruner, 1987; Labov, 1982) and these narrative forms are learned during the preschool years (Fivush & Hamond, 1990; Nelson, 1992). Before children have control over these narrative forms, their memories will not be coherently organized and therefore they will be inconsistent (Fivush et al., 1991). Is it the case that children's verbal recounts are becoming more narratively organized across the preschool years?

Coherence of Recall

To tell a coherent story, one must go beyond reporting what happened (referential information). One must also place the event in context by telling

when and where it occurred and who was present (orientation). Most important, one must provide an evaluative framework for understanding the story
(evaluation). Why is this event interesting and important to recount? What is
the personal meaning of this event for the teller or for the listener? Following
from theories of narrative structure (Labov, 1982; Peterson & McCabe, 1983),
we analyzed all of the children's recounts for narrative organization. Each
statement was coded as expressing one of three major narrative functions: (a)
orientation information, which includes information specifying the spatial or
temporal context of the event (e.g., "It happened last Halloween."), the
introduction of people present during the event (e.g., "And Adam and Billy
and me were all there."), and descriptions of the physical environment (e.g.,
"It was really cold."); (b) referential information, which included the actions
occurring during the event (e.g., "I watched the clowns."); and (c) evaluative
information, which included intensifiers (e.g., "And it was a really sharp
knife."), repetitions when used for emphasis (e.g., "We went on a long hike.
And it was really really long."), negations (e.g., "But I wasn't scared."),
attention-getters (e.g., "And you know what else?"), and dialogue (e.g., "And
my mom said, 'We have to go.' ").

Table 1.1 shows the mean proportion of propositions of each type at each
interview. What is most striking about these data is their similarity over time.
Even at the youngest age point, children are including information in all three
major categories, suggesting that their narratives are reasonably coherent. In
addition to telling the interviewer what happened during the event, children
are placing the event in context by providing orienting information and
informing the listener about the significance of the event by including evaluative information. And the proportions of orienting, referential, and evaluative information remain relatively stable over time.

It is important to stress that not only are children's narratives coherent from
an early age but that, when recalling the same event after a 6-month or 1-year
delay, they are able to recount that event just as coherently as they had on the
initial recall. That is, time since occurrence of the event does not seem to lead
to a less organized recount. A few examples of children's recounts will illustrate just how coherent children's recall remains over time. Note several things
about these examples. First, while the narratives are surprisingly coherent for
children this young, they are not exactly stellar stories. Children in this study
are still having some trouble expressing their memories in a completely
coherent form. But even so, to an outsider with no knowledge of the event,
these stories make sense. The listener can follow the narrative, know what

Table 1.1   Proportion of Propositions in Each Major Narrative Category Over Time

| Time Point (age) | Narrative Category | | |
	Orientation	Referential	Evaluation
Time 1 (40 months)	.28	.42	.26
Time 2 (46 months)	.29	.44	.24
Time 2 (46 months)	.26	.47	.28
Time 3 (58 months)	.36	.38	.27
Time 3 (58 months)	.10	.49	.43
Time 4 (70 months)	.25	.47	.22

happened, and even know how the child felt about it. Second, notice in reading children's narratives about the same event over time how little consistency there is in the information recalled, as discussed earlier. So although the stories remain coherently organized, the stories are not stable. The first example is from our youngest age group. This child first recalls seeing a Christmas parade when she is 3 years 4 months old (an ellipsis indicates the interviewer made an intervening comment):

> (Unintelligible) in downtown. It was in winter. There were all sorts of things going. And first they had wheels! And an old car that they used in the olden days. . . . Clowns with all different colors of hair. . . . They gave me little bags. You could put anything you like in those bags.

The child begins the recall by placing the event in spatial and temporal context for the listener. She then describes the various things that she saw at the parade, embellishing each item with rich, descriptive detail. Six months later, when asked to recall this event again, she recounts:

> It was cold. And my grandmother came with me. She was wearing a black furry coat all the way down to here. My friends came with me, and my mommy and my daddy. We shook hands and they were holding balloons. I was shown a man with a picture of a spider and he was by there flying balloons. And we saw a star balloon that the man was holding. And then we saw, umm, we, uh, we saw, it was too late to see the (unin.). . . . It was too late to see the rest of it. Because otherwise in the freezer, umm, in the freezer, in the freezer, I, I, it was too cold in the freezer so, so we went home.

Again, she begins her recount with temporal orientation information, but this time she also includes information about the participants. And again she recalls various things that she saw at the parade in great detail, but she obviously reports different parade items than previously. Finally, she has some trouble verbally expressing herself at the end of the story, presumably confusing "being in a freezer" with "being freezing." But after several false starts, she is able to get her meaning across and end the story. To give a sense of how children are recounting events as they get older, the next examples are from the last two time points. This child first recounted going to Sea World when she was 4 years 10 months old:

> First, umm, my mom didn't know it was (unin.), but, but she kinda knew. She, and she didn't know where she was. So then she saw the sign called "Sea World." And then, umm, then she went to him and she said, "This is Sea World." And then we saw, umm, the sea stuff and then a few hours after that, umm, umm, I had like a little drink, and then. . . . And then, umm, what happened was my mommy said, "It's time to go." And we said no, (unin.) tiny bit more. And then we went.

Her story begins with how they got to Sea World and, in fact, focuses on the fact that her mother wasn't quite sure how to get there. She then summarizes everything that happened during their visit in one statement ("we saw sea stuff"), and ends the narrative. A year later, at the age of 5 years 10 months, she recalls:

> Oh, it was fun when we went to Sea World. It was real fun. We saw, umm, a whale show. And, umm, the whale show, if you sat, ummm, by the whales, you'll get all splashed. And I was wet, 'cause we were sitting in the second row, and we got all wet. But if you were sitting like way up high, you won't get as wet. And we saw, ummm, Shamu. And, ummm, we, ummm, and what else did we see? We saw a really bird, a white bird. That was at (unin.). This white bird that was walk-, and I was, see we had lunch there and mom took a picture of a white bird. It was a real pretty white bird. Ummm, that was a long time ago.

Now the child begins her story with an overall evaluation of the experience, and then reports in much more detail than previously what happened while they were there. Of interest, she ends the story by commenting that they went to Sea World a long time ago.

Unexpectedly, then, given previous research documenting development in narrative coherence across the preschool years (Hudson & Shapiro, 1991; Peterson & McCabe, 1983), children in this study were already giving relatively coherent accounts of personal experiences at a very young age. Perhaps the difference is due to the importance of the event to the child. Indeed, Miller and Sperry (1988) have shown that even 2-year-old children will include evaluative information in their spontaneously produced personal narratives. When it is personally important to report an event, even very young children seem able to recount that event in a way that communicates effectively to the listener.

Integrating Content, Consistency, and Coherence

The findings from this study are really quite surprising. As has been found previously, young children are recalling a good bit of information about their personal experiences. Moreover, their recall is relatively well organized. Even at the youngest age points, children's recounts include critical narrative elements for organizing and recounting the past. In addition, they recall as much information in as organized a framework after a 6-month or 1-year delay as they had when first asked to recall the event. These findings might suggest that memory for highly salient personal experiences may be quite stable over the preschool years. But children's recall is extremely inconsistent over time. While the total amount of information recalled about specific events does not seem to change over time, children recall different information each time they recount an event. How are we to understand this pattern? And what implications can we draw for children's eyewitness testimony?

First and foremost, we must emphasize that only about half of the children asked to recall an event at a second interview that they had recalled at the previous interview recounted any information about the target event at all. Of those children who did not recall any information about the event over time, about half recalled an event different from the target event, although the confusion was usually understandable. For example, children asked about a particular amusement park often recalled a different amusement park, or children asked about a particular party event recalled a different party event. Because the interviewer did not provide any cues or prompts beyond the general open-ended question, children had difficulty focusing in on the event that the interviewer was asking about. The other children who did not recount any information simply said they could not remember the target event. Of course, it is entirely possible that, given more cues, all of these children could have remembered and recounted some information about the target event. So we cannot draw any conclusions about forgetting from these data.

However, it does seem possible that those events that were easily recalled with just an open-ended question were those events that, for some reason, were more salient to the child. That is, the events that children were easily able to recount after a 6-month or 1-year delay, with only a general open-ended question, may be a subset of extremely salient events. Examination of the events that were recalled does not reveal any systematic differences between these events and events not recalled. That is, some children did not remember seeing a parade, whereas others did; some children did not remember going to an amusement park, whereas other did; and so on. This suggests we must look beyond the type of event to understand why some events may be so memorable.

There are several possible explanations for why some events may be more salient than others. The first is that some events may be rehearsed more frequently, leading to better memory. Although we cannot estimate how often children thought about these events on their own, we did collect data from the parents on how frequently these events had been discussed, whether there were photographs of the event, and, if so, how often the photographs had been looked at. Overall, parents claim that they do not look at photographs very often with their young children, and time spent looking at photographs was unrelated to children's recall at any of the time points. However, parents did talk about these events with their children. Frequency of parent-child conversations about these events was unrelated to children's recall at the earlier time points, but at the last time point, when children were 5 years 10 months old, those events that had been talked about more frequently were more likely to be recalled than events talked about less frequently. This pattern suggests that talking about events with others may not play much of a role in keeping that event memory alive early in development but, toward the end of the preschool years, talking about events with others may begin to become a powerful tool for maintaining memories.

A second reason some events may be better remembered than others may be due to their distinctiveness. That is, the child who did remember going to a particular amusement park may have had only one such experience, whereas the child who did not remember going to a particular amusement park may have been to several similar amusement parks. Unfortunately, we did not gather any information that would allow us to evaluate this possibility. But certainly everything we know about personal memories, from childhood through adulthood, would suggest that, the more frequently one experiences an event, the more difficult it is to recall a single specific experience of that event (see Hudson, Fivush, & Kuebli, 1992, for a review and discussion). Still, this explanation would lead us to expect children with multiple experiences to recall the event but confuse details among the various instantiations, and we saw no evidence of this in our data. Rather, once children focused in on an event, whether it was the event the interviewer was targeting or not, they seemed to recall details of that particular event. Unfortunately, we did not assess accuracy systematically in this study, but, for that subset of events for which parents did provide accuracy information, it was the case that parents judged children's recall to be accurate to the specific event being recalled. And we must bear in mind that, in research that has systematically assessed accuracy, preschooler's memory is quite accurate about the details of specific experiences; about 90% of information children recall is judged accurate by parents (Fivush et al., 1987; Fivush et al., 1991; Hamond & Fivush, 1990).

A final reason some events may be particularly well remembered is because they are emotionally laden. The relationship between emotional tone and memory is quite controversial (see, e.g., Goodman, Rudy, Bottoms, & Aman, 1991; Terr, 1988, versus Peters, 1991). However, it seems that events that are highly emotional and, especially those that affect the child's physical well-being, may be particularly well remembered. The kinds of events studied here are quite different from the kinds of events that have been studied in the previous literature addressing this issue. Those studies have examined children's memories for highly stressful and disturbing events such as painful medical procedures and physical traumas. In this study, we focus on the other end of the continuum. Children were asked to recall events that were highly enjoyable and quite positive in emotional tone. Importantly, most of these events were also child centered. Children were most often asked to recall events in which they were central participants and, even more, these were events that were explicitly engaged in for the child's enjoyment (e.g., going to Sea World or going to the circus). Although children did not explicitly recall much affective information, they did include a great deal of evaluative information that indicated positive emotion, such as intensifiers and exclamations, as can be seen in the previous examples.

Of interest, the only other study in the literature to find no age or retention interval differences in children's autobiographical recall is a study of children's memories for a family trip to Disneyworld (Hamond & Fivush, 1990). Although that study used a cross-sectional rather than a longitudinal approach, it was the case that children ranging in age from $4\frac{1}{2}$ years to $6\frac{1}{2}$ years recalled a great deal of information about their experiences, and amount of recall was unrelated to whether the experience occurred 6 months ago or 18 months ago. Although there is really too little data to draw any firm conclusions as yet, it seems that highly emotional (whether positive or negative) and personally involving events may be very well remembered over long periods of time even for very young children. The problem is that this explanation is somewhat circular for explaining the present findings. Only about half of the children recalled the target event at the delayed interview. It is not clear that the events not recalled were less emotionally salient than the events that were recalled. Moreover, the same event may have very different emotional meaning for different children. Thus, to really assess the relationships between emotional tone and memory, we must have a way of determining the child's emotional involvement at the time of experience, and relate these measures to subsequent recall.

Of course, possible effects of rehearsal, distinctiveness, and emotional tone on memory are not mutually exclusive. There may be multiple reasons a specific event is well remembered, and if more than one of these factors is operating simultaneously, they may make an event even more memorable. But note that these explanations are all aimed at understanding why children's personal memories are so good. We must not forget that, although children recall the same amount of information over time, they recall different information at each recall. Why are children's personal memories so inconsistent? It does not seem to be the case that children's memories are inconsistent because they are unorganized and therefore not stable. In this study, the narrative coherence of children's memories was relatively good even at the youngest age studied and remained stable over time. Nor can inconsistency be explained as a developing focus on recalling different types of information. Again, in this study, the types of information that children recounted about events were stable across the age range studied.

Rather, to understand the inconsistency of young children's recall, we need to reconsider the fact that we are studying *verbal recounts* of personal experiences. Especially when the children in our study were very young, they may have had some difficulty expressing their memories verbally. Certainly, though their recounts were relatively organized, they were not extremely fluent, as evidenced by much hemming and hawing, false starts, and long pauses. It is possible that children are able to remember a great deal about a past event but have difficulty putting what they remember into words. This process may be difficult enough that it exhausts young children's ability to recount all that they remember.

This argument may seem puzzling given that even the youngest children's recounts were coherently organized. One might assume that children's ability to use a conventionalized narrative form, in even a rudimentary fashion, would lead to more consistent recall. Several theorists have argued that conventionalized narrative forms aid children in the retrieval of information by providing a "retrieval guide." That is, the narrative form itself carries with it information about what kind of information needs to be recounted about the event. But, clearly, this was not the case, as illustrated in the examples above. Although children consistently provide orienting, referential, and evaluative information, the information selected to fill these "slots" varies from one recall to the next. It seems that, although children can tell *a* coherent story about a personal experience, they have not yet developed *the* coherent story about that experience. What develops during the preschool years that might help explain the development of consistent recounts about past events?

For one thing, children seem to develop an interest in sharing their past experiences with others. Although children will submit to answering an interviewer's questions about the past when they are 2 and 3 years old, there is a real sense that they do not enjoy this activity. In addition to the qualitative impression one gets when interviewing a very young child, it is also the case that younger children go off topic more often, insist on more frequent breaks, and generally need to be cajoled more by the interviewer to keep talking than older children. But sometime between 4 and 5 years of age, children begin to enjoy these conversations much more. They are not only more willing to participate in these interviews, but they spontaneously bring up other related events to tell the interviewer about. The qualitative impression one gets during these interviews is of a child who is interested in sharing her past experiences with others.

Why might children become more interested in sharing stories of their experiences with others? We know that parents and children begin talking about past experiences together almost as soon as children begin to talk (Engel, 1986; Hudson, 1990a), but in these early conversations, the parent provides most of the content and structure. With increasing age, children begin to participate more and more in these conversations (Reese, Haden, & Fivush, 1993), but it is not just a matter of recalling more information over time. Children seem to develop an understanding of the purposes of engaging in these conversations (Fivush & Reese, 1992; Hudson, 1990a). Over the preschool years, children seem to be socialized into understanding that sharing past experiences is an important and valuable social activity. Talking about our past with others allows us to create interpersonal bonds based on a sense of shared history. The fact that those events that are talked about more frequently begin to be more easily remembered than events talked about less frequently by the end of the preschool years supports this argument. Children seem to be learning to value the activity of sharing their past, and those events that are talked about more often come to be seen as interesting and valuable enough to continue to share with others.

Implications for Testimony

Finally, we need to consider the implications of these data for issues involving children's ability to give credible testimony. Perhaps the most important finding to emerge from these data, and from other recent investigations of young children's personal memories, is that very young children are able to give accurate, detailed accounts of their personal experiences even after extended periods of time. However, we must be extremely cautious in generalizing these findings to the courtroom. First, in these studies, children are asked to recall special, emotionally positive events. We do not yet know if children's recall of negative events, the type of events children are most likely to be called on to testify about, follows the same pattern. Second, children were not cajoled into responding. Although the interviewer attempted to elicit recall with open-ended prompts, if the child indicated lack of memory, the questions ended. And, most important, no misleading or suggestive information was introduced.

Still, the emerging picture of the preschooler's ability to recount personal experiences is impressive. Children between the ages of 3 and 6 years are able to give coherent, detailed accounts of past events after long delays. Thus, at least as far as basic memory abilities go, preschool children are competent to testify. However, their recounts are likely to be highly inconsistent on different recall occasions. While inconsistency does not mean inaccuracy, it may prove to be a problem for investigators interested in children's testimony. In this situation, the child is most often being asked to report very specific aspects of the event—those aspects most relevant for legal judgment. So the question becomes one of determining the best way to focus the child on that aspect of the event that needs to be recounted without providing leading questions. Thus research needs to focus on finding better ways to elicit what we now know young children are able to recall.

On a more speculative level, we need to consider the social functions of recounting our past to others. Early in development, recall may be quite inconsistent because the child has no particular agenda or reason for sharing her memories with others. But as children grow older and are socialized into the social functions of reminiscing, memories may come to take on a different kind of importance. Recounting the stories of our lives becomes an important way of communicating with others, and the stories of our lives may become more stable and consistent. To understand children's eyewitness testimony, we need to consider both the young child's basic memory abilities, which seem to be quite good, and the child's developing understanding of the reasons for recalling and recounting the past, which seems to change across the preschool years.

2

Tell Me Again and Again

Stability and Change in the Repeated
Testimonies of Children and Adults

DEBRA ANN POOLE

LAWRENCE T. WHITE

On a summer evening in 1985, in Beloit, Wisconsin, 9-year-old Anthony Darnell Wilson was stabbed repeatedly and then killed by a severe blow to the head. The next morning, when Darnell's body was found in a garden next to his grandmother's house, 5-year-old M. L. told her stepaunt that she knew "who hurt Darnell." The events that followed illustrate what Whitcomb (1992) identified as two of the most frustrating aspects of our criminal justice system: the need for witnesses to repeat their stories over and over again, and the lengthy delays involved in the adjudication process. Over the following year, M. L. was interviewed by police investigators, a social worker, a school psychologist, a psychiatrist, and attorneys and investigators for the prosecution and the defense. During this period, M. L. identified more than a dozen perpetrators and four different murder weapons. Despite these inconsistencies, three children—ages 14, 12, and 11 years—were charged with the murder and, in three separate trials, found guilty of the murder of Darnell Wilson.

The interview techniques that M. L. experienced are typical of criminal investigations: multiple interviews, suggestive questions, and questions repeated within interviews in apparent attempts to elicit contradictions in the testimony. At the time of Darnell Wilson's murder, little was known about the stability of eyewitness testimony across multiple retellings. Consequently, there were no guidelines to use in judging whether the inconsistencies in M. L.'s testimony were typical for a young child who had been repeatedly questioned.

Recently, however, many researchers have included multiple testing sessions or repeated questions within sessions in studies of eyewitness performance. Their interest in the stability of eyewitness reports reflects both practical and theoretical concerns. On the practical side, there is an increased awareness that repeated questions are common in criminal investigations. Service providers estimate that most child victims are interviewed at least a dozen times during the course of an investigation (Whitcomb, 1992). Some critics have argued that multiple interviews serve as training sessions, whereby "the child learns more about what the interrogator expects and learns what to say or do that will get a positive response from the interrogator" (Underwager & Wakefield, 1990, p. 15). Psychologists also have noted that interviewers often pressure children by asking them identical or similar questions repeatedly within a session (see Ceci & Bruck, 1993a; Underwager & Wakefield, 1990, for excerpts from selected interviews). Therefore researchers have included repeated questions to create interview environments that more closely resemble the experiences of actual witnesses (e.g., Cassel & Bjorklund, in press; Poole & White, 1991).

On the theoretical side, researchers have built repeated questioning into eyewitness studies to explore whether phenomena from laboratory studies of memory and memory development will generalize to the recall of personally experienced events. For example, if repeated recall increases performance on list-learning tasks (due to either retrieval relearning or storage-based mechanisms; see Brainerd, Reyna, Howe, & Kingma, 1990; Howe, Kelland, Bryant-Brown, & Clark, 1992; Payne, Hembrooke, & Anastasi, 1993, for discussions), will repeated questioning also refresh eyewitness memories? Recommendations to avoid repeating questions have been curiously juxtaposed with claims that repeated testing preserves memories and increases the amount of information reported (see Brainerd & Ornstein, 1991; Dent, 1991; Goodman & Clarke-

Stewart, 1991). These seemingly contradictory recommendations underscore the need to distinguish between the influence of repetition on event *memory* versus the influence of repetition on event *reporting* (e.g., Warren-Leubecker, 1991). Although one hopes that witnesses will answer questions by accessing their memories, social and linguistic factors also come into play because witnesses no doubt attach some meaning to the fact that questions are being repeated over and over again. In some everyday contexts, for example, repetition signals us to suggest a plausible answer in the absence of knowledge (e.g., "When will the meeting be over?"), to change our answer from a previous response (e.g., "Did she really say it exactly like that?"), or to acquiesce to a suggestion about which answer the questioner prefers (e.g., "Are you sure I don't look better in the black dress?").

Our goal in this chapter is to review studies that have examined the eyewitness performance of children and adults across repeated questions. We first consider the impact of across-session repetition, or multiple interviews, followed by a review of within-session repetition. In each section, we begin by describing the empirical or theoretical bases for predicting that repetition will enhance or degrade testimony, and then compare those predictions with findings obtained from studies of eyewitness performance. Existing studies have not tackled all of the important issues that face legal professionals who work with witnesses. We therefore conclude our chapter with a discussion of unresolved issues and suggestions for future research.

Multiple Interviews

Recent findings on children's delayed recall underscore the need to identify procedures that minimize forgetting and memory distortion over time. For example, in one study, the proportion of total information that was inaccurate in the reports of 6- and 9-year old children doubled from 9% 1 day after the event to 18% 5 months after the event (Flin, Boon, Knox, & Bull, 1992). In contrast, adults maintained a constant error rate over this period (10% after 1 day versus 8% after 5 months). We recently discovered a similar pattern in a study of children ages 4 to 8 years and adults (Poole & White, 1993). One week after witnessing an ambiguous event, children and adults reported comparable proportions of inaccurate information (7% on average). Two years later, however, 20% of the information reported by children was inaccurate, whereas adults maintained their earlier error rate. In both studies, children reported smaller amounts of accurate information while maintaining constant amounts of inaccurate information.

Children as young as 5 or 6 sometimes report few inaccurate details about witnessed events, even after a 2-year period (Pipe, 1992). Nevertheless, we still should be concerned about the impact of long delays on children's testimonies. In our 2-year delay study (Poole & White, 1993), 21% of the children attributed actions to one assistant during free recall that had actually been performed by another assistant—an error pattern with serious legal implications. None of the adults made similar errors. Our transcripts also included other disturbing inaccuracies, such as one child who correctly described the white perpetrator shortly after the event but later identified him as "black."

To minimize the likelihood of further trauma to child witnesses, some researchers have recommended that the legal system limit the number of times a child is interviewed (see Goodman, Taub, et al., 1992, for a discussion of the emotional consequences of testifying). In terms of memory, however, there is little doubt that discussing an experience can dramatically improve the ability of children and adults to recall it at a later time. Studies of basic memory processes have identified three benefits of multiple testing.

First, testing shortly after exposure to the to-be-remembered material may attenuate forgetting during a delay. As Brainerd and Ornstein (1991) concluded, "perhaps the most fundamental principle of memory is that repetition facilitates performance" (p. 15). Intervening tests bolster subsequent recall of textbook passages (Foos & Fisher, 1988), word lists (Howe, Kelland, Bryant-Brown, & Clark, 1992), and series of paired comparisons (i.e., A > B; Fisher & Chandler, 1991). Similarly, children who repeatedly discuss a salient event with their families are more likely to recall details about the event at a later time (Hamond, 1988, described in Hudson, 1990a), although verbal recall alone may not influence specific memories until about 33 to 42 months of age (Hudson, 1990a). Howe, O'Sullivan, and Marche (1992) concluded that, although the specific cues that trigger trace reinstatement may change with age, "the fact is that simply reencountering cues in the environment serves to inoculate memory against forgetting at all ages" (p. 248).

A second benefit of multiple testing is the possibility of reminiscence (i.e., the recall of previously unreported information). Howe, O'Sullivan, and Marche (1992), for example, found that roughly 20% of the items that were not recalled during a first session were retrieved 2 weeks later. Although laboratory studies have revealed no clear age trend in reminiscence with verbal materials (Howe, O'Sullivan, & Marche, 1992), preschool children generally display less consistency in their repeated autobiographical reports than school-age children or adults. (See Fivush & Shukat, this volume, for a discussion of this phenomenon.) Hence it is not surprising that police investigators often interview children numerous times in the hopes of eliciting additional information.

A final benefit of repeated testing is that young children may learn through repeated conversations to engage in memory talk or, as Hudson (1990a) described, to shift their focus from one of answering questions to actively remembering and spontaneously offering information. Children who are accustomed to conversing with adults may therefore require fewer specific prompts to adequately recount an event (Rogoff & Mistry, 1990).

In sum, laboratory studies of memory for verbal materials and children's accounts of autobiographical events suggest that child and adult witnesses who are frequently interviewed will, on average, recall more than witnesses who are not frequently interviewed. Unfortunately, it is not possible to verify this prediction by evaluating the testimonies of actual witnesses because the number of interviews is confounded with the passage of time in individual cases. Consequently, we will only discuss eyewitness studies that have (a) included two or more groups of subjects, (b) varied either the number or the type of interview, and (c) interviewed all subjects after a fixed period of time. (We will not discuss the many studies that have examined the effect of suggestive questions on the testimonies of children and adults. See Ceci and Bruck, 1993a, for an excellent review.)

In their groundbreaking article, Dent and Stephenson (1979) reported two frequently cited experiments. In the first study, 10- and 11-year-old children individually viewed a film depicting a theft. All of the children were interviewed on five occasions: immediately after the film and 1 day, 2 days, 2 weeks, and 2 months later. The children were assigned to one of three conditions for their first and second interviews: free report (e.g., "Tell me everything you can remember from the film."), 10 general questions (e.g., "Tell me as much as you can about what the man in the white mac looked like and what he was wearing."), or 46 specific questions (e.g., "What color hair did the man in the white mac have?"). All of the children answered only specific questions in the last three interviews. As numerous studies have since replicated (e.g., Dent, 1986; Goodman & Reed, 1986; Marin, Holmes, Guth, & Kovac, 1979), free recall elicited smaller amounts of correct and incorrect information than general or specific questions. The children who initially answered free-recall questions did not, however, report fewer errors than the other groups in interviews 3, 4, and 5, when all children answered specific questions. Thus initial free-recall attempts did not inoculate children against volunteering erroneous information to later specific questions, nor did early interviews with specific but nonleading questions predispose children to recall more false information after a long delay.

In their second study, Dent and Stephenson (1979) explored the possible benefits of interviewing shortly after a witnessed event. As in the first study, 10- and 11-year-old children viewed a film depicting a theft. One group of children was interviewed on five occasions: immediately after the film and 1 day, 2 days, 2 weeks, and 2 months later. A second group was interviewed twice: 2 weeks and 2 months after the film. A third group was interviewed only once: 2 months after the film. In every interview, children were asked to free recall (e.g., "Tell me everything you can remember from the film."). Although the amount of incorrect information did not vary as a function of number of prior interviews, children who participated in earlier interviews reported more correct information.

Findings from subsequent studies lead us to conclude that early interviews, if properly conducted, can consolidate memories for an event without introducing errors into testimony. Baker-Ward, Hess, and Flannagan (1990), for example, exposed triads of first- and fourth-grade children to 21 different activities. Some children were interviewed immediately after the activities and again 1 week, 2 weeks, and 3 weeks later; other children were interviewed immediately after the activities and 3 weeks later. Unlike the infrequently interviewed children, children who discussed the events weekly maintained their original level of recall over the 3-week period.

Other studies also have documented the benefits of repeated testing. Hudson (1990b) reported that 4- and 5-year-old children who were interviewed immediately after a day's activities recalled more after 4 weeks than did children who were interviewed only once at the end of 4 weeks. Similarly, Tucker, Mertin, and Luszcz (1990) reported that 5- and 6-year-old children who were interviewed 1 day after receiving an inoculation recalled more after 1 week than did children who were interviewed only once at the end of the week. Even children as young as 2 years benefit from intervening tests that cue them to reenactment events (Fivush & Hamond, 1989; also see Rovee-Collier & Shyi, 1992, for a discussion of the impact of physical reminders on long-term retention in infancy).

In contrast, Goodman, Bottoms, Schwartz-Kenney, and Rudy (1991) detected no impact of an interview conducted 2 weeks after an inoculation experience on correct or incorrect information freely recalled after a 4-week delay. Baker-Ward, Gordon, Ornstein, Larus, and Clubb (described in Ornstein, Gordon, & Baker-Ward, 1992) also found no benefit from a 1-week delayed interview on reports after 3 weeks among 3-, 5-, and 7-year-olds who were questioned about a physical examination.

Timing of the initial interview thus appears to be critical. When the initial interview occurs 1 week or more after an event, its benefit as a "memory consolidator" may be attenuated, presumably because too much time has elapsed and memory has begun to decay. Another explanation is also possible. Early interviews may have little impact on the ability of children to freely recall a single event (e.g., an inoculation) because children tend to report only the gist of the interaction on free-recall tests regardless of how much they remember. Evidence for this explanation can be found in the study by Goodman, Bottoms, et al. (1991) mentioned earlier: Children who reported twice were more accurate on specific questions about the person, room, and possible abuse than children who reported only once, indicating that prompting may sometimes be necessary to detect the benefits of a prior interview.

The adequacy of the initial interview appears to be another contributing factor in determining the benefits of additional interviews. For example, in Flin, Boon, Knox, and Bull's (1992) study, children who were initially given a cognitive interview recalled more 5 months after an event than did children who were initially given a cued-recall interview or not interviewed at all. Compare this finding with our study of 4- to 8-year-old children and adults (Poole & White, 1991). Our interviews included little probing for details, and children who reported immediately after the event did not recall more information 1 week later than children who reported for the first time after a 1-week delay. Adults in our study, however, benefited from the earlier interview, presumably because they—unlike the children—spontaneously reported substantial amounts of information in the earlier interview.

Although procedures that push witnesses to recall details may enhance later event reports, we cannot recommend the use of multiple interviews with specific questions, especially for children who will be testifying after relatively long delays. The major problem with specific questions, of course, is that they elicit more inaccurate information (e.g., Dent & Stephenson, 1979). This is partly because children and adults frequently attempt to answer specific questions even when they have not been exposed to the relevant information (Poole & White, 1991, 1993). In fact, young children rarely give "I don't know" responses (e.g., Poole & White, 1991; Rudy & Goodman, 1991), and instructing children that they can say "I don't know" does not always increase accuracy (Moston, 1987).

A recent study illustrates the potential for early interviews with inappropriate questions to contaminate the accuracy of later reports. Cassel and Bjorklund (1993) designed their procedures to simulate the kinds of interviews that witnesses experience during pretrial preparation, including exposure to leading questions. Subjects in three age groups (6 years, 8 years, and adults) viewed a short videotape and immediately answered questions similar to those used by police officers in initial investigative interviews. Specifically, each witness first answered questions designed to establish rapport between the interviewer and the witness, followed by free recall of the videotape, and, finally, a series of specific, unbiased questions that probed for information not previously mentioned by the witness. One week later, some subjects repeated their free-recall testimony and then answered either 20 "positive leading" questions (i.e., questions that suggested a correct response) or 20 "negative leading questions" (i.e., questions that suggested an incorrect response). One month after the videotape was viewed, all subjects were interviewed for a final time. This interview contained free-recall questions followed by positive leading and negative leading questions posed by two different interviewers.

Cassel and Bjorklund's (1993) results illustrate the peculiar independence of narrative accounts versus answers to specific questions. When asked specific questions during the initial interview, children were more likely than adults to report inaccurate information, but this information was not incorporated into their subsequent free-recall narratives. The detrimental influence of leading questions in this study was limited to subjects' answers to subsequent leading questions.

Comparable findings can be found in Goodman's study discussed earlier (Goodman, Bottoms, et al., 1991) and in analyses of conversations between toddlers and their mothers (Hudson, 1990a). In Goodman's study, children who answered misleading questions during an initial interview reported no more errors during subsequent free recall than children who had not answered misleading questions. Similarly, after talking with their mothers, preschool children typically do not incorporate information discussed by their mothers into their later conversations, although they do include new, previously unreported information. Goodman and Reed (1986) found occasional intrusions from misleading questions, but only two 6-year-olds and two adults of 32 subjects reported misinformation even though free recall immediately followed the misleading questions.

At this point, we are tempted to conclude that free-recall accuracy is uninfluenced by multiple interviews and is relatively immune to contamination from inappropriate (i.e., misleading) questions. However, few investigators have simulated the intensity of leading and misleading information to which the typical witness is exposed. Notable exceptions are two recent studies by Ceci and his colleagues. In Ceci and Desimone's (1992, described in Ceci, Leichtman, & White, in press) delightful "Sam Stone" study, 3- to 6-year-olds were exposed to conversations about Sam Stone that depicted him as clumsy and prone to breaking things. After an uneventful visit by Sam, the children were asked suggestive questions during four biweekly interviews. When an unfamiliar interviewer subsequently questioned the children, 72% of the 3- and 4-year-olds said Sam had ruined one of the suggested items and, upon further questioning, 45% said they had actually seen Sam damage the item. Moreover, some of the children spontaneously embellished their reports with false details.

In a second study (Bruck, Barr, Ceci, & Francouer, 1993), an experimenter talked with preschool children and read them a story during a visit to a pediatrician for routine inoculations. Then, 4 to 18 months later (average interval = 11 months), a different experimenter visited the children on four occasions over a 2-week period. During the first three visits, the experimenter played with the children and discussed the inoculation visit. Some of the children were given positive feedback about the experience (you were brave, you didn't cry); other children were given neutral feedback. In addition, some of the children were given misleading information about five actions completed by the pediatrician and/or the research assistant. In the final interview, misled children gave more false information in response to specific questions but, more important, they also made more spontaneous errors in initial free recall.

These two studies illustrate that even free recall can be contaminated by frequent exposure to misinformation, with young preschoolers being less resistant to suggestions than older children (Ceci & Bruck, 1993a). It is also clear, however, that information elicited by free-recall questions is surprisingly stable across retellings among children and adults who have not been exposed to an unusual amount of pressure to alter their reports, at least over short delays. When a witness's narrative accounts are characterized by major inconsistencies, we should closely inspect the witness's motivation, ability to recount the events, or exposure to outside influences. For example, children will omit information initially if they are embarrassed (e.g., reports of genital contact; Saywitz, Goodman, Nicholas, & Moan, 1991) or have been encouraged to conceal a crime (e.g., Pipe & Goodman, 1991). On the other hand, expert witnesses who analyze interview transcripts might be justified in ignoring inconsistencies that appear only in response to inappropriate questions, because young children are more likely than adults to acquiesce to specific suggestions (Cassel & Bjorklund, 1993; Warren, Hulse-Trotter, & Tubbs, 1991).

Despite the fact that psychologists often recommend frequent testing as a method for preserving memory, rarely are multiple interviews conducted in legal settings with that purpose in mind. Rather, multiple interviews typically are conducted in the hopes that new information will be recalled. The following excerpt, from a police report in the Darnell Wilson murder, explains why a school psychologist was asked to interview M. L., the key witness for the prosecution:

> I spoke with . . . who is a psychologist . . . and he indicated that he would be more than happy to assist in any way he could and I briefly told him about the 5-year-old . . . and felt that she possible [sic] was holding something back or blocking it from her mind for whatever reason and he indicated this would have to come out sometime and explained he would interview the child if so desired using the school facilities, etc.

Despite this detective's conviction that any new information is valuable, reminiscence is not always viewed positively. According to Cassel, an experienced attorney, reminiscence can be used to discredit a child on the basis that the new facts must have been "planted" by an intervening event (Cassel & Bjorklund, 1993). Unfortunately, researchers rarely code data to separate old information from new information across retellings, so it is not clear whether repeated interviewing is generally an effective strategy for eliciting additional accurate information. The 6- and 8-year-olds in Cassel and Bjorklund's (1993) study rarely reported additional (i.e., new) information (although repetition was somewhat effective in eliciting additional information from adults). In contrast, when Hudson and Fivush (1987, described in Fivush & Hamond, 1990) asked 6-year-olds to describe a museum trip 1 year after it occurred, 38% of the information they reported was new. The amount of reminiscence by young children is highly variable and probably depends on the complexity of the event, the children's degree of involvement, and the extent to which changes in verbal abilities and knowledge base during the retention interval support more elaborated narratives. Recent evidence indicates that, when interviews are separated by 1 or 2 years, new information provided by children is less accurate than their repeated information (Pipe, 1992). Given the fact that young children involved in the legal system are interviewed many times, we recommend additional research to establish guidelines about the usefulness of "evidence" that comes to light only after repeated questioning.

In summary, laboratory simulations of eyewitness testimony offer strong corroborating evidence that multiple testing sessions preserve memories over time. Although children may benefit less than adults when early interviews do not encourage them to report details, there is no evidence that frequent retelling is more likely to introduce inaccuracies than other techniques for supporting delayed testimony such as the use of dolls to minimize verbal demands (e.g., Boat & Everson, 1993) or props to provide retrieval cues (e.g., Pipe, Gee, & Wilson, 1993). We are aware of no studies in which multiple interviews with nonsuggestive questions were associated with increases in the amount of inaccurate information recalled by children or adults. Misleading information, suggestive questions, or memory reconstructions due to prior stereotypes or the passage of time (see Ceci & Bruck, 1993a), rather than multiple interviews per se, seem to be responsible for introducing errors into testimony. These conclusions—distilled from numerous studies representing diverse methodologies—receive further corroboration from a comprehensive project by Warren and Lane (this volume). Unfortunately, we do not yet know enough to guide professionals in their interpretation of reminiscence. Until further evidence is available, we believe that professionals who work with witnesses should be cautious about the validity of details that are reported for the first time after multiple interviews.

Within-Session Repetition

Most people are surprised to learn that the verbal exchanges between attorneys and child witnesses in trial proceedings rarely approximate normal conversation. One of the greatest differences between the two is the degree to which questions are repeated. The direct examination of 5-year-old M. L. by a prosecuting attorney illustrates a typical exchange:

Q: How was he hurt?
A: Who?
Q: Darnell. What part of his body was hurt?
A: His arm.

Q: His arm?
A: (Witness nods affirmative.)
Q: Was there anybody else with you?
A: Uh-huh.
Q: Who?
A: My mommy.
Q: Was your mommy out there when Darnell got hurt?
A: Huh-uh.
Q: Did you see anybody hurt Darnell's head?
A: Uh-huh.
Q: Who hurt—Who hurt Darnell's head?
A: Sarah.
Q: Who else, if anybody?
A: Only Sarah.
Q: Sarah hurt his head?
A: (Witness nods affirmative.)

M. L.'s testimony illustrates three recurring questions about the impact of repeated questioning within a single session. When young children respond with minimal answers, is repeating questions a useful technique for eliciting additional, accurate information? Are children and adults generally consistent across repeated questions? Is consistency correlated with accuracy; that is, do changes in testimony indicate that a witness is not credible or that memories for the original event are seriously degraded?

Two separate lines of research make different predictions about the impact of repeating questions within a single session. In the memory literature, repeated recall is often associated with hypermnesia (i.e., more complete recall across multiple attempts) and/or reminiscence (i.e., the recall of previously unreported information; see Howe, O'Sullivan, & Marche, 1992; Payne, 1987; and Roediger, Wheeler, & Rajaram, 1993, for reviews). The ability of repeated testing to elicit more or new information has been demonstrated for a wide variety of stimuli (e.g., words, pictures, faces) and methods of testing (e.g., cued recall, recognition, free recall). Current debates center on establishing the boundary conditions for obtaining these phenomena (e.g., delay between retests; Roediger et al., 1993) or on the relative contribution of various mechanisms to the observed effects (e.g., storage versus retrieval mechanisms; Brainerd et al., 1990). However, the basic observation that repeated testing alone is sufficient to enhance recall for discrete items or item clusters is uncontested and age invariant (Howe, O'Sullivan, & Marche, 1992). An important caveat is the danger of forcing subjects to recall: When instructed to guess so as to produce a required number of responses, adults will later recall some of their guesses as presented items (Roediger et al., 1993). In the absence of pressure to speculate, however, there is nothing in the literature on hypermnesia and reminiscence that raises concerns about repeating questions to eyewitnesses.

Although repetition often improves memory, studies of cognitive development have found that children's general knowledge is underestimated when experimenters repeat questions. Question repetition has been associated with poorer performance on a variety of tasks, including class inclusion (Winer, 1980), tests of numerical competence (Gelman, Meck, & Merkin, 1986), and conservation of number (McGarrigle & Donaldson, 1974; Siegal, Waters, & Dinwiddy, 1988). The major difference between these procedures and the typical memory paradigm is the degree to which knowledge is tested within a conversational context. Experimenters working within the Piagetian tradition often develop rapport with a child and then pose a series of questions about materials that are manipulated by the experimenter and/or the child. Although Piaget was concerned about the impact of repeated questioning and suggested that interviewers rephrase successive questions, he generally ignored the potential for mismatches between the adult's and the child's interpretation of a question's intent (Siegal, 1991). In Piagetian studies, the finding that answers to initial questions are generally more accurate than those to subsequent answers has been taken as evidence that children intentionally change responses because, in normal conversation, a repeated request implies that the original answer was insufficient in some way (see Siegal, 1991, for a review).

Professionals who are unfamiliar with language development may erroneously assume that young children respond only to the literal meaning of questions and are incapable of making subtle inferences about interviewers' needs or intents. It is now widely accepted, however, that children as well as adults are sensitive to conversational rules. For example, young children and adults adjust their speech according to listener characteristics (Shatz & Gelman, 1973) and cooperate by offering answers to incongruous and illogical questions (Pratt, 1990; Winer, Rasnake, & Smith, 1987). Children assume that a speaker's message will be motivated by what Siegal (1991) summarizes as "cooperativeness, non-redundancy, truthfulness, relevance, and clarity—conventions of communication that have been noted by philosophers of language" (p. 30). Even preschool children show impressive abilities to negotiate conversations: They position address terms to gain attention, use repetition to maintain conversation, and respond appropriately to rising versus falling intonation in clarification requests (e.g., "What?"; see Cox, 1991, for a non-technical discussion of these conversational competencies). Additionally, children in eyewitness studies alter their testimony based on the emotional tone (Goodman, Bottoms, et al., 1991; Goodman & Clarke-Stewart, 1991) and age of the interviewer (Ceci, Ross, & Toglia, 1987b).

Because forensic interviews are simultaneously memory tests and conversations, it is difficult to predict how repetition will influence testimony. Although repeated questioning can improve recall, repetition may introduce errors if it is interpreted by the witness as a request to change an answer or to speculate in the absence of information. It is safe to assume that repetition effects will not be uniform but will be dependent on variables that alter witnesses' interpretations of repeated requests. Possible mediating factors include witness age or familiarity with the format of investigative interviews, the tone of the questioner, the positioning of repeated requests (immediately or after several intervening questions), and the presence of instructions that clarify the reason for repetition.

There have been only a handful of studies to date on repeated within-session questioning with eyewitness procedures. Researchers at three independent labs found that adults increased the amount of accurate information they reported about complex events across successive recall attempts. The impact of repetition on inaccuracies, however, was inconsistent across studies. Using a written recall procedure, Scrivner and Safer (1988) found only minor increases in inaccuracies over trials. Eugenio, Buckhout, Kostes, and Ellison (1982) and Dunning and Stern (1992) both elicited oral reports and encouraged subjects to report more information (e.g., "Is there anything else you can remember?"), yet their results were not comparable: Eugenio and his colleagues found that multiple-recall attempts produced greater amounts of inaccurate information, whereas Dunning and Stern detected no significant increase in inaccurate information even after 3-day and 1-week delays. In contrast, Tanenbaum (1991) found no hypermnesic effect over trials, but adult subjects did recall a significant amount of new information with repeated testing. Most important, fewer than half of the subjects reported more than one erroneous detail despite being asked to recall six times.

These studies document that repeated questioning is useful for recovering additional information in eyewitness contexts, although it is not yet clear which procedures produce concomitant increases in intrusion errors. Intuitively, it makes sense that witnesses who repeat a story will quickly review what they previously reported and then begin to flesh out the story with new details. Please note, however, that the procedures in the aforementioned studies were more similar to those used in traditional memory experiments than those used in forensic interviews. Specifically, subjects recalled information but did not engage in a back-and-forth dialogue involving general and specific questions. Nonetheless, it is encouraging that—at least for adults—repeated recall even with prompting (e.g., "Please go on.") did not greatly increase speculation.

The value of repeated questioning diminishes when laboratory procedures drift away from resembling memory tests and toward more conversational, interactive styles of prompting. In our first repetition study (Poole & White, 1991), we individually exposed children (4-, 6-, and 8-year-olds) and adults to an ambiguous, live event during which a male assistant snatched a pen from the subject's hand and squabbled with the female research assistant. An interviewer subsequently asked each subject a few questions to establish the topic for the interview, followed by open-ended questions (e.g., "What did he look like?" and "What happened when he came into the room?"), specific yes-no questions (e.g., "Did the man hurt Melanie?"), and questions the subject could not answer without speculating ("What does the man do for a living? What is his job?"). The interviewer repeated each set of questions three times in succession. Half of the subjects were interviewed immediately after the event and 1 week later, and the other half were interviewed only once, 1 week after the event.

Despite the large age range in our study, we found little reason to be concerned about repeating general, open-ended questions. Subjects reported slightly less information as questioning continued, probably because they became somewhat bored and tended to summarize. Children and adults were highly accurate on open-ended questions (93% and 94% accurate information, respectively), and there was no increase in the amount of inaccurate information reported across trials. Reminiscence occurred at all ages, although the payoff for repeated recall was clearly greater for the adults than for the children: Within a single session, adults averaged 16.3 new units of accurate information on the second round of questions and 8.3 on the third round, compared with the children's averages of 3.9 and 1.5, respectively. Information that was volunteered for the first time during the third round of questions was surprisingly accurate—94% for the children versus 92% for the adults.

In contrast to the stable reports associated with general questions, our subjects' responses to specific questions raised some concerns. Four-year-olds were less consistent on yes-no questions than the older children and adults, replicating the response shifts that have been reported in conservation studies with preschool children (e.g., Siegal et al., 1988). In addition, subjects of all ages tended to use fewer uncertainty qualifiers (e.g., "I'm not sure but . . .") with repetition, even when speculating about a specific question they could not possibly answer. It is interesting that the adults speculated more than the children.

Two years later, we invited our subjects back to the laboratory, ostensibly to participate in a study of "routine events" (Poole & White, 1993). In fact, we first asked questions about the event they witnessed 2 years earlier. The unusually long delay provided us with an excellent opportunity to explore whether repetition with nonleading questions encourages subjects to specu-late when memory traces are weak. Contrary to expectations, the impact of repetition was identical to the patterns observed 2 years earlier. All age groups (now 6-, 8-, and 10-year-olds and adults) maintained good consistency on yes-no questions within a session, but the children repeated the answers they gave 2 years earlier on only half of the questions. As in the original study, subjects of all ages reported slightly less information and used fewer uncer-tainty qualifiers as questioning continued, but repetition did not increase the proportion of inaccurate information they reported. Finally, some subjects who initially said "I don't know" to the unanswerable question offered a speculative answer as questioning continued. Whether immediately after the event or 2 years later, the major "costs" associated with within-session repeti-tion were that subjects appeared more confident about their responses and had more opportunities to speculate. Although children's reports were less accurate than adults' reports after 2 years, repeating questions did not exac-erbate age differences.

In our studies, repetition created problems only when questions were mildly suggestive: yes-no questions and specific questions about a detail the witnesses could not possibly report. Two studies that included misleading questions provide additional evidence that repetition acts synergistically with procedures that are inherently suggestive to degrade witness testimony. Moston (1987) asked 6-, 8-, and 10-year-old children a series of 16 questions about a live event. The children were more accurate on the first round of questions (69%) than the second (54%), leading Moston to conclude that "when ques-tioning children, one should be prepared to accept their first answer, since this is probably the best response that they can give" (p. 77).

Similarly, Warren et al. (1991) read a story to first- and sixth-grade children and adults, followed by a free-recall session and two presentations of 20 questions, 15 of which contained misleading cues. To further increase social pressure, subjects were instructed after the first set of specific questions that they had not performed very well, so it would be necessary to go through the questions again. Confirming previous research (Ceci et al., 1987b), the first graders were more affected by misleading questions than the older children and adults, and they changed more responses after negative feedback, even to nonleading questions. The sixth graders performed as well as the adults on misleading questions initially, but after negative feedback, they (like the first graders) shifted more of their responses. Age differences in this study were mediated by initial levels of recall: Controlling for the amount of free recall resulted in nonsignificant correlations between age and measures of acquiescence.

These findings on within-session repetition follow logically from the pragmatic function that repetition serves in normal conversation. Open-ended questions are often repeated in daily interactions (e.g., "What was that you said you did in school today?"), and children as well as adults generally respond to such requests by repeating their original story with surprisingly little variation. Repeating open-ended questions appears to be an innocuous procedure, and one that may lead witnesses to recall a useful piece of additional information. The conversational "implicature" (Grice, 1975) of repeating a specific question is quite different, however (e.g., "Are you sure you don't want something to eat?"), and children are more prone than adults to change answers to yes-no questions, specific leading questions, and nonleading questions following negative feedback. Adults are actually more likely than children to speculate about specific questions when they have the knowledge base to generate a plausible response (Poole & White, 1991), although when children do speculate their answers are often unrelated to the context of the observed event (Poole & White, 1993). Overall, these findings suggest that children and adults interpret forensic interviews as both conversations and memory tests. For example, whereas children frequently fail to respond to questions in everyday conversations (e.g., 90% of the wh- questions were not answered by preschoolers in one study; Dimitracopoulou, 1990; see also van Hekken & Roelofsen, 1982), they rarely say "I don't know" or fail to respond in eyewitness interviews (e.g., Poole & White, 1991; Rudy & Goodman, 1991).

How shall we answer the questions posed at the beginning of this section? First, repeating questions within a session can elicit useful additional information, provided the interviewer asks general, open-ended questions in a nonsuggestive way. When these guidelines are followed, children and adults generally maintain accuracy across recall trials. But what about the relationship between consistency and accuracy?

Despite the fact that inconsistency lowers witness credibility in the eyes of jurors (Ross, Miller, & Moran, 1987), judges, and attorneys (Fisher & Cutler, 1992), we are aware of only a few studies that have included correlations between consistency (i.e., absence of explicit contradictions) and overall accuracy. Fisher and Cutler (1992), in a series of four experiments, computed correlations between the number of inconsistent details across two interviews and overall accuracy (proportion correct details) in describing various target individuals. Four out of eight correlations were nonsignificant (range = .01-.10); the remaining four were statistically significant but small (range = .26-.33). Similarly, we recently found no significant correlations between children's consistency on yes-no questions and their overall accuracy or completeness in describing a complex event (Poole & White, 1993).

The limited data that are available suggest that the number of inconsistent details reported across multiple sessions has little value for diagnosing the overall accuracy of a witness's statement. But in the Warren et al. (1991) study, which elicited within-session response changes by informing subjects that they had not performed very well on the first round of questions, there were significant negative correlations between the amount of information reported during free recall and inconsistency on both suggestive ($r = -.65$) and non-suggestive questions ($r = -.55$). The correlations remained large even when age was statistically controlled, indicating that witnesses may succumb more to social pressure when their memories for the event are poorly elaborated.

Summary and Conclusions

Repeating questions is neither a harmless remedy for failed recall nor an inherently suggestive procedure to be strictly avoided. Across-session repetition generally delays forgetting for subjects of all ages; exposure to misleading information or suggestive questioning, rather than multiple interviews per se, is responsible for significant memory reconstruction over time. The consequences of within-session repetition are more complex. Children and adults who have no motive to conceal information generally maintain accuracy across answers with nonsuggestive procedures and primarily open-ended questions. Preschool children are more likely to change answers to yes-no questions, and children in general show performance decrements across repetitions when they have difficulty understanding or remembering the target material or when interviews contain numerous specific and misleading questions. Because repetition elicits additional information and is a relatively innocuous procedure when appropriate questions are used, sweeping recommendations to avoid repetition are not warranted.

Despite remarkable consistency across studies in the effects of repetition, several interesting conundrums remain. Rather than attempting a comprehensive list of unresolved issues, we will close by discussing three areas of concern that are noteworthy for the challenges they pose to research psychologists and for their potential to inform the legal community.

First, research psychologists recommend that investigators use primarily general, open-ended questions with small children (e.g., Bull, 1992), and the data on repetition effects clearly support this guideline. In practice, however, it is exceptionally difficult to get children to volunteer information with general questions. Psychologists often bemoan the inability of small children to organize memory retrieval despite the fact that many of us are confronted daily with our own children's lengthy autobiographical stories (Nelson, 1990). We clearly need to be more creative in identifying the social and linguistic environments that foster extended narratives by small children. For example, one strategy described by Fisher and Geiselman (1992) involves asking children to discuss a topic about which they are an expert, followed by an interview about the target event.

A second unresolved issue is the significance of inconsistencies across multiple retellings. We are limited in making recommendations from available research because laboratory studies typically have not exposed subjects to personally embarrassing or threatening events and then followed up with repeated questions. Researchers are beginning to study children's testimonies about traumatic medical procedures (e.g., Goodman, 1993; Ornstein, Baker-Ward, Gordon, & Merritt, 1993), and these paradigms provide an excellent opportunity to analyze the stability of repeated reports under highly emotional circumstances.

Finally, psychologists have recently tackled the difficult issue of coaching and exposure to misleading conversations (e.g., Bruck et al., 1993). In some circumstances, such as sexual abuse in group-care settings or allegations raised during custody battles, this type of misleading information may have a more significant impact on children's testimonies than suggestive interviews. Concern about the source of information is not limited to sex abuse cases. For example, in the investigation of Darnell Wilson's murder, M. L. claimed that she did not disclose the actual perpetrators in early interviews because she had been told to substitute other names. Serious inconsistencies (e.g., identifying multiple perpetrators) should raise questions about the possibility of coaching, yet we know little about children's ability to accurately identify the source of their knowledge (e.g., personal experience, overheard conversations, and so on) in everyday settings or after they have been interviewed multiple times. (For reviews of the extant literature on memory-source monitoring, see Johnson, Hashtroudi, & Lindsay, 1993, and Lindsay, 1994.) If multiple interviews consolidate memories for events, might they also consolidate misinformation when a child has been coached, thereby increasing the chance that the child will subsequently report the suggestive conversations? By adding repeated interviews and source-monitoring tests to future studies of coaching effects, delayed recall, and emotion-memory relationships, researchers will be conducting studies that better represent the experiences of many child witnesses.

3

Effects of Timing and Type of Questioning on Eyewitness Accuracy and Suggestibility

AMYE R. WARREN

PEGGY LANE

Recently, Brainerd and Ornstein (1991) suggested that repeated questioning has the potential to facilitate children's eyewitness memory, stating that "the most fundamental principle of memory is that repetition facilitates performance" (p. 15). They based this conclusion on traditional laboratory memory research that has shown enhanced memory performance with repeated questioning, using word lists as the memorial material (e.g., Brainerd, Reyna, Howe, & Kingma, 1990; Howe, Kelland, Bryant-Brown, & Clark, 1992). Flin (1991) challenged Brainerd and Ornstein's suggestion because of "ethical, emotional, and motivational factors" (p. 22). She stressed that the results of enhanced memory for word lists in the laboratory cannot and should not be

AUTHORS' NOTE: This research was funded in part by a University of Chattanooga Foundation Faculty Research Grant. Portions of this work were conducted by the second author for her master's thesis. We gratefully acknowledge the assistance of Audrey Buhrman, Debby Hulse, Carole Snider, and Susan Thoeming in data collection and scoring, and the helpful comments of Charles J. Brainerd and Debra Poole on an earlier version of this chapter.

generalized to repeatedly interviewing child witnesses, and stated that practitioners in the field believe that repeated questioning can be emotionally disturbing to children and can compromise the quality of their testimony. Present guidelines for professionals who interview child victims therefore recommend minimizing the number of interview sessions and videotaping early interviews to reduce the need for further questioning and court appearances by child witnesses (Flin, 1991).

However, repeated questioning of witnesses seems to be the norm in our judicial system (Cassel, 1991; Eugenio, Buckhout, Kostes, & Ellison, 1982). It is therefore vitally important to know if the potential benefits of repeated interviews outweigh their possible liabilities. Unfortunately, studies on the effects of repeated questioning on memory for a witnessed event have not yet produced conclusive answers to this question.

One consistent finding of repeated testing research in the laboratory has been that material not recalled on initial tests can be "reminisced," or recalled, on subsequent tests without additional study (for reviews, see Payne, 1987; Richardson, 1985). In fact, sometimes the amount of information reminisced on later memory tests exceeds the amount forgotten, a phenomenon known as "hypermnesia" (Payne, 1987). Studies have shown that repeated testing produces hypermnesia and/or reminiscence for word lists (Brainerd et al., 1990; Madigan, 1976; Richardson, 1985; Slamecka & Katsaiti, 1988; Wilkinson & Koestler, 1983) and pictures (Erdelyi & Stein, 1981). Typically, reminiscence is produced by a series of tests given immediately after the material is presented. However, even when the initial test is given after a lengthy retention period, it seems to refurbish memories, producing superior results on subsequent tests (Brainerd et al., 1990; Howe, Kelland, et al., 1992).

In addition to reminiscence, a test administered shortly after acquisition can cause resistance (inoculation) to forgetting (Brainerd et al., 1990; Fivush & Hamond, 1989; Howe, Kelland, et al., 1992; Slamecka & Katsaiti, 1988). The early initial test may facilitate the consolidation of the memory for the to-be-learned material (Richardson, 1985).

On the other hand, negative consequences of repeated testing are commonly noted in basic laboratory research. For example, perseveration of errors across repeated trials was demonstrated by Kay (1955). He found that errors produced on an earlier free-recall test tended to recur on later trials even after the original material was presented for further study. Cooper and Monk (1976) concluded that "a test trial consolidates the learned material in some way leading to resistance to forgetting in delayed recall and a stereotyping of the responses" (p. 136).

Sanders and Warnick (1980) questioned the generalization of findings in basic learning and memory research to eyewitness memory, and Flin (1991) has echoed these concerns. Davies (1991) and Warren-Leubecker (1991) have also asserted that materials other than word lists should be used before leaping to conclusions regarding the advantages and disadvantages of multiple interviews in forensic settings. However, studies on repeated questioning in eyewitness memory research have produced both negative and positive results, consistent with the basic laboratory findings.

Several eyewitness studies have shown positive results of repeated neutral questioning with adults. Scrivner and Safer (1988) showed subjects a videotape of a burglary, then immediately tested the subjects three times and again 48 hours later. Subjects experienced hypermnesia across the four trials with 77 of 90 subjects recalling more details on the last trial than on the first. Poole and White (1991) tested half their subjects twice—immediately and 1 week later—and half the subjects only once, at the 1-week interval. They found that the subjects questioned for the second time at 1 week remembered considerably more than those tested for the first time at 1 week.

The beneficial effects of repeated interviewing also appear to hold for children's event memory. For example, Howe (1991), using repeated questioning with children, found that "reminiscence occurred across test trials and increased the probability of correct factual recall" (p. 746). Fivush and Hamond (1989) reported that very young children who twice reenacted an event demonstrated more complete and accurate memories than those who had reenacted it only at the latter session. Tucker, Mertin, and Luszcz (1990) found a similar pattern when comparing children interviewed both 1 and 7 days after an inoculation with those interviewed only once after 7 days.

Unfortunately, repeated questioning, even when it is completely neutral, can have unanticipated harmful consequences. In studying hypermnesia to a witnessed crime, Eugenio et al. (1982) found that some witnesses produced a significant number of intrusions after three recall trials, indicating that, with repeated questioning, subjects may construct additional details even after they have told all they can remember. Fivush and Hamond (1989) found that those children who twice reenacted an event made more errors than those who reenacted it only once. Memory reports appear to become more complete with repeated interviews, but both accuracies and inaccuracies increase.

Tucker et al. (1990) asked children to recall an immunization experience 1 and 7 days later; 67% of the errors of commission made at Time 1 were repeated at Time 2. Further, Poole and White (1991) repeatedly asked open-

and closed-ended questions about a staged event. Children were more likely than adults to change their answers to closed-ended (yes/no) questions. Further, one of the open-ended questions involved the occupation of one of the actors even though this information had not been presented in the event. Adults who speculated on the answer to this question became more certain of their answers with repetition.

Repeated neutral questioning thus appears to have both beneficial and detrimental effects on memory for witnessed or experienced events. But how often do witnesses encounter solely neutral and completely unbiased questions and interviewers? Even those who stress the positive aspects of repeated neutral questioning (e.g., Brainerd & Ornstein, 1991) acknowledge that exposure to misinformation and inaccurate suggestions are likely to increase with repeated questioning. In reviewing the literature concerning misleading post-event suggestions on memory for natural events, Hall, Loftus, and Tousignant (1984) stated that "a considerable body of psychological research, . . . seems to indicate that under certain circumstances rehearsal of information can interfere with rather than enhance recollection. In particular, interference is likely to occur if rehearsal trials include exposure to new potentially misleading information" (p. 124).

Warren, Hulse-Trotter, and Tubbs (1991) suggestively questioned adult and child subjects two consecutive times, giving negative feedback ("You did not get all of those questions exactly right. Let's try it again.") between trials. Subjects of all ages changed answers on the second trial, and children were significantly more likely to change their answers than were adults. Cassel (1991) showed adults and 6- and 8-year-olds a brief video and shortly afterward asked specific, but neutral, questions about all critical details. One week later, two thirds of the subjects were questioned with either positively leading (suggesting the correct answer) or misleading questions. One month later, all subjects were suggestively questioned, in both correctly leading and misleading ways. The 6-year-olds were more likely than the older children or adults to be misled by the negatively suggestive questions and were more likely to change their minds when questioned first one way and then the other. However, adults rejected both the correctly leading questions (resulting in lower accuracy) and the misleading questions.

Schooler, Foster, and Loftus (1988) had subjects view a slide presentation of a burglary. After a delay of 10 minutes, they introduced misleading information in the answers to a forced-choice test and gave a final forced-choice test 5 minutes later. They found that the selection of a distractor on the initial forced-choice test reduced accuracy on the final test. Schooler et al. (1988) concluded that "the act of committing to an incorrect response causes subjects to falsely remember that information . . . which later causes interference that impairs the subjects' ability to remember the original details" (p. 249).

The timing of suggestive interviews, rather than just their frequency, may also be critical for accuracy in testimony. Lipton (1977) had subjects view a film of a crime, then questioned them immediately or 1 week later. The delayed-test subjects recalled less material and were less accurate. Loftus, Miller, and Burns (1978) required subjects to view a series of slides, answer questions (half consistent with the original information/half misleading), and take a final forced-choice (correct answer or misleading answer) recognition test. The questionnaire was given either immediately following the slide presentation or just before the final test, which occurred after a retention interval of 20 minutes, 1 day, 2 days, or 1 week. The misleading information had a greater impact when presented just prior to the final test than when presented immediately after acquisition. Belli, Windschitl, McCarthy, and Winfrey (1992) presented subjects with misinformation either immediately, 5 days, or 1 week after viewing a slide series. Misinformation had no effect when given immediately but a strong effect when presented after a longer retention interval.

It is possible that misinformation presented at some delay from an event is even more harmful to children than to adults, given that recent research has documented developmental differences in both completeness of event encoding and in forgetting rates (Brainerd et al., 1990). In other words, children's memory traces for events may not be as strong as adults' from the beginning and will fade more quickly over time. In support of this idea, Tucker et al. (1990) found that children who were suggestively questioned 7 days after an event were more likely to agree with the suggestions than children who were questioned only 1 day after the event.

Summarizing, both basic laboratory and eyewitness research have demonstrated that repeated testing/interviewing preserves error (Tucker et al., 1990), confirms speculation (Poole & White, 1991), increases intrusions (Eugenio et al., 1982), and produces inconsistencies (Warren et al., 1991) while also producing hypermnesia (Scrivner & Safer, 1988), reminiscence (Eugenio et al., 1982; Howe, 1991), and inoculation against forgetting (Brainerd et al., 1990). Studies also indicate that misleading information has a stronger effect if presented after a delay (Belli et al., 1992; Loftus et al., 1978). Because repeated questioning, with the increased possibility of exposure to misleading information, is prevalent in eyewitness situations, we need to understand how interview timing (soon after or at some delay after an event) and interview repetition (the sheer number of interviews conducted) may interact, and how each of these factors may relate to age. However, few studies that combine these factors have been conducted.

In our laboratory, we have been interested in several questions related to this interaction between interview number and timing. For example, although it has been well documented that early neutral testing can inoculate against forgetting, is it possible that it could also inoculate against susceptibility to misleading information encountered in later questioning? To our knowledge, no prior study has directly investigated this issue. Further, could initial misleading questioning freeze error, causing subsequent neutral questioning to be ineffective, or will later neutral questioning enable subjects to recover accurate memories? An answer to this question could prove especially helpful to those who must question a witness who has already been "contaminated" by a prior leading interview. Will a delay in the initial questioning make testimony not only less complete and accurate but also more susceptible to later misleading information? Prior work with adults certainly suggests that this is the case, but we have yet to see this finding replicated with children. The study we report in this chapter was designed to provide preliminary answers to these fundamental questions.

The Present Study

SUBJECTS

Subjects were 279 student volunteers (198 females and 81 males, 243 whites and 36 minorities) from introductory psychology classes who received extra credit for their participation. The mean age of these adult subjects was 22 years. Approximately 30 adult subjects were randomly assigned to each of 9 experimental conditions and tested in groups. A second sample of subjects was composed of 63 third- and fourth-grade children (32 females, 31 males, all white; mean age = 9 years 4 months) from a nearby parochial school. Children were randomly assigned to one of three experimental conditions, with 21 children in each.

MATERIALS

Video. All subjects viewed a short, $2\frac{1}{2}$-minute video depicting an incident involving a mother, her daughter, and a boy from her daughter's class at school. The mother was doing the dishes while the children were studying at the table. When the mother went to answer the door, the children got something to drink. While the boy's back was turned, the girl took some money off the counter and put it in her pocket. The children returned to the table and resumed studying. The mother came back into the room to get the money to pay for Girl Scout cookies that were being delivered, and found it missing. She asked if either child had seen the money, but neither admitted seeing it. The mother then sent the boy home and said she would look for more money in her purse (although this activity and her purse were not shown).

Questions. The video was shown to a group of graduate and upper-class students in the psychology department. They were asked to give free recall immediately after viewing. From the free-recall protocols, 25 open-ended questions were developed to be used as base questions for three conditions: neutral (neutral and positive leading questions), misleading (neutral and negative misleading), and final (all neutral, designed to detect the effect of the misleading questions). These questions concerned both central ("Who took the money?") and peripheral ("What color was the boy's shirt?") information, although the centrality or salience of the information was not empirically determined a priori. Of the 25 base questions, 7 were selected as target questions while the other 18 remained neutral and identical across conditions. For the 7 target questions, three versions were developed: one misleading, one neutral, and one "final" neutral (e.g., "Where was the mother when the boy took the money?" versus "Where was the mother when someone took the money?" versus "Who took the money?"). The misleading and neutral versions of each question were parallel in content, form, and the cognitive demands made on the subjects (e.g., if a misleading question required a generated answer, the parallel neutral question did also). There was one extra question in the misleading condition that had no parallel in the neutral condition, as it misled about an item not present in the film, and it was presented as the last question ("What type of purse did the mother have?" becoming, in the final version of the question, "Did you see the mother's purse?"). In the neutral condition, no question positively led (i.e., contained the correct target information) on critical items in a parallel misleading question. For example, the neutral question, "What was the name of the person who delivered *something* to the door?" did not contain the correct answer (Girl Scout cookies) to the final target question, "What was delivered to the door?" The final condition thus contained 26 questions, 18 of which related to the 18 neutral questions, whereas the remaining 8 concerned the target information about which some subjects had been misled previously.

PROCEDURE

All adult subjects were tested in groups, whereas children were tested individually. At Time 1 all subjects viewed the video and then completed a 10-minute filler task. Then approximately one third of the subjects received a second filler task (the "no questioning" condition), one third received the neutral questions, and one third the misleading questions.

One week later (Time 2), adult subjects were again randomly assigned to one of the three questioning conditions. After being questioned neutrally, suggestively, or completing a filler task (for the "no questioning" condition), all adult subjects were given a 20-minute written filler task, followed by a final set of questions (all neutral and open ended) regarding the video (Time 3) and free recall. The child subjects were all suggestively questioned at Time 2, then performed a filler task followed by free recall and the final neutral questions.

We predicted that the 18 neutral questions presented at the initial session—whether as part of the neutral or misleading condition—would consolidate memories resulting in more accurate memories for these facts (relative to those of subjects who were not questioned at Time 1 at all). We also expected that suggestive information presented at the initial session would result in less accurate memory for that target information, but that suggestive questioning at Time 2 would be even more detrimental to performance. Further, we predicted that subjects neutrally questioned at Time 1 would be more resistant to later (Time 2) suggestive questioning compared with subjects who either were not questioned or were suggestively questioned at Time 1. No significant age differences or interactions with age were expected for suggestibility or accuracy, based on reviews of large numbers of studies that find school-aged children to be no more suggestible than adults (e.g., Ceci & Bruck, 1993a).

Results

SCORING

We scored the responses to the questions for accuracy at the final session. For example, the correct answer to the question, "What color was the girl's hair?" was "blonde." We further subdivided incorrect answers to the eight target questions into three categories: those reflecting the misleading information (e.g., "brown hair" from the misleading question, "The girl's brown hair was long, wasn't it?"), those that were incorrect in another way (e.g., "black hair"), and "don't know" or blank responses. To achieve interrater reliability, 10% of the subjects' answers were scored independently. Interrater agreement exceeded 95%. We also scored the free-recall protocols for the three conditions common to adult and child subjects. We determined that 33 details had been either asked about or included within the questions, and these 33 details were therefore examined in free recall. All free-recall protocols were scored by three scorers, and disagreements were resolved through discussion. Free-recall accuracy scores denote the number of accurate details reported, divided by the 33 total possible correct details. Free-recall suggestibility scores denote the number of suggested details (those implied in the misleading questions) present in the subjects' reports, divided by the 8 total misleading details.

ACCURACY OF ANSWERS TO FINAL QUESTIONS

We analyzed adults' accuracy on the final neutral questions (summed across all 18) using a 3 (Type of Time 1 Questioning: none, neutral, suggestive) by 3 (Type of Time 2 Questioning: none, neutral, suggestive) ANOVA. Only a significant effect of Time 1 (T1) questioning was found, $F(2, 270) = 44.69, p < .0001$. Table 3.1 indicates that those who were questioned either neutrally or suggestively at T1 were significantly more accurate on the final neutral questions than those who were not questioned initially. A similar pattern was found in the children's data. A one-way analysis of variance with Time 1 type of questioning as the grouping variable revealed a significant effect, $F(2, 60) = 3.29, p < .04$ (see Table 3.2). Both groups of children questioned at T1 answered more final neutral questions correctly than children not questioned initially.

When the children and adults were directly compared, we excluded neutral questions not common to both child and adult subjects (children had been

Table 3.1   Adults' Percentage of Accuracy and Suggestibility on Final Questions by Condition

Condition			Accuracy		Suggestibility	
Time 1	Time 2	n	Mean	(SD)	Mean	(SD)
None	None	32	71.2	(10.0)	8.3	(11.2)
None	Neutral	30	70.0	(7.9)	12.1	(12.4)
None	Misleading	31	65.3	(9.7)	33.1	(20.5)
Neutral	None	34	82.2	(9.2)	7.0	(9.9)
Neutral	Neutral	30	83.2	(9.2)	7.9	(10.6)
Neutral	Misleading	35	79.5	(12.2)	18.5	(20.1)
Misleading	None	29	80.8	(10.0)	22.9	(19.5)
Misleading	Neutral	29	77.8	(11.2)	13.8	(13.1)
Misleading	Misleading	29	81.1	(9.5)	26.3	(22.8)

NOTE: Differences in accuracy greater than approximately 7.9% and in suggestibility greater than 16.7% are significant at $p < .05$ according to Tukey's HSD post hoc tests.

asked two questions that were not asked of the adults, and adults were asked three questions that were not asked of the children). Thus 16 total final neutral questions shared by all subjects were examined. A 2 (Age) × 3 (T1 Condition) ANOVA was conducted, revealing a significant effect of condition, $F(2, 152) = 30.77$, $p < .01$. We found neither an age main effect nor an interaction of age and condition.

Table 3.2   Percentage of Accuracy and Suggestibility on Final Questions by Age and Time 1 Condition

	9-Year-Olds		Adults	
T1 Condition	Accuracy	Suggestibility	Accuracy	Suggestibility
None				
M	70.2	38.8	66.1	33.1
(SD)	(11.5)	(18.1)	(9.6)	(20.5)
Neutral				
M	78.3	32.8	78.9	18.5
(SD)	(10.0)	(19.1)	(12.1)	(20.1)
Misleading				
M	81.5	39.9	81.4	26.3
(SD)	(8.9)	(17.5)	(9.4)	(22.8)

NOTE: Differences in accuracy greater than approximately 7% and in suggestibility greater than 15% are significant at $p < .05$ level according to Tukey's HSD post hoc tests.

SUGGESTIBILITY IN ANSWERS TO FINAL QUESTIONS

We conducted a 3 (T1 Condition) by 3 (T2 Condition) ANOVA on the adults' suggestibility on the eight misleading (target) questions. Significant main effects of both T1 and T2 conditions were found, and a significant interaction was also revealed, $F(4, 270) = 3.708$, $p < .006$ (see Table 3.1). Post hoc tests indicated that those subjects who were not questioned at T1 and were suggestively questioned at T2 (no/mis), those who were suggestively questioned twice (mis/mis), and those misled at T1 and not questioned at T2 (mis/no) were equally suggestible, and all of these groups were significantly more suggestible than those who were never misled (with one exception—see Table 3.1). Further, in examining the interaction, we saw that the no/mis group was more suggestible than the mis/no group, while the neut/mis subjects were more suggestible than mis/neut subjects, indicating that suggestive questioning at T2 was more detrimental than the same type of questioning at T1. Also, neutral questioning at T1 or T2 did result in a reduction of susceptibility to misleading information—in fact, the no/mis group was significantly more suggestible than the neutral/mis group, and those who were neutrally as well as suggestively interviewed were no more suggestible than subjects who never were misled.

The children's data revealed a different pattern. No significant effect of T1 questioning was found in a one-way ANOVA comparing the three groups' tendencies to answer the final target questions with misleading information (see Table 3.2). However, when a 2 (Age) by 3 (T1 Condition) ANOVA was conducted on suggestibility, an interaction between age and condition emerged, $F(2, 152) = 3.52$, $p < .05$. This interaction indicated that those child subjects who were misled at T1 and those who were not questioned initially were equally suggestible at the final session, and more suggestible than children neutrally questioned at T1. For adult subjects, on the other hand, all three groups were significantly different, with no initial questioning resulting in greater suggestibility than initial misleading questioning, which, in turn, produced greater suggestibility than initial neutral questioning. Also, the differences between adult groups were much larger than those between child groups. Further, a main effect of age was found, $F(1, 152) = 14.52$, $p < .001$. Overall, children were more suggestible than adults (see Table 3.2). In fact, the most suggestible adults (those not questioned at T1) were no more suggestible than the least suggestible children (those neutrally questioned at T1).

Table 3.3   Free-Recall Percentage of Accuracy and Suggestibility by Age and Time 1
Condition

	9-year-olds		Adults	
T1 Condition	Accuracy	Suggestibility	Accuracy	Suggestibility
None				
M	17.3	11.8	30.2	7.7
(SD)	(9.5)	(10.3)	(11.1)	(10.5)
Neutral				
M	23.0	6.3	43.3	4.3
(SD)	(11.3)	(9.8)	(13.3)	(7.4)
Misleading				
M	21.4	20.6	42.2	8.2
(SD)	(8.5)	(17.8)	(10.8)	(10.2)

NOTE: Differences in accuracy greater than approximately 9.1% and in suggestibility greater
than 9% are significant at $p < .05$ according to Tukey's HSD post hoc tests.

ACCURACY IN FREE RECALL

The analysis of number of correct details reported in free recall revealed
main effects of age—$F(1, 144) = 90.24, p < .0001$—and condition—$F(2, 144)$
$= 9.39, p < .0001$. As Table 3.3 indicates, children reported fewer accurate
details in free recall than did adults. Further, subjects not questioned at Time
1, regardless of age, reported significantly fewer correct details than subjects
who had been either neutrally or suggestively questioned at Time 1. The
condition effect mimics that found in the answers to specific questions.

SUGGESTIBILITY IN FREE RECALL

The analysis of suggested details reported in free recall revealed main effects
for both age—$F(1, 144) = 10.87, p < .0012$—and condition—$F(2, 144) = 8.17$,
$p < .0004$. As Table 3.3 shows, children were more suggestible than adults
overall, and subjects questioned neutrally at T1 were less suggestible than
those not questioned at T1, who in turn were less suggestible than those
questioned suggestively at T1. However, the analysis also revealed a significant
($p < .05$) interaction between age and condition, $F(2, 144) = 2.98$. It appears
that adults who were suggestively questioned twice were not significantly
different from those who were not questioned initially and then suggestively

questioned 1 week later. However, children suggestively questioned twice were significantly more suggestible than their peers (see Table 3.3).

PROPORTION OF ACCURACY IN FREE RECALL

To obtain a sense of the overall ratio of accurate details to total details reported in free recall, we divided the accuracy scores by the sum of accuracy and suggestibility scores for each subject. The ANOVA on this measure revealed significant main effects of age—$F(1, 144) = 28.23$, $p < .0001$—and condition—$F(2, 144) = 6.24$, $p < .0025$. Overall, children were less accurate than adults (84.7% versus 95.6%), and subjects questioned suggestively and those not questioned at Time 1 were less accurate than those neutrally questioned at Time 1 (87.6% versus 95.2%). There was also a trend ($p < .09$) toward an interaction, which indicated that the children showed greater condition differences than the adults. In fact, the children neutrally questioned at Time 1 had an accuracy proportion (92.8) virtually equal to that of the adults in any condition (neutral = 97.6%, none = 94.1%, and misled = 95.1%), whereas suggestively questioned children and children not questioned at T1 were a full 10% lower in accuracy (79.8% and 81.5%, respectively).

Conclusions and Implications

As predicted, both child and adult subjects questioned initially were more accurate on final neutral questions and they reported more correct details in final free recall. This result clearly supports the hypothesis that questioning or testing shortly after an event results in inoculation against forgetting (Brainerd & Ornstein, 1991). Not only is memory accuracy greater if assessed soon after an event, the early assessment itself helps to maintain that accuracy over a longer period. However, it is unclear just how long such an inoculation may be expected to last. Ornstein, Gordon, and Baker-Ward (1992) reported that children who were interviewed both immediately and 3 weeks after a doctor's exam had no advantage over their peers who were interviewed only at the second session. Flin et al. (1992a) found that, when children and adults were interviewed both shortly after an event and 5 months later, the adults maintained their initial recall levels over the delay, but children's recall levels decayed and were ultimately no different from those of children interviewed only after the delay. Considering the extensive delays routinely encountered between witnessing an event, initial questioning about that event, and later courtroom testimony, it would be premature to conclude that initial questioning confers any meaningful, forensically relevant, long-term advantages. Perhaps "booster shots" of neutral questioning sessions during the long retention intervals are necessary to maintain high levels of accuracy (Brainerd & Ornstein, 1991). There are at least two problems with this suggestion, unfortunately. First, our data indicate that later neutral questioning is not nearly as effective as early neutral questioning (for increasing accuracy). Adults who were not questioned initially but neutrally questioned 1 week later were no different from those not questioned at either time, and adults who were questioned neutrally both times were no different from those questioned neutrally only the first time. Second, the likelihood of subsequent, multiple *neutral* interviews may be quite low in the "real world" of eyewitness testimony.

Cassel (1991) argues that in certain cases, such as bystanders witnessing a car accident or a crime, the first interview may well be primarily neutral, as the investigating officer is simply attempting to determine what has occurred. Follow-up questioning by attorneys, on the other hand, is likely to be leading, with attorneys from opposing sides asking questions that may lead in differing directions. Our results indicate that initial neutral questioning does in fact reduce susceptibility to later suggestion for both children and adults (although more so for adults than for children). Further, neutral questioning following suggestive questioning also reduces ultimate suggestibility.

There are many possible theoretical explanations for these findings, but our study design does not allow us to rule out alternatives. For example, perhaps the initial questioning creates stronger traces that are either more resistant to overwriting by postevent information or simply more accessible than competing postevent information traces (see Zaragoza, Dahlgren, & Muench, 1992, for an overview). In any case, the fact that neutral questioning reduced susceptibility to suggestion seems to have encouraging implications for the real world of child witness testimony. Again, however, there are several obstacles preventing us from wholesale application of these findings to legal settings. Unlike the bystander witnesses described by Cassel (1991), child abuse witnesses (the primary concern of most child witness researchers and practitioners today) may not be initially interviewed until months or even years past the events in question. Thus these interviews may occur well past the time that any "trace strengthening" benefits would accrue. In Cassel's own (1991) study, all children were originally neutrally questioned, yet they were quite suggestible a week or a month later. Moreover, the initial interview in child abuse cases is just as likely to be suggestive as neutral. We must therefore examine the extent to which the effects of suggestive questioning depend on the delay since the event.

Replicating the results of prior studies (e.g., Belli et al., 1992), we found that our adult subjects were more adversely affected by suggestive questioning if it occurred 1 week after as opposed to immediately following the event. The most suggestible subjects were those who were not questioned at Time 1 and were suggestively questioned at Time 2, although subjects suggestively questioned twice were close behind. This result again highlights the potential importance of memory strength. If subjects are questioned shortly after an event, they may more easily notice discrepancies between postevent information and their own recollections. As forgetting occurs over the delay, subjects may become less confident of their own memory of the event and thus more willing to accept another's interpretation (see Belli et al. for other possible explanations of the retention interval effects).

Because we did not include all nine adult conditions in our study of children, we cannot directly test the effects of timing of suggestive questioning on children. However, it is interesting to note that, unlike the adults, children suggestively questioned at Time 1 were equally suggestible at the final session to those who had not been questioned at Time 1. Further, children suggestively questioned twice reported many more suggested details in their free-recall reports. This partly contradicts the results of Tucker et al. (1990), who found that children (mildly) suggestively questioned twice, 1 day and 7 days after an event, were less likely to agree with suggestions than children questioned only after the 7-day interval. Another interesting hint from our data that children did not differentially respond to suggestive questioning based on time of administration came from examining performance at Times 1 and 2. It appears that children suggestively questioned both times were just as suggestive the first time as they were the second. In other words, suggestibility did not increase with the second administration of misleading questions, and children did not appear better able to notice and thus reject discrepancies at the shorter rather than the longer delay. Recent research suggests that children may be less capable of monitoring postevent information for discrepancies, and of distinguishing which information came at which time from which sources (e.g., Lindsay, Johnson, & Kwon, 1991). However, given the limitations of our design, much further analysis and research will be required to definitively address this issue.

Contrary to our own predictions and others' claims (e.g., Ceci, Ross, & Toglia, 1989) that school-aged children and adults are equally suggestible, the

9-year-olds in this study were significantly more suggestible than adults. The reasons for the children's greater suggestibility are not clear. It does not appear to be due to generally weaker memory, because the children and adults were equally accurate on the final neutral questions, both those concerning central and those concerning peripheral details. Further, our preliminary analyses of accuracy on neutral questions at Times 1 and 2 indicate no age differences. Typically, children's free recall is just as accurate, but not as complete, as that of adults (e.g., Dent, 1991). Our child subjects were neither as complete nor as accurate in free recall. Unless they had been neutrally questioned shortly after witnessing the event, the children were more suggestible than adults both in responses to specific questions and in their free-recall reports. This "carry-over" of suggested details into free-recall reports is not typically found and is particularly troublesome. It should be kept in mind, however, that children's free-recall reports were given immediately after their Time 2 misleading questioning, whereas adults' free recall occurred following their Time 3, neutral final questions.

We were concerned that children's greater overall suggestibility might be attributable to only a small subset of the eight suggestive questions, perhaps only those dealing with more peripheral details. The children and the adults were equally resistant to misinformation concerning one central activity in the video (the child actors were doing math homework), but the children were suggestible about a central event; they were more likely than adults to answer that the boy, rather than the girl, had taken the money. More surprising was the fact that children were not clearly more suggestible than adults regarding peripheral details, such as the girl's hair color and shirt color.

Yet another potential explanation of the children's relatively high level of suggestibility concerns the type of witnessed event we used. Rudy and Goodman (1991) found that children who merely observed were more suggestible than children who actively participated in an event, although observers and participants were equally accurate in free recall and answers to specific questions. Nonmemorial, social factors also play a significant role in the children's suggestibility. Even if children can remember an event as well as do adults, and can clearly monitor and distinguish their own recollections from postevent misinformation, they may be more likely to comply with an adult authority's contradictory suggestion. As Ceci and colleagues have observed (Ceci et al., 1989; Toglia, Ross, Ceci, & Hembrooke, 1992), children are more suggestible when credible or authoritative figures present the misinformation. In our study, the interviewers were seen as knowledgeable sources, as they had been present during the to-be-remembered event. Additionally, the children were individually interviewed, whereas the adults were questioned in groups, which may have diminished the interviewer's authority status for adult subjects and exaggerated the age differences in suggestibility.

In summary, the type, timing, and number of interviews interact in complex ways with one another and with age. Our preliminary work provides support for the common practice of interviewing both child and adult witnesses as soon as possible following an event, as such interviews appear to inoculate against forgetting and attenuate suggestibility. For adult witnesses, even early suggestive interviews may be relatively harmless, given that memories and confidence may still be strong enough for contradictory information to be noticed and rejected. Given the realities of most child abuse cases, however, an initial interview may be weeks, months, or even years after an event. Our data suggest that even neutral interviews given 1 week after an event are helpful, but far less so than immediate interviews, and that suggestive interviews after a lengthy interval are quite damaging—possibly even more damaging than early, repeated suggestive interviews. Although still in its early and speculative stages, our work suggests that interview repetition (a factor that may be controlled in real-world contexts) may be less important than interview timing (a less easily controlled variable) to the eventual integrity of an eyewitness account. Depending on the timing of their administration, multiple neutral interviews may confer no additional benefits, and multiple suggestive interviews may do no additional harm. If these conclusions hold true in further research, we would be wise to heed Flin's (1991) recommendation to minimize the number of interviews, thereby minimizing the stress placed on the eyewitness.

4

How Shall a Thing Be Coded?

Implications of the Use of Alternative Procedures
for Scoring Children's Verbal Reports

LYNNE BAKER-WARD

PETER A. ORNSTEIN

BETTY N. GORDON

ANDREA FOLLMER

PATRICIA A. CLUBB

In response to the unprecedented involvement of very young witnesses in the legal system, research on children's testimony has mushroomed in

AUTHORS' NOTE: We thank Karen J. Saywitz for providing us with invaluable consultation in the reanalysis of our original data and Gabrielle Albert, Elaine Burgwyn, Beata Janssen, and Lauren Shapiro for their technical assistance. This work was supported in part by grant MH 43904 from the National Institute of Mental Health.

recent years, as evidenced by the studies reported in this volume (see also Ceci, Ross, & Toglia, 1989; Ceci, Toglia, & Ross, 1987; Doris, 1991; Goodman & Bottoms, 1993; Goodman, Taub, et al., 1992). This work has contributed greatly to our understanding of the factors that affect children's reports of personally experienced events and has begun to bring about changes in the treatment of child witnesses in legal settings (see Part II of this volume). These advances notwithstanding, relatively limited attention has yet been directed to the coordination of findings across investigations.

The integration of results obtained in different settings is particularly important when young children's eyewitness testimony is under consideration. Recent formulations of memory development (Baker-Ward, Ornstein, & Gordon, 1993; Folds, Footo, Guttentag, & Ornstein, 1990; Ornstein, Baker-Ward, & Naus, 1988) emphasize the extent to which memory performance in preschoolers and younger elementary school-age children is dependent on aspects of the context in which remembering is assessed. Even very young children can appear highly competent in remembering past events under certain circumstances (see Fivush & Shukat, this volume). In contrast, under other conditions, children's reports can be very limited and are not always reliable indicators of their experiences (e.g., Lindsay, Gonzales, & Eso, this volume). Cognitive developmentalists increasingly have come to view a range of performance as characteristic of the mnemonic capabilities of young children and to conceptualize memory performance as a continuum of competence. The likelihood that a particular child's report will fall along a given point on such a continuum is determined by a range of factors characterizing the particular event (see Ornstein, Larus, & Clubb, 1991) as well as the child's developmental level (see Garbarino & Stott, 1991) and personal characteristics (e.g., temperament; see Gordon et al., 1993).

The context specificity of children's memory renders the pervasive problem of determining what a child knows particularly salient in assessments of children's memory for events. Researchers are faced with many procedural decisions in designing investigations, any one of which can have profound implications for the descriptions of children's performance that emerge from their work. Clinicians, as consumers of an often apparently contradictory literature, may find it difficult to draw conclusions in delivering expert testimony or predicting a young witness's probable level of performance. As Flin argues in Chapter 12, the need to provide valid generalizations for the legal system amidst the variations and complexities of individual cases is a critical challenge for psychologists concerned with children's testimony. As developmental and clinical child psychologists long concerned with assessing children's reports of personally experienced events in both research and practice, we have often struggled with the fundamental issue of cognitive diagnosis (see Flavell, 1985; Ornstein et al., 1991) in evaluating memory performance. Specifically, how can we be sure that our impressions of a child's report under given circumstances provide a reasonably accurate description of her capacity to remember a particular event? In this chapter, we examine one important—if rather prosaic!—issue in evaluating a child's report: the criterion set for accepting an often incomplete or unclear statement as evidence for memory of a particular aspect of an event. Specifically, the consequences of the procedures used to code recall performance are investigated, using our own work on children's memory for a physical examination as a case study. In interpreting the impact of different coding schemes or "rules of evidence" in laboratory investigations, we consider the extent to which characterizations of age-related patterns in children's reports are likely to be robust across different studies. This consideration, we believe, is a necessary step in the consolidation of the burgeoning literature on children's testimony.

The Nature of Children's Memory for Events

Children's testimony requires the retention of experienced or observed events and the report of information concerning these events at a delayed interview. The information is acquired in an incidental manner, as of course the child is not told in advance that a memory interview is forthcoming and does not engage in strategies to increase the likelihood of information storage (Ornstein, Gordon, & Baker-Ward, 1992). Although the first report of an event is a case of incidental memory, this incidental recall subsequently turns into a deliberate memory task, as the child is urged to try to remember as much information as possible.

When the child is interviewed regarding an event, she may provide information with little intervention by the examiner, or she may only respond to the interview's questions about aspects of the event. Recall, or the provision of information with only very general prompts, is of great importance in legal settings, both because it is most frequently demanded in such contexts (Myers, 1987) and because it is seen as having greater credibility than information provided in response to specific queries (Wehrspann, Steinhauer, & Klajner-Diamond, 1987). Hence children's recall abilities are of particular interest to those concerned with children's testimony. Despite the fact that free recall is generally regarded as credible, children's unstructured accounts of an event may nonetheless be imperfect indicators of their experiences, at least under some circumstances (see Ornstein et al., 1991). Several factors may limit the completeness of the child's report, and hence there is a need to rely on prompted recall to some extent. Clearly, to be recalled, information must be initially encoded in memory and subsequently maintained over time; but it is apparent that neither of these processes operates perfectly. In addition, even when information is maintained over time, children may fail to report all that they know, either because of embarrassment or fear (Batterman-Faunce & Goodman, 1993; Saywitz, Goodman, Nicholas, & Moan, 1991), or because they do not understand the interview process (Ornstein et al., 1991). Finally, the accuracy of the child's memory may be affected by her experiences in the interval between the event and the report that may distort information stored in memory (Brainerd & Ornstein, 1991).

In addition to free recall, cued recall is typically involved in children's testimony (see Batterman-Faunce & Goodman, 1993; Dent & Stephenson, 1979). In cued recall, information is provided in response to questions whose contents serve to prompt retrieval. In some cases, these questions may provide fairly general cues, for example, in directing the child's attention to a particular action or individual. In others, these questions may convey the very information under consideration and require that the child confirm or deny the target action or description, providing in effect a test of recognition memory. Thus specific questions may be direct or may be misleading in the sense of implying that an event occurred. Although specific questions may be considered to be "leading" in a court of law, they may be necessary to elicit information from young children. Clearly, the information conveyed in the question itself is of considerable importance in evaluating memory performance.

In the growing literature on children's memory for personally experienced events, methodological issues most often arise in the assessment of cued recall but are clearly relevant concerns in any attempt to measure free-recall performance as well. How do the decisions researchers make in quantifying memory performance affect (or even partially determine) our emerging understanding of children's abilities to provide accurate accounts of their experiences? This issue is explored below within the context of an investigation from our continuing research program on children's memory for medical procedures. The impact of (a) modifying the stringency of the coding criterion in the analysis of cued (or specific) recall and (b) changing the unit of analysis involved in measuring free (or open-ended) recall is considered in detail. Finally, the implications of these methodological issues for determining children's competency as witnesses are discussed.

Children's Memory for a Pediatric Examination

To examine children's retention of the details of a salient, personal experience, we have for some years conducted research addressing memory for well-child physical examinations (see Baker-Ward, Gordon, Ornstein, Larus, & Clubb, 1993; Gordon et al., 1993; Ornstein, Gordon, & Baker-Ward, 1992; Ornstein, Gordon, & Larus, 1992; Ornstein et al., 1991). Within this paradigm, it is possible to explore children's recall of a complex, naturally occurring event involving some degree of stress. Further, investigations of memory performance can be conducted under conditions in which some degree of experimental control is possible (see Baker-Ward, Ornstein, & Gordon, 1993). Through the cooperation of the medical professionals who provide the examinations, the children's experiences at the time of encoding can be specified. In addition, children at different ages can be randomly assigned to conditions differing in the length of the retention interval, use of alternative techniques for assessing recall, and other variables of interest.

Procedure. The data considered below were collected by Baker-Ward, Gordon, et al. (1993) in a study of the effects of age and delay interval on children's long-term retention and forgetting. Parents of children who were scheduled for physical examinations at two private pediatric practices were recruited for the study prior to their appointments. The final sample consisted of 187 children, distributed approximately equally at three age levels: 3-, 5-, and 7-year-olds. Within each age level, the children were randomly assigned to one of three groups differing with regard to the length of the delay between the initial and the follow-up interviews, or to a control group interviewed only on one occasion, 3 weeks after the examination. Comparisons of performance between children in the control condition and those in the experimental conditions indicated that the initial interview did not affect subsequent recall performance. The same structured protocol was used for both the immediate and the delayed interviews. Each child's retention of 27 standard, predefined features of the examination (e.g., "nurse obtains urine sample," "doctor listens to chest with stethoscope") was assessed. A series of hierarchically structured probes was employed, in that the child was first given the opportunity to report the feature in response to a very general question, followed by increasingly specific probes if the feature was not generated.

General coding procedures. All interviews were videotaped and the tapes were transcribed for subsequent coding. Each child's recall was coded with reference to the particular features of the examination that were reported. In addition, the level of specificity of the probes required to elicit information was categorized. *Open-ended questions* were those that could be correctly answered by reporting many different features of the examination; that is, these probes did not direct the children's attention to any particular detail of their experiences. Open-ended questions included both the very general queries used to initiate the interview (e.g., "Tell me what happened during your checkup." "Tell me what the doctor [or nurse] did.") as well as more focused questions referring to specific parts of the examination (e.g., "Tell me what parts of your face the doctor checked."). *Specific questions*, in contrast, requested only the child's verification of information, including the presence of particular features of the examination (e.g., "Did the doctor check your eyes?") and the action involved in carrying out certain procedures (e.g., "Did the doctor shine a light in your eyes?"). In some analyses, as described below, the specific questions were subdivided into two categories and considered separately. The more direct specific questions, as illustrated by the first example above, were categorized as *yes/no questions*, whereas those containing elaborative detail, such as the one in the second example above, were classified as *leading questions.* Interrater reliability was determined on the basis of the agreement between two raters who had independently coded 25% of the interviews. Agreement within categories of recall for each feature was calculated using the kappa statistic (Landis & Koch, 1977), and ranged from .62 to .96, with a median of .85. Because there were some variations in the children's examinations and interviews, the data were considered as the percentage of features recalled that were present in the examination and addressed in the interview.

Standard scoring procedure. Both Ornstein, Gordon, and Larus (1992) and Baker-Ward, Gordon, et al. (1993) used an identical set of scoring rules in coding children's reports of visits to the physician. As the application of this criterion has constituted our typical coding procedure, this scoring system will be referred to as our Standard Criterion; it is, in fact, a fairly liberal approach to assessing memory performance. The Standard Criterion allows scoring a feature as correctly recalled if the child reports it spontaneously or in response to any probe. In this system, features reported in response to very specific follow-up questions (leading questions) as well as the more direct yes/no questions are scored as correctly recalled. As an example of the application of the Standard Criterion, consider the following sequence. After a child can provide no additional information in response to the open-ended questions, she is asked, "Did the doctor check your mouth?" and she responds in the negative. The interviewer then asks, "Did he put a stick into your mouth?" and the child responds affirmatively. Using the Standard Criterion, the child's recall of the feature "checks mouth" would be scored as being correct at the level of a specific question. Hence total recall included features affirmed only in response to leading questions, in addition to those provided in response to general probes and direct questions. Further, within the context of the Standard Criterion, the children's spontaneous elaborations of the features, defined as the provision of detail concerning the action, location, or instrument involved, are not considered. (In our current work, the extent to which elaborative information accompanies a child's report of a feature is examined in separate analyses.) Figure 4.1 presents a diagram that summarizes the procedure for scoring specific recall with reference to the Standard Criterion. Note that this representation applies only to features that were not reported in response to open-ended probes earlier in the interview.

Results obtained through standard scoring. The major findings reported by Baker-Ward et al. are illustrated in Figure 4.2. It is apparent from the inspection of this figure that the overall level of performance was impressive, with 75.1%, 82.2%, and 92.2% of the features of the examinations recalled at the initial interview by the 3-, 5-, and 7-year-olds, respectively. The use of analysis of variance techniques confirmed age effects in total recall performance at both the initial and the delayed interviews, and preplanned contrasts indicated that all differences among the three groups were significant. Moreover, it is important to note that, on each interview occasion, there were significant age-related differences in the efficacy of the open-ended questions about the physical examination, with the older children reporting a greater percentage of information in response to the general probes.

Forgetting over the course of the 6-week delay was examined by calculating the difference between immediate and delayed recall for each child in the experimental condition. The resulting difference scores were then compared

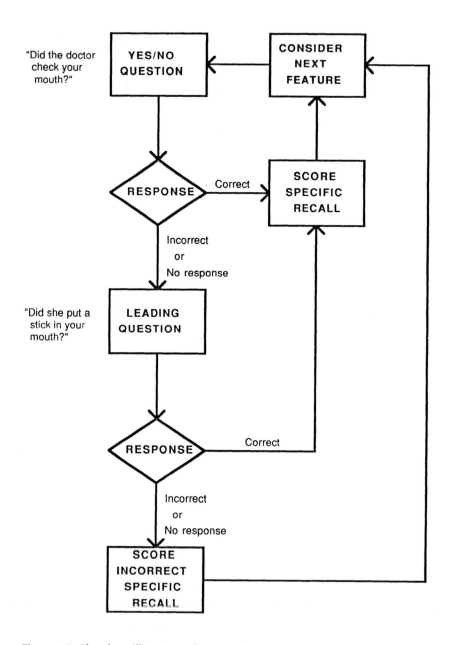

Figure 4.1. Flowchart illustrating the procedures involved in scoring responses to specific questions using the Standard Scoring Criterion.

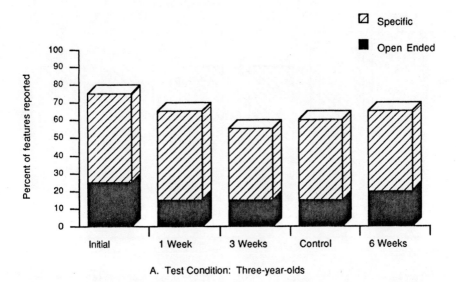

Figure 4.2a. Percentage of features correctly reported in response to open-ended and specific probes by test condition at ages 3 (panel A), 5 (panel B), and 7 (panel C) years as scored by means of the Standard Scoring Criterion.

SOURCE: From Baker-Ward, Gordon, Ornstein, Larus, and Clubb (1993); © The Society for Research in Child Development, Inc. Used by permission.

NOTE: The data presented for the initial test are averaged across the three delay groups.

with the 0% that would be expected on the assumption of no forgetting. Among the 3-year-olds, significant memory loss was observed at 1 and 3 weeks, but not at 6 weeks, reflecting an unexpected improvement in performance at the longest delay. At age 5, forgetting was observed at delays of 3 and 6 weeks, but not at 1 week. The 7-year-olds did not evidence forgetting at any delay interval.

Interpreting memory performance. We have interpreted these findings as evidence of a level of memory performance in young children that can be considered surprisingly strong in comparison with traditional laboratory assessments of preschoolers' mnemonic competence (e.g., see Ornstein, Gordon, & Baker-Ward, 1992; Baker-Ward, Ornstein, & Gordon, 1993). It should be noted, however, that the strength of the performance of the younger children is dependent on the provision of specific questions. Further, it is clear

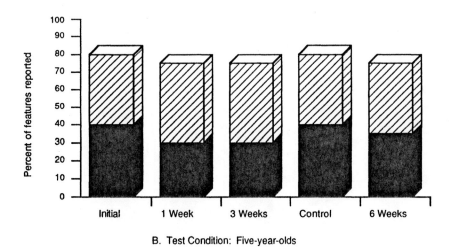

Figure 4.2b. Percentage of features correctly reported in response to open-ended and specific probes by test condition at ages 3 (panel A), 5 (panel B), and 7 (panel C) years as scored by means of the Standard Scoring Criterion.

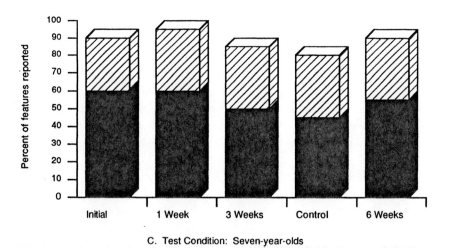

Figure 4.2c. Percentage of features correctly reported in response to open-ended and specific probes by test condition at ages 3 (panel A), 5 (panel B), and 7 (panel C) years as scored by means of the Standard Scoring Criterion.

that the coding criterion used in the Baker-Ward et al. investigation is only one of several possible and reasonable scoring systems. As discussed above, we consider our Standard Criterion to be fairly liberal, because children's responses to even very detailed yes/no questions are accepted as evidence of memory. Accordingly, one can ask if the findings summarized above are influenced by the specific coding rules that we applied to the children's reports. Are the impressions of children's competence that emerge from a consideration of the Baker-Ward et al. findings artifacts of one of several possible scoring systems? To evaluate the generalizability of our findings and to explore the impact of applying different decision rules in scoring recall, we conducted an extensive rescoring of the Baker-Ward et al. data and repeated the major analyses as described above using these recoded data.

Alternative Scoring of Specific Questions

Using a more conservative criterion. The entire set of interviews generated in the study was rescored using a more conservative coding criterion. More stringent rules were applied to the scoring of both open-ended recall as well as specific recall. With regard to open-ended recall, features were not considered as correctly recalled if they were accompanied by incorrect spontaneous elaboration. However, because incorrect elaboration was quite rare, this change had no appreciable effect on open-ended recall. With this one revision, the scoring of free recall was consistent across the two criteria. In contrast, as can be seen below, the coding of specific recall within the context of the More Conservative Criterion differed in several regards from the procedures involved in the application of the Standard Criterion. Further, these changes had a major impact on the impressions of young children's memory that emerged from consideration of the recoded data.

When applying the More Conservative Criterion to the specific recall data, features were scored as correctly recalled only when they were reported initially in response to the yes/no question. If both the yes/no question and the leading question (i.e., the question about the details of a particular procedure) were presented to the child, she was required to have responded affirmatively to both questions to receive credit for having recalled the feature. These decision rules contrast with the procedure applied to the same response within the context of the Standard Scoring Criterion as described above, in which correct responses to the leading questions were accepted as evidence of memory for the feature. Hence, for example, if a child responded yes to the question, "Did the doctor check your eyes?" but no to the next question, "Did the doctor shine a light in your eyes?" the feature would not be counted as recalled when the More Conservative Criterion was used in scoring. Similarly, a correct response only to the latter question following no response or "don't know" to the former question would be considered insufficient evidence of recall to justify scoring the feature as correctly remembered. Both of these responses, however, would be acceptable when the Standard Criterion is used in scoring. Figure 4.3 presents a flowchart that summarizes the scoring rules embodied in the More Conservative Criterion.

Performance as assessed with the More Conservative Criterion. The results obtained through the use of this alternative criterion are presented in Figure 4.4. As illustrated, in comparison with the levels obtained in the original analysis, total recall appears depressed among the younger children. This is especially true for the 3-year-olds, who reported only 47.0% of the features at the initial interview, representing a level of performance that is less than two thirds of that obtained through the application of the Standard Criterion. In contrast, the performance of the 7-year-olds seems relatively unaffected. The lower levels of responding—not a surprise—can be attributed to the lower scores for specific recall obtained when the more stringent criterion was applied. Open-ended recall performance, however, was virtually unchanged, reflecting the general absence of incorrect elaboration accompanying the spontaneous recall of the features, as mentioned above. Hence, as total recall decreases when the More Conservative Criterion is employed, a larger percentage of features are reported in response to open-ended questions.

We conducted two sets of analyses to examine the impact of the changes in the scoring criterion.[1] First, we examined the effects of age on recall and forgetting in the rescored data to determine the extent to which the patterns of performance we originally reported were influenced by the use of a relatively lenient scoring criterion. Second, we evaluated the significance of the change observed in the levels of performance across the two sets of coding criteria.

Although the level of performance appeared to differ when the More Conservative Criterion was applied, the pattern of age effects in recall obtained through the standard scoring procedure was again observed. The use of analyses of variance procedures with the rescored data confirmed the presence of age effects in initial recall, with total recall increasing at each age

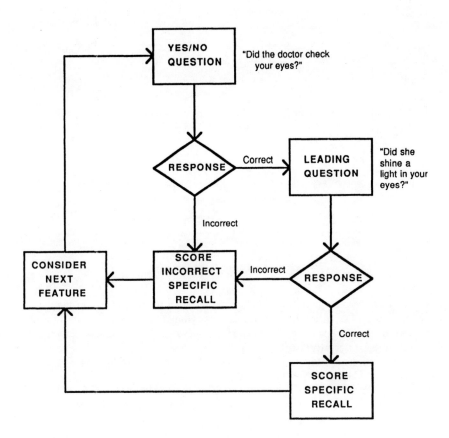

Figure 4.3. Flowchart illustrating the procedures involved in scoring responses to specific questions using the More Conservative Criterion.

level. Similarly, analysis of the delayed recall data verified the apparent effect of age, with increases in performance at each age level. The percentage of features reported in response to open-ended probes again increased with age, with significant increases at each age level. Forgetting was once more assessed by determining whether or not the differences between percentages of recall at the initial versus the delayed interviews differed from 0. Among the 3-year-olds, forgetting was again apparent at 1 and 3 weeks, but not at 6 weeks. A somewhat different pattern was observed among the 5- and 7-year-olds in the

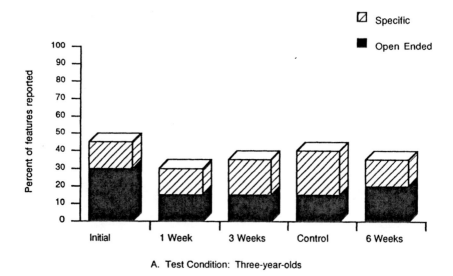

A. Test Condition: Three-year-olds

Figure 4.4a. Percentage of features correctly reported by the children in the Baker-Ward et al. (1993) study in response to open-ended and specific probes by test condition at ages 3 (panel A), 5 (panel B), and 7 (panel C) years as scored by means of the More Conservative Criterion.

SOURCE: From Baker-Ward, Gordon, Ornstein, Larus, and Clubb (1993); © The Society for Research in Child Development, Inc. Used by permission.

NOTE: The data presented for the initial test are averaged across the three delay groups.

reanalysis and in the original treatment of the data. For the 5-year-olds, forgetting was observed at 3 weeks in both analyses. However, when the Standard Criterion was used to score the data, forgetting was present at 6 weeks but not at 1 week, whereas the opposite pattern was revealed in the data scored by the More Conservative Criterion. Among the 7-year-olds, for whom no forgetting was previously observed, significant loss of information was confirmed at 3 weeks. In summary, our reanalysis of the original data with more stringent criteria revealed the same age-related increases in performance as we reported originally, although some variations in the pattern of information loss over time were observed.

Although age-related patterns of performance were similar under the two scoring criteria, a direct comparison of levels of recall revealed significant differences. In these analyses, we computed difference scores representing the

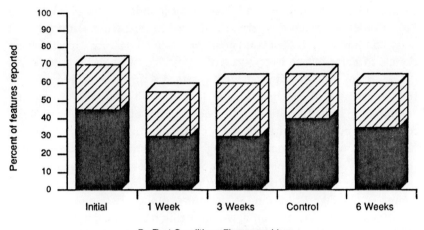

Figure 4.4b. Percentage of features correctly reported by the children in the Baker-Ward et al. (1993) study in response to open-ended and specific probes by test condition at ages 3 (panel A), 5 (panel B), and 7 (panel C) years as scored by means of the More Conservative Criterion.

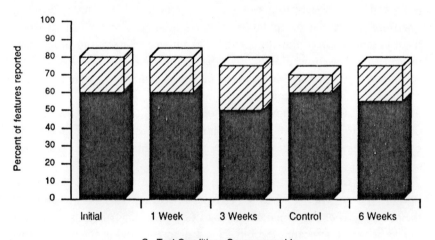

Figure 4.4c. Percentage of features correctly reported by the children in the Baker-Ward et al. (1993) study in response to open-ended and specific probes by test condition at ages 3 (panel A), 5 (panel B), and 7 (panel C) years as scored by means of the More Conservative Criterion.

change in information reported by each subject under the Standard and the More Conservative coding criteria. The mean difference scores within age and delay conditions were then compared with 0, the difference expected if no change in performance were observed across the two scoring criteria. No differences in open-ended recall were observed at any delay within any age. In contrast, all of the comparisons of specific recall under the two scoring conditions indicated significant differences. In each of the nine cells resulting from the combination of three levels of age and three levels of delay, the children demonstrated significantly higher levels of memory performance in response to yes/no questions under the Standard Scoring Criterion than with the More Conservative Criterion. Further, as is also readily apparent in a comparison of Figures 4.2 and 4.4, the impact of the selection of a particular scoring criterion is greater among younger children than older children.

Implications of the results obtained through the use of the two alternative scoring criteria. The application of the More Conservative Criterion clearly indicates that the general patterns of effects reported by Ornstein, Gordon, and Larus (1992) and Baker-Ward, Gordon, et al. (1993) were not simply artifacts of a relatively liberal scoring system. The relatively conservative scoring system examined in this investigation removed items reported in response to "leading questions" from the computation of total recall and scored as incorrect features reported in conjunction with the acceptance of inaccurate descriptive information. The application of this criterion did not change the effects of age and specificity of probe revealed in the analyses. Further, levels of open-ended recall performance were comparable under the two scoring systems. The use of the alternative rules, however, did result in a noteworthy change in the observed performance: All of the children appeared more "competent" in responding to specific questions when the Standard Scoring Criterion was applied.

Although, with the exception of forgetting at some delays, the *pattern* of findings did not change when the alternative scoring criterion was applied, the overall *level* of performance was markedly altered. Further, this decrease in specific recall appeared to be the most dramatic among the 3-year-olds, reflecting their reliance on specific prompts (see also Dent & Stephenson, 1979). The 5- and 7-year-olds, in contrast, demonstrated a relatively modest, although still significant, decline in performance when the more stringent scoring criterion was applied to their data. Indeed, when the youngest children's memory performance as scored by the More Conservative Criterion is considered, our earlier description of their recall as "impressive" seems quite inappropriate.

Do these results call into question the use of 3-year-olds as witnesses in legal settings? On the one hand, given the limited extent to which they typically provide information spontaneously (see Klajner-Diamond, Wehrspann, & Steinhauer, 1987; Wehrspann et al., 1987), younger preschoolers may not be seen as credible witnesses. On the other hand, it should be noted that the information that 3-year-olds do provide in response to open-ended questions is quite accurate (Gordon & Follmer, 1994). However, little information may be forthcoming from a 3-year-old when she alone knows the particular details of the event in question, resulting in a greater dependence on specific forms of questioning. Further, it appears that the impact of fairly subtle changes in evaluating the accuracy of a child's responses to specific questions may be greater among young preschoolers, relative to children beyond kindergarten age. To the extent that variations in the real-world context within which a child's report is evaluated (such as more forceful instructions to the jury) have effects similar to those created by increased stringency in assessments of recall in research settings, particular care is indicated in presenting evidence involving only the responses of very young children to specific questions.

Consideration of the two criteria employed here suggests that information obtained in response to highly specific probes presented to the youngest children must be regarded very cautiously. Recent work conducted in our laboratory by Clubb and Follmer (1993) supports this interpretation. These researchers examined the retention functions across a 12-week period that were generated by 222 children included in three separate studies of memory for a visit to the doctor. As most of the recall demonstrated by the 77 3-year-olds in the combined sample was elicited by specific questions, the accuracy of their responses was of particular concern. Clubb and Follmer noted substantial variability in the recall performance of the 3-year-olds. Moreover, examination of patterns of performance on an individual basis enabled them to identify two subgroups of 3-year-olds who apparently experienced difficulty in adapting to the interview context. The first subgroup consisted of seven 3-year-olds who exhibited high probabilities of saying "no" to all types of specific questions, including those "lure" items addressing features of the physical examination that were not experienced; these children appeared to be in a "no" response set. Five other 3-year-olds tended to respond affirmatively to all specific questions, in a pattern characteristic of a "yes" response set. As would be expected, these apparent response biases had a profound impact on assessments of recall performance. When responses to total present features were tabulated, the children in the "no" response subgroup scored significantly below the mean for their age level, whereas those in the "yes" subgroup appeared to outperform even the 7-year-olds! Of interest, Clubb and Follmer found that the overall level of recall performance for the 3-year-olds did not appear to be altered by the presence of the two subgroups, because the artificially high performance of the "yes" group was offset by the lowered level of correct responding observed by the "no" subgroup. It is quite possible, however, that the ratio of children who appear to have a "yes" compared with a "no" response set could differ in other investigations, thus affecting overall recall performance. Future research efforts will examine the extent to which individual differences among children in temperament and other factors are related to apparent response biases as well as the stability of these patterns of performance. Nonetheless, it is clear that response bias is an important concern in assessing young children's competence in remembering. The possible presence of individual subjects with "yes" or "no" response sets should be evaluated in assessing group results in response to specific questions. If such subgroups are present in the sample, the impact on group performance of the data contributed by subjects who may "just say no" (or yes) to specific questions must be examined carefully. To avoid increasing the likelihood of false diagnoses of remembering, analyses should be repeated without the inclusion of the data derived from subgroups with apparent response sets.

We have concluded that the responses of young children, particularly 3-year-olds, should be interpreted with caution. It should be noted, however, that our advocacy of particular care in evaluating young children's cued-recall performance is not an indictment of such assessments. The following considerations are relevant in examining our results. First, the design of our interview protocol may have contributed to the generally poor specific recall performance of the younger children. As discussed above, the interviews used in our research are hierarchically structured, so that increasingly specific probes are presented. If a child does not spontaneously report a feature, she is presented with more directed but still open-ended questions, followed by increasingly specific probes when information is not reported. Because only information that has not been forthcoming in response to more general queries is requested through specific recall, our specific questioning may be directed only toward relatively weak memory traces. Hence the levels of responding that we observe may underestimate children's ability to respond to direct questions in interview contexts in which all information is requested through specific questions (e.g., see Saywitz et al., 1991). Second, although the presence of response bias is an important consideration in evaluating levels of specific recall, it should be noted that only a minority of the 3-year-olds examined by Clubb and Follmer—a total of 12 from a group of 77—appeared to demonstrate a response set. Hence, whereas both researchers and clinicians should be aware of the apparently increased likelihood of false positive or negative response among 3-year-olds relative to older children, the majority of young preschoolers do not appear to perseverate with "yes" or "no" answers.

Alternative Units of Analysis

Given the difficulties associated with the interpretation of children's responses to specific questions, it is clear that assessments of free recall in response to open-ended questions are particularly desirable. Although free recall does not present many of the concerns associated with cued recall, other methodological issues are relevant. Most significantly, researchers must determine just how free recall is to be implemented. The first step in devising a coding scheme is to determine the unit of analysis to be used in measuring recall, and this decision may have important consequences for characterizing memory performance and for subsequently integrating the results of different investigations.

As described above, the basic unit of analysis selected for use in our studies of children's memory for medical investigations is the *feature of the event*, defined as discrete acts performed by nurses or physicians and typically included in a well-child checkup. Within this framework, "doctor checks heart with stethoscope" would be considered one feature—that is, one unit of recall—and free recall is analyzed as the percentage of present features that were reported by the child in response to general (e.g., "What did the doctor do when you had your checkup?") questions. It should be emphasized, however, that this unit of analysis is only one possible choice. Indeed, another approach to the analysis of children's memory for medical procedures has been taken by Goodman and her colleagues (Goodman, Hirshman, Hepps, & Rudy, 1991) and by Saywitz et al. (1991), who have defined free recall in terms of the *units of information* contained in the child's verbal response to a very general probe. These units reflect the number of actions and descriptions reported by the child. For example, a child who reports, "The doctor listened to my heart," provides four units of information, one each for "doctor," "listened," "heart," and "my." Each unit of information can be further categorized as correct or incorrect when the details of the child's experience are known to the researchers.

These alternative approaches to the assessment of recall each offer distinct advantages. The use of units of information appears to be particularly appropriate in explorations of children's competency as witnesses. This measure is clearly sensitive to the degree of elaboration contained in the child's report, one of the three major criteria referenced by clinicians as important in judging the credibility of children's reports (Wehrspann et al., 1987). Although the extent of elaboration accompanying children's reports of features may be considered as a separate measure, as we have done in our more recent research (e.g., Gordon & Follmer, 1994; Gordon et al., 1993), the feature as a unit of analysis is not sensitive to elaboration. Further, the units of information measure appears to emphasize the child's fluency in providing a report. This emphasis may be particularly appropriate in investigating the extent to which aspects of the event or the interview increase a child's hesitancy in disclosing the details of her experience (e.g., Saywitz et al., 1991).

The feature as a unit of analysis, in contrast, appears to offer some advantages in examining questions related to the memory of an event. The set of specific features that describe an event is defined before memory for the event is examined. Hence the comparison of recall performance on different occasions permits the determination of specific components of information that are lost or weakened over time as well as the evaluation of the degree of consistency of the child's report. In addition, by referencing a predefined set of features, the relative completeness of the child's account, at least with reference to adults' perspective of the event, can be considered. In contrast, the use of units of information does not easily allow these assessments, because the event is not defined in terms of specific components. Hence the same number of units of information could be provided in two interviews that reflect very different content.

Clearly, the use of either of these units of analysis may be appropriate, given the questions under consideration in a particular investigation. But do the depictions of children's memory performance obtained through the application of the different assessment techniques correspond? To examine this question, we applied the scoring scheme used by Saywitz et al. (1991) to code units of information in free recall to the data obtained by Baker-Ward, Gordon, et al. (1993). We were primarily interested in examining the impact of the alternative coding technique on our characterization of free recall. However, similarities in the two investigations permit us to consider the generalizability of recall findings as well. Saywitz et al. were particularly interested in children's reports of genital contact, investigated within the context of a physical examination. Half of their subjects, however, experienced checkups that did not include genital touch and were similar to the physical examinations received by the subjects in our study. Moreover, both investigations included groups of 5- and 7-year-olds whose recall of the physical examination was assessed after a 1-week delay interval.

We returned to the original transcriptions of the interviews of the 5- and 7-year-olds in the 1-week delay condition in our earlier investigation, thus selecting groups corresponding to those included in Saywitz et al.'s study. We also modified our definition of general probes so that it would be consistent with that used by Saywitz and her colleagues. That is, we considered information provided in response to the very broad queries included in both investigations (e.g., "Tell me what the doctor did to check you.") but for this analysis did not consider items reported in response to our more focused but still open-ended probes (e.g., "Tell me what parts of your face the doctor checked."). We then rescored the children's open-ended recall in terms of the units of information provided in their reports, using the coding scheme devised by Saywitz et al. We also recoded free recall in terms of the percentage of features that were reported by the child in response to the most general prompts as defined by Saywitz et al. This represented a somewhat more rigorous definition of features reported in free recall than presented in our original report. The units of correct and incorrect information provided by the children, as well as the percentage of features reported in free recall, are shown in Table 4.1.

The data presented in Table 4.1 indicate that 5-year-olds report fewer correct units of information than 7-year-olds, as well as a smaller percentage of features, and that very little incorrect information is provided at either age level. These general impressions are consistent with the findings reported by Saywitz et al. for the group of subjects who did not experience genital contact during their examination. It should be noted, however, that the levels of performance when correct units of information are considered are rather divergent across the two investigations. The 5- and 7-year-olds in our sample reported 6.35 and 24.82 units of correct information, respectively. The corresponding data for the children in the nongenital examination condition in the

Table 4.1   Correct and Incorrect Units of Information and Percentage of Features
(and standard deviations) Contained in the Open-Ended Recall of 5- and
7-Year-Old Children in the 1-Week Delay Condition in the Reanalysis of
Baker-Ward, Gordon, Ornstein, Larus, and Clubb (1993)

Children	Correct Units	Incorrect Units	Features
5-year-olds ($n = 17$)	6.35 (5.13)	0.97 (1.48)	8.71 (7.33)
7-year-olds ($n = 14$)	24.82 (16.82)	0.64 (2.13)	24.50 (14.23)

Saywitz et al. study were 16.69 and 35.94 units at ages 5 and 7, respectively—a
standard deviation above the level of performance we observed. It seems likely
that this discrepancy in apparent levels of performance results from differences in the procedures employed in the two studies. As our investigation was
not designed to consider units of information, our interview procedures may
have limited the children's free recall in some instances. For example, when
the interviewer posed a follow-up question that asked for a particular elaborative detail, the child's prompted response could not be considered in this
assessment of free recall, although the information might have been forthcoming. Further, only information that could be verified is considered correct,
and our checklists, which were designed to record predefined features of the
examinations, were sometimes incomplete in that they did not include information concerning details of the examination or the setting reported by the
children. Given these considerations, the fact that the level of performance is
different in the two investigations is not surprising.

For the present purposes, the most relevant concern is the impact of the
particular mode of analysis employed in implementing free recall in the
assessment of memory performance. To examine this issue, we evaluated the
degree of correspondence in the rank orderings of children's levels of free
recall as determined through the use of the two alternative units of analysis:
features and information units. The Spearman correlation coefficient we
obtained was quite impressive: rho = .91, $p < .0001$. Saywitz (personal communication) has also noted a convergence in the depictions of children's recall
of a videotaped event obtained when the same protocols were coded in terms
of units of information as defined above or with reference to an a priori
determination of the number of possible propositions contained in a complete account of the event (see Saywitz & Snyder, 1993, for a brief description

of this propositional analytic system). Hence it seems unlikely that general findings obtained in investigations of free recall are simply artifacts of the particular coding schemes selected by researchers. Although procedural differences across investigations may result in different descriptions of the level of memory performance, patterns in recall appear to be robust across variations in coding methodology.

Implications for Scoring and Interpreting Children's Memory Performance

It is clear that even moderate changes in the rules used for scoring recall can result in substantial differences in the likelihood that young children will be credited with reporting information in response to specific questions. Further, given the youngest subjects' reliance on memory probes, these changes would appear to have the greatest impact on the characterizations of their performance. The generalization of findings concerning children's responses to specific questions thus requires considerable attention to the methodologies involved in different investigations. In contrast, our examination of free-recall performance suggests that children's spontaneous reports are quite robust. Open-ended recall was unaffected by the stringency with which the information was evaluated and appeared to be quite consistent across assessments using different methodologies. The results of our reanalyses would suggest that even fairly significant changes in coding schemes are unlikely to affect the impressions of children's memory competence as indicated in their free recall performance. Further, even changing the unit of analysis used to implement recall resulted in consistent rank orderings of children's performance. Although other aspects of the interview context may affect children's recall performance (see, e.g., Gordon, Schroeder, Ornstein, & Baker-Ward, in press), variations in the coding and scoring of open-ended recall should not be expected to impose major limitations on the generalizability of recall findings.

Given the impact of the scoring criterion selected on assessments of specific recall, should researchers use relatively liberal or conservative scoring techniques? It would be inappropriate, of course, to advocate the use of one scoring system over another in any absolute sense. It should be noted that the selection of a scoring criterion is clearly an aspect of cognitive diagnosis, involving careful assessments of the relative risks of false positive and false negative classifications (see Flavell, 1985; Ornstein et al., 1991). Indeed, the particular purpose for obtaining children's reports must determine, in part, the selection of a criterion for assessing the accuracy of the information provided by children (see Garbarino & Stott, 1991). In some real-world settings, the need to generate all possible leads from a child (e.g., in an inquiry phase of a legal proceeding) mandates a lenient decision rule for determining what constitutes useful information. In others, the grave ramifications of mistakes require certainty "beyond a reasonable doubt."

Just as the nature of the issue under consideration must determine the choice of the coding system, the purposes of the investigation should dictate the stringency with which children's reports should be evaluated. In some research settings, it may be highly appropriate to consider information obtained through leading questions and even to incorporate recognition measures in assessing memory (e.g., Geddie, 1993). Such techniques enable the examination of basic questions concerning the operation of the memory system. In other circumstances, only information provided spontaneously or accompanied by elaboration may be considered as evidence of recall. Such rigid assessments may be most appropriate when issues concerning the credibility of children's reports are central to the investigation. It should be noted that researchers, unlike jurors, have the luxury of assessing memory performance repeatedly, through the means of alternative criteria. In some cases, it may be desirable to use multiple criteria to examine directly the implications of alternative scoring systems. Patterns of results that are not robust across methodological variations should be interpreted cautiously, if at all. Careful consideration should be given to the extent to which levels of performance (and subsequent impressions of children's memory competence) are affected by changes in the selection of dependent measures.

Ultimately, of course, knowledge regarding children's event memory is accrued through the careful review of many investigations representing converging evidence obtained through multiple methodologies. Coding criteria, like statistical analyses, are useful in determining the evidence that can be admitted for consideration, not in determining the truth of the findings. The rules selected for scoring recall thus function as a judge, determining what is admissible for consideration; the scientific community remains the jury, charged with getting to the truth of the matter.[2] Good outcomes, of course, depend on the successful functioning of both of these components. Frequent and public review of rules of evidence, we believe, must be an important part of scientific as well as judicial decision making.

Notes

1. Due to space limitations, these statistical findings are briefly reported. Complete results are available from the authors.

2. This analogy was originally presented by Mark Appelbaum in an introductory statistics class held at the University of North Carolina in Chapel Hill during the fall semester of 1978.

5

Aware and Unaware Uses of Memories
of Postevent Suggestions

D. STEPHEN LINDSAY

VALERIE GONZALES

KAREN ESO

One of the difficulties people face when trying to remember a particular past event is discriminating between memories of that event and memories of other, related events that may come to mind during the attempt to remember. For example, when trying to remember what a friend told you yesterday, memories of what that friend told you the day before, or of what another friend told you that day, may come to mind. Sometimes memories from one source are mistaken as memories from another source (e.g., we think we are remembering something Liz said when we are really remembering something Kathy said). This problem may be particularly great for eyewit-

AUTHORS' NOTE: The research reported here was supported by a Natural Science and Engineering Research Council operating grant to the first author. We thank Vincenza Gruppuso for her comments and suggestions on an earlier version of this chapter.

nesses called on to testify in court, because they are likely to have many memories that are directly related to the crime but that are not memories of witnessing it per se. One source of such memories is the witness's own thoughts and statements about the crime (e.g., the witness may have made inferences about nonwitnessed aspects of the crime, or used a combination of remembering and fantasizing to imagine various alternative outcomes of the crime or to elaborate on and improve stories told to friends). Another origin of nonwitnessed memories is external sources, such as other witnesses' descriptions of the crime, newspaper accounts, or suggestive questions presented by police or lawyers.

The research presented in this chapter focuses on the question of how memories derived from external sources can influence eyewitness reports by children and adults. Psychological research in this area has a long history, dating back to turn-of-the-century work by Binet and others (see Ceci & Bruck, 1993a). Loftus and her colleagues (e.g., Loftus, Miller, & Burns, 1978) are credited with developing the modern approach to studying eyewitness suggestibility. The basic procedure involves three stages: witnessing an event, receiving postevent misinformation about details in the event (often misleading suggestions embedded in questions or in a narrative description of the witnessed event), and taking a memory test. For example, in studies reported by McCloskey and Zaragoza (1985), subjects first viewed a lengthy slide sequence that depicted an incident in which a maintenance man stole things from an office. For some subjects, one of the slides showed the maintenance man holding a hammer, and some of these subjects later read a narrative description that mentioned that the maintenance man had been holding a wrench. Subjects were later tested on their memory for which tool had been seen in the slides. Variations of this procedure have been reported in a large number of experiments (see Ceci & Bruck, 1993a).

We know from this research that misleading suggestions about details in a witnessed event often cause subjects to err when later questioned about those details. And we know that this "misinformation effect" (Loftus, 1979) is often larger in young children than in older children or adults (for review, see Ceci & Bruck, 1993a). What is less clear is *why* misled subjects perform more poorly than controls, and *why* young children are especially vulnerable to misleading suggestions.

One class of explanations for the misinformation effect focuses on the possibility of "aware" uses of memories of the postevent information. That is, when subjects base responses on memories of the postevent information, they may be aware that they are doing so. Aware uses of memory of postevent suggestions can be divided into two subtypes. In one subtype, subjects remember the postevent information and its source but do not remember the original event in detail and do not realize that the postevent suggestion is inconsistent with what they witnessed (e.g., "I don't remember what kind of tool was shown in the slides, but I remember that the experimenter later mentioned it was a wrench, so I'll say 'wrench.' "). In the second subtype of aware uses of postevent information, subjects recollect both the suggested detail and the original detail but base their responses on the former. Subjects might make such errors because they place greater trust in their recollections of the postevent information than in their recollections of the event itself (e.g., "I thought I saw a hammer in the slides, but the experimenter later said it was a wrench, and the experimenter must know better than I, so I'll say 'wrench.' ") or because they wish to comply with the perceived desires of the experimenter (e.g., "I know I saw a hammer in the event, but the experimenter evidently wants me to say it was a wrench."). The defining feature of aware uses of memories of suggestions is that when subjects base answers on the postevent information they are aware that they are doing so.

A second class of explanations for the misinformation effect focuses on the possibility of what Lindsay and Johnson (e.g., 1987, 1989a, 1989b) and Zaragoza and her coworkers (e.g., Zaragoza & Lane, 1994) have referred to as "source-monitoring" errors. According to the source-monitoring account, subjects may be genuinely confused about the origins of their memories of suggested details and think that they are remembering something they saw in the event when they activate memories of something they heard or read after the event.

Obviously, the explanation of the misinformation effect has important implications for the practical application of research findings in this area. If the misinformation effect reflects aware uses of memory of postevent information, the research may have little relevance to legal testimony; under oath and cross-examination, witnesses would be able to tell the court what they remember seeing in the event in question, "gating out" or qualifying material that they remember as hearsay. On the other hand, if the misinformation effect reflects genuine memory confusions in which people truly believe that they remember seeing things that were merely suggested to them, witnesses would sometimes confidently testify to suggested details as things they had seen with their own eyes.

The answer to the question about the nature of the misinformation effect also has implications for our understanding of young children's susceptibility to misleading suggestions. If the misinformation effect reflects aware uses of memory, one might frame hypotheses about the developmental pattern in terms of age-related changes in trust of authority figures and susceptibility to demand characteristics. On the other hand, if the misinformation effect reflects confusions about the origins of memories, one might focus on developmental changes in source-monitoring processes as an approach to understanding young children's susceptibility to suggestions.

In recent years, it has become clear that both aware uses of memory of postevent suggestions and genuine source-monitoring confusions contribute to the misinformation effect. Thus, as is so often the case, there is no single answer to the question about the nature of the misinformation effect. Likewise, there is no single answer to the question about the cognitive mechanisms that underlie developmental changes in suggestibility. Instead, developments in a number of cognitive, linguistic, and social skills contribute to age-related changes in the misinformation effect (Ceci & Bruck, 1993a; Poole & Lindsay, 1994).

In the following pages, we briefly review theories and evidence concerning source monitoring in adults and children, and describe evidence of the role of source-monitoring confusions in the misinformation effect. We then describe new research aimed at separately estimating the roles of aware and unaware uses of memories of postevent information in misinformation effects in adults and children.

Source Monitoring

According to the source-monitoring approach, memory records rarely include abstract, propositionlike tags or labels that directly specify their sources (e.g., where and when the event occurred, what people and objects were involved in the event, through what media and sensory modalities the event was perceived). Rather, memories consist of records of the cognitive processes that gave rise to and constituted the experience itself. As such, they include various kinds of information, such as information about the perceptual characteristics of the event or one's thoughts and feelings while experiencing the event. The sources of event memories are identified via decision-making processes performed when the events are recollected. Those decision-making processes use the available information, together with more general knowledge available in memory, to attribute the memory to a specific source.

People sometimes consciously struggle to identify the source of a recollection, but more often such attributions are made without conscious awareness of any decision-making processes. Thus, for example, you may identify an idea that comes to mind as a memory of something Sam said because it includes information about the sound of the voice and the appearance of the speaker, and you recognize the speaker's voice and appearance in the activated memory information just as you would recognize them in ongoing perception. Subjectively, this usually feels like simply remembering something Sam said—that is, the attribution process is made quickly and automatically.

Source-monitoring errors occur when a memory derived from one source is misattributed to another source (e.g., you recall something you heard Kathy say, and mistakenly remember the speaker as Liz). The likelihood of source misattributions varies with the amount and nature of the source-specific information in the memory record, the discriminability of different potential sources, and the stringency of the decision processes and criteria used during remembering. Thus, for example, you are more likely to mistakenly remember Liz saying something you actually heard from Kathy if the memory record is vague rather than clear, if the two people are similar to one another rather than dissimilar, or if the source attribution is made quickly and automatically rather than with careful deliberation.

Empirical support for the source-monitoring approach comes from studies in which subjects are exposed to information from two or more different sources and are later asked to identify the sources of particular pieces of information (e.g., to remember which of two speakers had made a particular statement or performed a particular act; see Johnson, Hashtroudi, & Lindsay, 1993, for a review). Such experiments have shown that source-monitoring errors are more frequent when potential memory sources are similar to one another in terms of their perceptual properties, modality of presentation, semantic content, or cognitive operations (orienting tasks). For example, subjects are more likely to misremember which of two people had talked about a particular event if the two storytellers were similar looking than if they were dissimilar (Lindsay, Johnson, & Kwon, 1991). Hasher and Griffin (1978) and Raye, Johnson, and Taylor (1980) reported studies indicating that the likelihood of source-monitoring errors varies with the stringency of decision-making criteria during recollection. Source discrimination has also been shown to improve with the amount of time subjects are given to respond to test probes (Johnson, Kounios, & Reeder, 1992) and with full as opposed to divided attention at study (Jacoby & Kelley, 1992; Jacoby, Woloshyn, & Kelley, 1989) and at test (Jacoby, 1991). In sum, there is considerable evidence to support the hypothesis that memories are attributed to particular sources via decision-making processes performed in the course of recollection.

Source-Monitoring Development

The relationship between age and source-monitoring ability is complex. Children as young as 5 years of age are as competent as adults at identifying the sources of their recollections in some situations, yet children as old as 9 years perform more poorly than adults in other situations. For example, Foley and Johnson (1985; Foley, Johnson, & Raye, 1983) found that young children performed as well as adults when asked to remember which of two other people had done particular things, but that children were more likely than adults to make errors when asked to remember whether they had actually done particular things or had merely imagined themselves doing those things.

Findings such as these led Foley and her colleagues (e.g., Foley, Santini, & Sopasakis, 1989) to propose that young children have special difficulty discriminating between actual and imagined self-generated acts ("Realization Judgments"). Broadening this hypothesis, Lindsay et al. (1991) argued that young children may be more likely than adults to confuse memories from different sources *whenever* those sources are highly similar to one another. Consistent with this hypothesis, Lindsay et al. (Experiment 3) found that, compared with adults, 8-year-old children were more likely to mistake memories of actions they had merely imagined another person performing as memories of actions they had actually seen that same person performing. Presumably, the fact that the same person was involved in the witnessed and imagined actions made the memories for the two types of events relatively similar and hence confusable, especially for the children.

A number of factors may contribute to the pattern of developmental change and invariance in source monitoring. It may be that children's ongoing experience (and hence the memory records of their experience) differs from adults' in ways that affect some kinds of source-monitoring discriminations but not others. That is, children and adults may attend to different aspects of events or may differently elaborate on them. Alternatively, it may be that the kinds of memory records that quickly and easily come to mind when remembering differ for children and adults. Finally, perhaps the most likely explanation is that age-related changes in source monitoring may be due to differences in the retrieval strategies children and adults use when they are uncertain of the source of a memory (e.g., Ackerman, 1985). That is, when adults feel uncertain about the source of a memory, they may perform effortful and strategic searches for additional memory information, whereas children may fail to do so. Developmental differences in strategic retrieval and conscious decision-making processes could contribute to age by condition interactions because the more difficult the discrimination the more likely that accurate performance would require special retrieval strategies.

Source monitoring is not a single skill that a child acquires at a particular age. Rather, source monitoring involves decisions about a number of different aspects of event memories (remembering who, remembering where, remembering how, remembering when, and so on). Furthermore, accurate source monitoring depends on a number of kinds of mental activities, such as perceptual analysis during encoding and retrieval of memory records and decision-making processes at test. Thus it is likely that developmental changes in source monitoring are gradual rather than sudden and domain specific rather than general. These considerations also suggest that source-monitoring development will reflect individual differences along a number of dimensions.

Source Monitoring and Suggestibility

According to the source-monitoring approach, memory records of postevent suggestions are sometimes misidentified as memories of the witnessed event itself. Memories of suggestions may be especially likely to be mistaken for memories of the event when source attributions are made quickly and automatically, without conscious awareness of decision-making processes, but such errors may also occur when subjects consciously deliberate about the source of a remembered detail. Further, source-monitoring errors may be more likely when only the suggested detail is recollected, because retrieval of both the suggested detail and the event detail would likely lead people consciously to deliberate about the sources of those memories, but source misattributions can nonetheless occur when both the suggested detail and the event detail come to mind. Finally, source-monitoring errors may contribute to memory impairment effects, in that, when a memory of a suggested detail pops to mind and is misidentified as a memory of an event detail, subjects are unlikely to continue searching memory for potentially retrievable information about the event detail.

The source-monitoring approach proposes that factors that increase the similarity between memories of the event and memories of suggestions increase the likelihood that memories of suggestions will be misidentified as memories of the event. By this view, the procedures typically employed in studies of suggestibility create good conditions for illusory recollections of eyewitnessing because of the similarities between the event and the postevent information: The event and the postevent information concern the same topic and are usually presented close together in time, in the same environment, by the same experimenter, and so on. These factors may lead subjects to experience compelling illusory recollections of witnessing things that were in fact merely suggested to them.

Suggestibility on source-monitoring tests. One straightforward way to assess the possibility that subjects sometimes misidentify memories of suggested details as memories of witnessed details is to ask them, at test, to specify the origins of their memories. For example, Lindsay and Johnson (1989a) and Zaragoza and Koshmider (1989) asked subjects to indicate, for each item on the test, whether they remember encountering that item only in the event, only in the postevent information, in both sources, or not at all. Other subjects were tested with a more standard recognition test, in which they were asked to make a yes/no judgment about whether they remembered seeing each item in the event. Subjects tested with the recognition test often claimed to have seen suggested items in the event. In contrast, those tested with the source-monitoring test correctly attributed their memories of suggested details to the postevent information. Lindsay and Johnson (1989a) viewed these findings as evidence that subjects tested with recognition tests sometimes misidentify memories of suggestions as memories of the event because they are using lax or inappropriate source-monitoring criteria. The source-monitoring instructions led subjects to use more stringent criteria and thereby correctly attribute memories of suggested details to the postevent information.

Follow-up studies demonstrated that even subjects tested with source-monitoring tests sometimes claim to have seen suggested details in the event, provided conditions make it difficult to discriminate between memories of the event and memories of the postevent information. For example, Zaragoza and her colleagues have shown that illusory memories of eyewitnessing are more likely to be obtained on a source-monitoring test if subjects are instructed to form visual images of the postevent information when it is presented (Carris, Zaragoza, & Lane, 1992) or if subjects are required to make their source-monitoring responses quickly (Zaragoza & Lane, 1991, 1994).

Jacoby's opposition procedure. Source-monitoring tests do not altogether elimi-nate the possibility that demand characteristics may contribute to apparent source-monitoring confusions. Subjects are led to believe that everything in the postevent information was also in the event, and they may wish to show that they paid attention to *both* the event and the postevent information. This may motivate subjects to claim that they remember things from both sources even if they really only feel that they remember them from the postevent information. Consistent with this demand characteristics account, subjects in these studies very rarely claimed that suggested details had been seen only in the event; rather, when they erred they claimed that suggested details had been in *both* the event and the postevent information.

More compelling evidence that subjects sometimes mistake memories of postevent suggestions as memories of the event itself comes from a study using Jacoby's (e.g., Jacoby et al., 1989) "opposition" procedure (Lindsay, 1990). In this experiment, conditions were such that the effect of knowingly using memories of the postevent information would be opposite to the effect of genuine memory source confusions. This was done by correctly informing subjects at test that the postevent information included misleading sugges-tions and that it did not include *any* correct answers to the test questions. That is, subjects were told *not* to report anything they remembered from the postevent narrative on the memory test, because any such answers would be wrong.

Acquisition conditions were manipulated such that remembering the sug-gestions and their source would be very easy for some subjects and relatively difficult for other subjects. In the Easy condition, subjects received the sug-gestions 2 days after viewing the event, minutes before taking the test, and under conditions that differed from those in which they viewed the event. Thus at test it would be easy for these subjects to remember the suggestions and their source. Subjects in the Difficult condition, on the other hand, received the suggestions minutes after viewing the event, under very similar conditions, 2 days before taking the test. Thus, at the time of the test, it would be relatively difficult for these subjects to differentiate between memories of the postevent narrative and memories of the event itself.

Subjects were given a cued-recall test with six questions: Three questions concerned details about which suggestions had been given and three questions served as controls. Before taking the test, subjects were explicitly and emphati-cally told *not* to report *anything* they remembered from the postevent infor-mation. It is clear that subjects understood and attempted to follow the injunction against reporting information from the postevent narrative, because subjects in the Easy condition showed no tendency to report suggested details more often on misled than control items. Nonetheless, subjects in the Difficult condition reported suggested details as things they recalled seeing in the event 27% of the time. Even though these subjects were specifically trying to avoid reporting memories from the postevent narrative, they frequently did report them.

This "opposition" study also provided evidence that misleading suggestions can impair subjects' ability to remember the corresponding event details. Although subjects in the Easy condition were able to identify the source of their memories of suggested details (and so did not erroneously report seeing them in the event), the misleading suggestions nonetheless hampered their ability to report event details: Correct recall of event details was significantly lower on misled items than on control items. Correct recall of event details was significantly impaired by suggestions even among those subjects in the Easy condition who never reported *any* suggested details.

Estimating Aware and Unaware Uses of Postevent Suggestions

As argued by McCloskey and Zaragoza (1985), and consistent with the results from the opposition test described above, standard tests of the misinformation effect overestimate genuine memory source confusions, because on the standard test aware uses of memories of the suggestions also contribute to reports of suggested details. On the other hand, the opposition procedure probably underestimates memory confusions. This is because, under the opposition instructions, even when misled subjects genuinely believe they remember seeing a suggested detail in the event, they will not use it as a test response if they also remember that it was in the postevent information. Comments made by Lindsay's (1990) subjects during debriefing indicated that the opposition procedure did underestimate source confusions: A number of subjects made statements such as "I could have sworn I saw a wrench in the slides, but I also knew I heard 'wrench' afterward, so I didn't write it down."

Jacoby (1991) recently introduced a technique, termed the *process dissociation procedure,* that allows one to obtain separate estimates of the simultaneous contributions of aware and unaware uses of memory to test responses (see Jacoby, Lindsay, & Toth, 1992, for a review). The work reported below applied that procedure to the misinformation effect.

In the standard misinformation procedure, subjects may base their test responses on the postevent information either because they knowingly remember it as part of the postevent narrative and assume it to be a valid basis for responding or, when they don't remember the actual source, because they believe they remember it from the event itself. This may be written as an equation:

$$p(\text{sugg} \mid \text{standard}) = \text{Narrative} + (1 - \text{Narrative}) \cdot \text{Event}$$

In the opposition procedure, in contrast, subjects should base their test response on the postevent information only if they do not remember that its source was the narrative and believe they remember it from the event itself. This too may be written as an equation:

$$p(\text{sugg} \mid \text{opposition}) = (1 - \text{Narrative}) \cdot \text{Event}$$

By doing an experiment that includes both the standard and the opposition tests, one can use these equations to obtain an estimate of the contributions of aware and unaware uses of memory for the postevent information. Subtracting the observed probability of using misleading suggestions as answers in the opposition condition from that in the standard condition yields an estimate of the contribution of aware uses of memories of postevent information. Using that estimate and simple algebra, one can calculate an estimate of the contribution of unaware uses of memories of suggestions. This procedure is illustrated in the following study.

Experiment 1: Adults' Suggestibility

Subjects viewed the McCloskey and Zaragoza (1985) slide sequence, which depicts an incident in which a maintenance man steals some things from an office. Subjects then listened to a tape-recorded narrative that reviewed the incident depicted in the slides. The narrative included misleading suggestions about three details in the slides and generic information about three other details (e.g., some subjects saw a hammer in one of the slides, and some of these later heard it described as a wrench, whereas others later heard it described as a tool). After a filled 15-minute delay interval, subjects were given two memory tests in succession. Each test asked them to recall the same six details from the slides (three misinformation target items and three controls in a random order). The instructions for the first test simply asked subjects to recall what they had seen in the slides (e.g., "What kind of *tool* did the man hide the calculator under in his tool box?"). Immediately after completing the first test, subjects were given the instructions for the second test. Subjects were informed that the narrative had included misleading suggestions and that there was no question on the test for which the narrative had mentioned the correct answer. Subjects were strongly and repeatedly instructed not to write *anything* they remembered from the tape-recorded narrative as an answer on the second test.

On the standard test, subjects reported seeing suggested items 55% of the time, compared with 12% on control items, $F(1, 267) = 296.37$, $p < .001$. Further, correct recall was poorer on misled items ($M = 15\%$) than on control items ($M = 24\%$), $F(1, 267) = 22.77$, $p < .001$. Thus the results on the standard test replicate the misinformation effect. On the opposition test, in contrast, subjects reported seeing suggested items only 13% of the time, which was statistically equivalent to the 11% (guessing) frequency of those answers on control items, $F < 1$. Further, on the opposition test, correct recall was equivalent on misled items ($M = 24\%$) and control items ($M = 23\%$), $F < 1$. Thus the same subjects who showed substantial misinformation effects on the standard test, in terms of both failing to report what they really did see and erroneously reporting what was merely suggested to them, did not appear to make such errors on the subsequent opposition test.

At first glance, these data would suggest that all of the effects of misleading suggestions in this study reflected aware uses of the postevent information: Once given the opposition instructions, subjects did not give suggested answers more often on misled items than on control items. As noted above, however, in the opposition condition, aware uses of memory of the suggestions may mask unaware uses of memory. That is, when subjects remember the source of memories of misleading suggestions, they can avoid reporting them on the opposition test, and avoidance of suggested details whose source is remembered would tend to push reports of suggested details below the guessing baseline. Indeed, perfect memory of the suggestions and their source would lead subjects to *never* use suggested details on the test, and consequently would push use of suggested details on misled items below the use of suggested details on control items (i.e., below the guessing baseline). Thus the fact that the frequency of reporting suggested details was equivalent for misled and control items does not necessarily mean that unaware uses of memory did not contribute to answering on the misled items.

The equations described above can be used to calculate estimates of the contributions of aware and unaware uses of memories of postevent information to responding. To obtain an index of the contribution of aware uses of memory of the misleading suggestions, the probability of answering with a suggestion on misled items on the opposition test (which should occur only when subjects do not remember that the postevent narrative was the source of those memories and believe that the event itself was the source) is subtracted from the probability of answering with a suggestion on misled items on the standard test (which may be based either on aware or on unaware uses of memories from the postevent narrative; .55 − .13 = .42). That is, in this study, aware uses of memory of the postevent suggestions contributed to responding on misinformation targets about 42% of the time. It is clear that subjects knew the source of these suggested answers, because when they were instructed to avoid reporting things from the postevent information, they did not report those items.

Given this estimate of the contribution of aware uses of memory of the misleading suggestions to responding, one can obtain an index of the contribution of unaware uses of memory of the suggestions using the equations described above and simple algebra. The equations hold that on the opposition test subjects will use suggested answers on misled items only if they fail to remember that the source of those answers was the postevent information and believe that their source was the event itself ([1 − Narrative] • Event). The observed probability of giving suggested answers on the opposition test was .13, and the estimate of aware uses of memories derived from the narrative was .42. Hence the estimate of unaware uses of memory, uncorrected for guessing, is

$$.13 \: / \: (1 - .42) = .22$$

This estimate must be corrected for the guessing baseline on the opposition test (i.e., the probability of generating a suggested answer in the control condition, which can only reflect guessing), which was .11. Thus approximately 11% of the time unaware uses of memories of the postevent information contributed to responding on misled items, even on the opposition test.

In sum, even though subjects did not more often report suggested details on misled items than on control items on the opposition test, unaware uses of memories of suggested details nonetheless contributed to responding on misled items on that test. Under the opposition instructions, unaware use of memories of suggestions is masked by the countervailing influence of aware memory of postevent suggestions. In this particular experiment, the combined influences of aware and unaware influences of memory of postevent information balanced each other out and therefore led to equivalent report rates for misled and control items. Unaware uses of memory of suggestions nonetheless contributed to responding on the opposition test: Suggested answers often came to mind, and about 11% of the time subjects were unaware of the true source of those answers.

Experiment 2: Children's Suggestibility

Whereas Experiment 1 used a within-subjects design for the test factor, our study with preschool and third-grade children used a between-subjects design (i.e., some children were given a standard memory test and others were given the opposition instructions). Further, in addition to age and the test instruction factors, we manipulated the timing of the presentation of the misinformation.

The materials were modeled on Ceci, Toglia, and Ross's (1987) "Loren" story. All subjects were told a story about a morning in the life of a little girl named Loren. The story was illustrated with nine drawings depicting various scenes in the story. Four of the pictures included critical details, all of which were mentioned in the accompanying story in generic terms (e.g., the story referred to Loren showing a toy to a friend, and the corresponding picture showed Loren holding a ball, a toy truck, or a doll).

All children were tested 3 days later. Misinformation was given either the day after presentation of the illustrated story and hence 2 days before the test (low-recency/low-discriminability condition) or 3 days later immediately before the test (high-recency/high-discriminability condition). The experimenter reminded the child of the story in general terms, then reviewed the details of the story, giving misleading suggestions about two of the critical details and generic information about the other two critical details (counterbalanced across subjects in each condition).

Children were tested individually by a new experimenter. In the standard condition, the experimenter explained that she understood that the child had heard a story and seen pictures about a little girl named Loren, but that she (the experimenter) did not know much about what happened in the story. (This was true in that the tester did not know what version of the illustrations individual children had seen or what misinformation they had received.)

Children were invited to recall whatever they could about the Loren story. They were then prompted with specific questions, beginning with easy-to-answer filler questions and proceeding to questions about the critical details (e.g., "One picture showed Loren feeding her pet. What kind of pet did you see in the picture?"). Finally, each child performed a three-alternative, forced-choice recognition test for each of the four critical details. The test required the child to select between the illustration he or she had actually seen, an illustration consistent with the misleading suggestion, and an illustration that differed from both the seen and the suggested illustrations.

In the opposition condition, the experimenter explained that the other experimenter, who had talked to the child about the Loren story (during the misinformation session), had accidentally said some things that were wrong. The tester took pains to communicate to the child that responses should not be based on anything the other experimenter had said. The rest of the test was the same as in the standard condition.

The preschool children ranged in age from 45 to 78 months (mean = 62.9 months, or about 5.25 years). The third graders ranged in age from 98 to 130 months (mean = 107.3 months, or about 8.75 years). There were 24 preschoolers and from 15 to 20 third graders in each condition. Only data from the picture recognition test are reported here. Those results are presented in Table 5.1.

Our interest focuses on how often subjects based their test responses on the misleading suggestions. Therefore we compared the proportion of recognition trials concerning misinformation targets on which subjects selected the picture that corresponded to the suggestion with the proportion of trials concerning control items on which subjects selected one of the two incorrect pictures (i.e., on control items, the score was the proportion of control items on which subjects selected either of the incorrect alternatives divided by 2). These data, which are depicted in Figure 5.1, were analyzed in a mixed-models analysis of variance, with age (preschool versus third grade), timing of the suggestions (2 days before the test versus immediately before the test), and test instructions (standard versus opposition) as the between-subjects factors and item type (misled versus control) as the repeated measure. The alpha level was .05, except where otherwise noted.

Preschoolers erred slightly more often than did third graders, although this effect fell short of statistical reliability, $F(1, 158) = 3.30$, $MSe = 0.043$, $p < .08$. Children in both age groups showed a reliable suggestibility effect; they more often selected the picture corresponding to a suggestion when they had been

Table 5.1   Three-Alternative Forced-Choice Recognition Performance (proportions)

Age and Condition	Misled Items			Control Items	
	Correct	Suggested	Other	Correct	Other[a]
Preschoolers					
High recency/discriminability					
Standard	.583	.354	.063	.771	.115
Opposition	.750	.146	.083	.920	.042
Low recency/discriminability					
Standard	.792	.188	.021	.938	.031
Opposition	.896	.104	.000	.875	.063
Third Graders					
High recency/discriminability					
Standard	.700	.300	.000	.925	.037
Opposition	.806	.194	.000	.972	.014
Low recency/discriminability					
Standard	.967	.067	.000	.967	.034
Opposition	.941	.029	.029	.941	.029

a. These values are the mean proportion of times subjects selected either of the two incorrect response alternatives on control items divided by 2.

given that suggestion (i.e., on target items) than when they had not (control items), $F(1, 158) = 29.15$, $MSe = 0.045$. Importantly, there was no hint of an interaction between age and item type; although third graders tended to outperform preschoolers in general terms, both age groups were equally affected by misleading suggestions, $F < 1$.

Children in both age groups performed more poorly when the misleading suggestions were given immediately before the test than when they were given 2 days earlier, $F(1, 158) = 12.57$, $MSe = 0.043$. As expected, there was a reliable interaction between timing of the misinformation and item type; the difference between misled and control items was greater when suggestions were given immediately before the test than when they were given 2 days earlier, $F(1, 158) = 8.68$, $MSe = 0.045$. Thus the recency of the suggestions affected responses concerning misled items, but not responses concerning control items.

Most important, both age groups benefited from the opposition instructions, in that suggestibility was reliably lower when children were told not to base their responses on what they had heard during the misinformation session, $F(1, 158) = 7.37$, $MSe = 0.043$. As expected, test instructions interacted

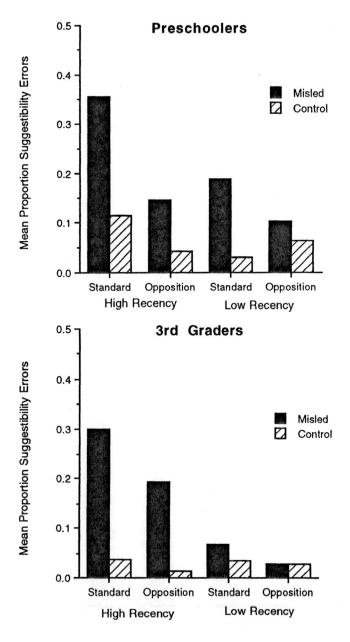

Figure 5.1. Proportion of subjects who based their test responses on misleading suggestions.

with item type; the opposition instructions substantially lowered errors on misinformation target items but had no reliable effect on control items, $F(1, 158) = 3.75$, $MSe = 0.045$, $p < .056$. Finally, there was a nonsignificant tendency toward an interaction between timing of the misinformation and test instructions, in that the difference between the standard and opposition test instructions tended to be larger when the suggestions were given immediately before the test than when they were given 2 days earlier, $F(1, 158) = 2.92$, $MSe = 0.043$, $p < .09$.

Several factors may contribute to the effects of the timing of the misinformation (e.g., greater effects of suggestions and of test instructions when the misinformation was given immediately before the test than when it was given 2 days earlier). It may be that some children simply forgot the misleading suggestions they had been given 2 days before the test. This seems unlikely, however, because, if the effect was due to forgetting, one might expect more forgetting, and consequently a greater reduction of the effect of suggestions, with delay among the younger subjects. In fact, however, the decrease in the effect of suggestions as a function of delay was greater for third graders than for preschoolers (although the three-way interaction between age, item type, and timing of suggestions was not reliable), $F(1, 158) = 1.96$, $MSe = 0.045$, $p < .17$. An alternative explanation of the effect of the timing of the misinformation is that the children more often detected discrepancies between what they had seen in the pictures and what was suggested during the misinformation session if the suggestions were given the day after the pictures were seen rather than 2 days later. Previous research indicates that discrepancy detection reduces suggestibility effects (e.g., Tousignant, Hall, & Loftus, 1986).

Overall, the results indicate that children were more affected by recent misleading suggestions than by ones that had been presented 2 days earlier, and that children given the opposition instructions can sometimes "gate out" suggested answers. Importantly, however, even under the opposition instructions, children of both age groups demonstrated a reliable suggestibility effect: Although these children were expressly told not to base any of their test responses on anything they had heard during the misinformation session, on target items they selected the picture compatible with the misleading suggestions 12% of the time (compared with 4% of the time on control items), $F(1, 81) = 7.04$, $MSe = 0.038$. This tendency was especially great when suggestions were given immediately before the test: Despite the opposition instructions, children in this condition based their responses on the misinformation an average of 17% of the time. These suggestibility effects were obtained even

Table 5.2   Estimates of the Contributions of Aware and Unaware Uses of Memory for Postevent Information

Age and Condition	Aware	Unaware
Preschoolers		
High recency/discriminability	.21	.14
Low recency/discriminability	.08	.04
Third graders		
High recency/discriminability	.11	.20
Low recency/discriminability	.04	.00

NOTE: The estimate of the contribution of unaware uses of memory was corrected for the guessing rate by subtracting the mean proportion of trials on which subjects selected one of the incorrect response alternatives on control items.

though the children demonstrated excellent memory for which pictures they had seen when they were not given misleading suggestions (an average of 91% accurate on control items).

The process dissociation equations were used to calculate estimates of aware and unaware uses of memory of the postevent information among children of each age group in the two delay conditions. Those estimates are shown in Table 5.2. In the current experiment, the estimates of the contributions of aware and unaware uses of memory are crude approximations at best. Each subject received only two misleading suggestions, and variability within conditions was quite high. Further, we cannot ascertain whether or not all subjects understood and attempted to follow the opposition instructions (although it is clear that subjects as a group were quite responsive to them). Thus for some children aware uses of memory may have contributed to selections of suggested items even in the opposition condition.

With these caveats in mind, the estimates suggest some interesting possibilities. One clear pattern is that both aware and unaware uses of memory for postevent information were greater when the suggestions were given immediately before the test than when they were given 2 days before the test. The pattern also suggests, contrary to our initial expectations, that preschoolers' responses were more often based on aware uses of memory for postevent information than were third graders' responses. This suggests that preschoolers often accepted the suggestions as correct (and consequently those in the standard test condition often based their test responses on them) even though they often knew that the source of their memories of those answers was the postevent information (because they often filtered out those answers when given the opposition test instructions). The third graders, on the other hand, less often based their test responses on memories that they knew were derived from the postevent information; they were just as affected as preschoolers by the suggestions, but that effect was more often mediated by unaware uses of those memories. Finally, although it is risky to compare across studies, the estimates hint at the possibility that, compared with adults, the children's suggestibility less often reflected aware uses of memory for the postevent information and more often reflected unaware uses of memory.

Given the problems with using the equations in this experiment, the patterns in the estimates cannot be taken as clear evidence for these claims about age differences in the contributions of aware and unaware uses of memories of postevent information but instead can be taken as grounds for speculations that may warrant further study. In future work, we plan to increase statistical power and develop means of assessing children's understanding of the opposition instructions so as to shed more light on these issues. At present, our primary aim is to demonstrate how the process dissociation procedure can be used to explore the contributions of aware and unaware uses of postevent information to the suggestibility effect.

Summary and Conclusions

This chapter has introduced a new method for obtaining separate estimates of the contributions of aware and unaware uses of memories of postevent information. The experiment with adult subjects indicates that aware uses of postevent information make a large contribution to responding on standard tests of the misinformation effect, but that unaware uses of suggestions also contribute to responding. Future studies using the process dissociation procedure will explore factors that affect the contributions of aware and unaware uses of memory.

The findings of Experiment 1 differed from those of Lindsay (1990) in that on the opposition test misleading suggestions did not reduce the frequency with which subjects provided correct answers. An important difference between the two experiments is that in the earlier study there was a 2-day delay between seeing the event and taking the opposition memory test, whereas in Experiment 1 subjects took the opposition test approximately 20 minutes after viewing the event. Longer delays between seeing the event and trying to remember details from it may increase susceptibility to memory impairment (Belli, Windschitl, McCarthy, & Winfrey, 1992). Another potentially important difference between the two studies was that, whereas subjects in Experiment 1 performed a filled 15-minute delay between hearing the postevent narrative and taking the memory test, and took the standard test before the opposition test, subjects in Lindsay's (1990) Easy condition (the critical condition for the memory impairment finding) took the test immediately after receiving the misleading suggestions. Shorter delays between hearing the misinformation and taking the test may increase the blocking effect of postevent suggestions (as is also suggested by the findings of Experiment 2).

The results of Experiment 2 indicate that unaware uses of memory for postevent information have almost as great an impact on preschooler's responding as do aware uses of those memories. Stated somewhat more cautiously, the results indicate that young children may be less able than adults to control their use of memories derived from postevent information. Children in the opposition condition less often selected the suggested items on the picture recognition test than did children in the standard condition, but even in the opposition condition a reliable suggestibility effect was obtained. As noted above, a good deal of additional research is needed before we can confidently interpret the children's performance. One possibility is that young children are more likely than adults to mistake memories of the postevent information for memories of the event itself. Another possibility is that young children have more difficulty than adults understanding the opposition instructions—that is, they may not understand that they are to avoid basing their responses on the suggested information. Of course, both of these explanations are potentially interesting and important, and teasing them apart is a central part of our ongoing research efforts.

The process dissociation procedure (Jacoby, 1991) is a new method, and our application of it to this domain is very much a work in progress. One potential problem with the procedure is that the equations assume that aware and unaware uses of memory for postevent information make independent contributions to responding. This is probably not a defensible assumption in this case, because the opposition instructions may increase the probability of retrieving information from the event, which would in turn reduce the likelihood of responding with information from the postevent narrative. Thus our use of the process dissociation procedure probably underestimated the influence of unaware uses of memory of postevent suggestions. We are working on ways to address this problem and hope soon to complete studies in which the assumed independence between aware and unaware uses of memory is more plausible. An important component of our planned work will be to present empirical evidence for the independence assumption. For present purposes, the estimates are probably inaccurate but are clearly a substantial improvement over traditional measures (see Lindsay & Jacoby, 1994).

Another limitation of the procedure as described here is that we have only applied it to aggregate data (i.e., means from each condition), rather than obtaining estimates of the contributions of aware and unaware uses of memory of postevent information for each subject. Given that one uses a within-subject design (as in Experiment 1), individual estimates can be derived provided that one has a sufficient number of misled and control items. Given estimates for individual subjects, one can then statistically analyze the contributions of aware and unaware uses of memory under varying conditions and in different subject groups. We are currently working on materials that will allow us to obtain such individual estimates.

Finally, both studies reported here used rather impoverished materials for the to-be-remembered events (i.e., slides and story illustrations). There is no reason that our procedure could not be applied in more complex and naturalistic situations, and we hope to explore this approach in the near future. It is clear that one cannot make sweeping generalizations about children's memory abilities, and we expect to find that different patterns of results will be obtained under varying conditions.

In summary, the important points presented in this chapter are as follows: (a) The influence of unaware uses of memories of postevent information is generally overestimated by standard tests of the misinformation effect and generally underestimated by opposition tests, and much more accurate (albeit probably imperfect) estimates can be obtained by comparing responses on the two types of tests with the process dissociation equations. (b) Under the conditions of Experiment 1, the misinformation effect in adults is often based on aware uses of memory of the postevent narrative, but unaware uses of memory also contribute to the misinformation effect. (c) Under the conditions of Experiment 2, preschoolers and third graders were able to control their use of memories of the postevent information to some extent, but even those given the opposition instructions showed a reliable suggestibility effect, and the children were especially influenced by suggestions presented immediately before the test rather than 2 days earlier. Future studies will explore the generality of these findings and the cognitive, developmental, and situational factors that mediate them.

Readers whose interest focuses on practical and applied issues may find these conclusions somewhat academic. From the applied perspective, perhaps the most important finding reported here is that, even when expressly told that they had been given false information during the misinformation session, and that they should not base any of their test responses on any of that information, children nonetheless sometimes claimed that they remembered seeing the pictures that fit with the suggestions rather than the pictures they had actually seen (e.g., children given the opposition instructions made such suggestibility errors an average of 17% of the time in the high-recency/discriminability condition). These findings indicate that children may find it difficult to escape the effects of misleading suggestions even when the interviewer warns the children against them.

PART II

Improving Children's Testimony

In this second part of the book, the emphasis is on empirical research findings that illustrate the capabilities and limitations of children thrust into an adult legal system. The authors who contribute to this part concentrate primarily on children's communication and memory capabilities as two areas that require special attention when eliciting testimony from children. With the capabilities of young children in mind, the authors discuss various techniques that have been developed for use in improving children's testimony.

At the root of all successful testimony is communication of information from the event in question. Even the most detailed memory of an event essentially becomes irrelevant if one is unable to communicate this information to the appropriate legal professionals. Thus a primary means of improving testimony comes from an understanding of effective communication. For children, special attention to communication is especially crucial given that their language skills are generally less advanced than those of adults.

In general, effective adult-child communication can be construed as operating at two related levels. At the first level is the adults' ability to effectively communicate to the child. In a legal setting, this consists of adults questioning children to elicit information about an event. The chapter by Saywitz emphasizes the need for legal professionals to phrase their questions according to what is known about children's language capabilities to give the child the best opportunity to communicate what he or she knows. According to Saywitz, there are numerous studies that suggest that legal professionals often expect children to understand questions that contain complex sentence structures and require sophisticated reasoning skills. For example, many of the questions that children face in legal situations have an ambiguous, overly complex structure (e.g., "When you were in the third grade, and you were on vacation at your grandma's house, did _____ happen to you?"). Moreover, much of the language children encounter in court contains vocabulary they do not understand (e.g., *court, jury, allegations*) or abstract concepts that children often fail to use correctly (e.g., time, weight, perspective). The use of such complex language can lead children to appear incompetent despite the fact that they may be able to provide valuable information in situations where age-appropriate language is used.

At the second level of communication is the child's ability to communicate relevant information to the adult. Recently there has been a movement to provide alternative ways for children to communicate experiences that they may be unable or unwilling to describe in words. A popular alternative has been to allow sexually abused children to communicate through the use of anatomically correct dolls. Recent surveys suggest that 90% of the professionals who work with abused children have used anatomical dolls in their investigative interviews with children (Ceci & Bruck, 1993b). While the use of such techniques appears to be a step taken toward adjusting for the limitations of young children, it may be a step taken without solid empirical backing from basic developmental research. The work of DeLoache on young children's understanding of symbolic representation questions the appropriateness of using anatomical dolls to interview very young children. In her research, DeLoache consistently finds that very young children have difficulty realizing that models, such as dolls, function as both an object and a representation of a real object. Without an understanding of the dolls' symbolic nature, one must question young children's ability to use dolls to effectively communicate their experiences to adults. Thus DeLoache's chapter highlights the need for practical techniques to be well grounded in developmental theory and research.

In addition to paying special attention to children's communication, legal professionals must also be sensitive to the unique memory capabilities of children. Just as memory is irrelevant without effective communication, communication becomes incidental if there is no memory for the details of the experience in question. While research suggests that children tend to encode a lot of information in memory (as evidenced by the free narrative reports discussed by Fivush and Shukat, this volume), there is evidence to suggest that children have difficulty retrieving the information that they have stored. To the extent that it is the retrieval stage of memory that poses the problem in a child's remembering, then their testimony may be improved by employing techniques that support retrieval processes.

The chapter by Fisher and McCauley as well as the chapter by Saywitz suggest several techniques that may be used to adjust for children's deficits in retrieval. For example, Fisher and McCauley suggest that the mnemonic techniques that comprise the cognitive interview, such as re-creating the original context of the event and using mental imagery to guide recall, have the potential to aid retrieval processes in children and thus lead to more complete recall. With the same intention, Saywitz suggests that the use of external cues (generic pictures) that represent forensically relevant categories (e.g., actions, affect, setting) can be used to elicit details that children may otherwise neglect to retrieve from memory. Thus the work of these authors shows how basic research in memory and its development can be used to develop techniques for improving the accounts provided by young children.

Finally, Bull's chapter summarizes Britain's recent attempt to formalize techniques for interviewing children by developing the *Memorandum of Good Practice*. As Bull's chapter points out, Britain's intent in formulating the *Memorandum* is to provide legal professionals with guidelines on a variety of interviewing techniques that can be employed when working with young children.

Taken together, the contributions to this second part of the book illustrate a variety of findings from basic research that have been used to formulate techniques for interviewing children involved in legal proceedings. As the authors point out, empirical tests of these techniques have suggested that there are several that are successful in improving children's testimony. Continued attempts to develop and assess the efficacy of these methods promise to be an important direction for eliciting the most complete and accurate information from children in our courts.

JENNIFER K. ACKIL

Improving Children's Testimony

The Question, the Answer, and the Environment

KAREN J. SAYWITZ

In cases of alleged sexual or physical abuse, children are often the only sources of vital information. There is rarely definitive physical evidence or an adult witness to verify a child's report. Without corroborating evidence, legal professionals rely heavily on the accounts of children, in and out of the courtroom, to discover the truth. Children bring both capabilities and limitations to the task. This chapter addresses the need to capitalize on their strengths, compensate for their weaknesses, and create an optimal environment for their remembering and communicating. Such efforts are important because the usual methods of collecting evidence are often inimical to the

AUTHOR'S NOTE: This chapter was supported by a grant to Karen J. Saywitz from the National Center for Child Abuse and Neglect, Department of Health and Human Services. Much of the data reported would not be possible without the invaluable efforts of many parents, teachers, children, research assistants, and colleagues. Special thanks go to Lynn Snyder, Mike Espinoza, Brenda Burke, Rebecca Nathanson, Richard Romanoff, Vivian Lamphear, Patricia Savich, Susan Moan-Hardie, Lorinda Camparo, Gail Goodman, Sarah Romanoff, Anna Romanoff, and the Torrance, Redondo Beach, and Santa Monica-Malibu school districts of southern California.

developmentally sensitive process necessary to elicit information from children. Consequently, children may not be able to provide information in pretrial interviews or courtroom questioning at the optimal level of which they are capable. Improving the quality of evidence that children provide would advance the fact-finding process and reduce the number of cases dismissed due to children's credibility. This would further the course of justice, protecting children from physical danger and adults from false accusations.

The bulk of past child witness research has described children's strengths and weaknesses, primarily enumerating their deficits (Doris, 1991). This approach is limited as a means of generating improvement in children's testimony. Methodologies and theories need to address the relationships between the child as respondent, the adult as questioner, and the physical-psychological environment in which questioning occurs rather than viewing witness reliability as a function of the child alone. Within this framework, several avenues of change suggest themselves. For example, improvement could result from child development training for legal professionals, adequate preparation of child witnesses, and child-sensitive court procedures.

In this chapter, I define *testifying* as remembering and communicating in the forensic environment. Barriers to effective communication, limitations on memory performance, and environmental concerns are identified. Three approaches to improvement are considered: (a) increasing the developmental sensitivity of questions to promote effective communication, (b) maximizing children's answers with memory strategy instruction, and (c) modifying the physical-psychological environment in which questioning occurs. The chapter concludes with a discussion of the need to expand theory and methodology to understand the effect of emotion and motivation on memory performance.

Effective Communication: The Questions

Studies have not produced a single "proper" method for interviewing child witnesses that can be held out as the standard by which all questioning should be conducted. Protocols and guidelines have been proposed (American Academy of Child and Adolescent Psychiatry, 1985; American Professional Society on the Abuse of Children, 1990). The bulk of them are untested. A few exceptions appear promising but require more research on their intended and unintended effects (Boat & Everson, 1988a; Jones & McQuiston, 1988; Saywitz, Geiselman, & Bornstein, 1992). For the most part, the clinical and forensic literatures on questioning children fail to address the role of communicative competence in eliciting reliable testimony. Similarly, the majority of child witness research has been centered on the accuracy of children's memory and the veracity of their reports, neglecting the fact that accurate reports are, in part, a function of children's communication skills as well as the communication demands of the legal system environment.

The ability to testify requires translation of memories into words and sentences that must be communicated within the constraints of legal process and procedure. Thus witnesses are required to remember and communicate according to a host of invisible rules for sociolinguistic interaction and under less than ideal psychological conditions. In the courtroom, communication is confined to a question-answer format in an unfamiliar setting, continually interrupted by the objections of authority figures. Children must produce language that can be understood by adults unfamiliar with the event in question. This includes not only formulation of words and sentences but, for example, comments that orient the listener appropriately to the topic and provide a frame of reference. It also requires comprehension of adult grammar, vocabulary, paralinguistic expression (intonation, facial expression), and conversational rules. Further, these production and comprehension skills must be deployed in an unfamiliar environment where fears of public speaking, the unknown, embarrassment, and recrimination may interfere with communication efforts (Dent, 1977; Peters, 1991; Sas, 1991; Saywitz, 1989; Saywitz, Goodman, Nicholas, & Moan, 1991; Saywitz & Nathanson, 1993). It is also an environment that could be modified to facilitate communication with special court procedures, such as closing the courtroom to spectators or allowing the presence of support persons (Goodman, Taub, et al., 1992).

Selected studies are discussed below to determine the degree to which the structure and content of adult questions match children's levels of language and cognitive functioning. Children's apparent lack of credibility may have as much to do with the competence of adults to communicate with children as it does with children's abilities to remember and relate their experiences accurately.

VOCABULARY

Recent studies regarding legal terms commonly used with children in court suggest that many terms are unfamiliar to or misinterpreted by children under 10 years of age (Flin, Stevenson, & Davies, 1989; Melton, Limber, Jacobs, &

Oberlander, 1992; Warren-Leubecker, Tate, Hinton, & Ozbek, 1989). In one representative study, sixty 5- to 12-year-olds' knowledge of legal terminology was tested (Saywitz, Jaenicke, & Camparo, 1990). Terms were chosen from transcripts of child witness testimony. Some terms were well understood by 5- to 12-year-olds (e.g., *truth, lie, promise, remember*); some terms were too difficult for children in this age range (e.g., *charges, allegation, defendant, minor*); and some terms showed age-related trends (e.g., *testify, evidence, attorney, jury, witness, facts*).

An error analysis revealed that younger children tended to make auditory discrimination errors, mistaking the unfamiliar legal term for a similar sound-ing familiar word, such as interpreting *jury* as *jewelry* ("Jury is that stuff my mom wears around her neck and fingers.") or *journey* ("a trip"). This is not surprising because auditory discrimination skills are not fully developed until 8 years of age (Ingram, 1976). Additionally, 5- to 6-year-olds made homonym errors by assuming a familiar nonlegal definition was the only definition, insisting terms could not have a different meaning in a courtroom, and failing to recognize that they had insufficient knowledge. "Court is a place to play basketball." "A hearing is something you do with your ears." "Charges are something you do with credit cards." Older children admitted lack of knowl-edge and recognized the potential for alternative meanings dependent on context. Findings suggest that children think they understand meaning when, in fact, they have a different meaning in mind from the adult questioner. When asked, "Do you know what an allegation is?" a young child is likely to answer "yes" but may be thinking about alligators.

Such studies illustrate that age-appropriate word choice is an important factor in eliciting reliable testimony from children. They suggest that one way to improve the quality of children's testimony is to closely match the vocabu-lary of the question to the child's ability. Normative studies of vocabulary development can suggest guidelines. For example, children master monosyl-labic words before multisyllabic words; thus the younger the child, the fewer syllables per word comprehended and produced. Similarly, children are slow to master the use of pronouns (e.g., *he, her, they*) and referents (e.g., *this, that, here, there*), that is, terms that refer to different people, places, and objects at different points in time. Preschoolers can be confused about the meaning of such terms even though they use them in their speech. Only repetition of the antecedent ensures that the child and adult have the same one in mind (e.g., "What did you do with *Mary and Bob*?" instead of "What did you do with *them*?").

One implication of the error analysis described above is that questioners will need to ask children to define potentially unfamiliar terms in their own words. Asking if they know what a word means (a yes/no question) is not enough. When asked, "Do you know what *testify* means?" a child may answer "yes" but be thinking about taking a paper and pencil *test*. Another implication of these studies is that child witness preparation should include learning the meaning of unfamiliar legal terms. Two recent studies suggest that young children can be taught relevant aspects of the investigative and judicial process (Sas, 1991; Saywitz, Nathanson, Snyder, & Lamphear, 1993, Experiment 7).

LINGUISTIC COMPLEXITY

Recent studies suggest that there are many types of grammatical constructions that are not mastered by young children but that are replete in the conversation of the courtroom (Walker, 1993). In one study, transcripts of 6- to 15-year-old child witnesses testifying were reviewed (Brennan & Brennan, 1988). Age-mates' abilities to repeat selected and randomly drawn questions from the transcripts were tested in the laboratory. Repetitions were categorized by the degree to which error in repetition (i.e., rephrasing) captured the sense of the original question. As expected, the results revealed children's misunderstanding of many common courtroom questions.

Studies of language acquisition suggest that lengthy compound sentences with embedded clauses and other linguistic complexities are beyond the comprehension and memory of many children under 8 years of age (see Reich, 1986, for a review). Yet, such overloaded utterances are endemic to the investigative and judicial process. Problems often arise when one question contains a number of previously established facts: "When you were on vacation the summer of third grade and you visited your maternal grandmother's house, did your uncle take you to his apartment, and what happened there?" Such utterances need to be broken into several short questions requiring short answers to assess the credibility of a child's response. Also problematic are questions that allow multiple interpretations and options but restrict answers to yes or no without qualification. "Did he push you into the car and make you do that three times?" "No." Listeners cannot interpret whether the response refers to the push, the car, the action, or the number of instances.

Similarly, atypical uses of the negative are frequent in court but create communication barriers with children (Brennan & Brennan, 1988). "It happened on Sunday, did it not?" Is this question asking the child to confirm that it happened on Sunday or that it did not happen on Sunday? "Is that not true?" could easily be rephrased as "Is that true?" Double negatives can be equally confusing. "Didn't your mother tell you not to go over to his house?" Unclear references often confuse young children. "Are you sure you told *those things* to the policeman?" The child may have a different antecedent for "those things" from the adult, but he knows he has to take his turn in the conversation. A question's grammatical construction is an important factor in eliciting reliable responses from children.

The illustrations above demonstrate that increased knowledge of the norms of syntactic development by questioners could improve the quality of evidence children offer. Table 6.1 displays sample considerations for talking to young children derived from the language acquisition literature. For example, grammatical constructions that are mastered early, such as noun-verb-object, are easiest for children to comprehend. It would not be unreasonable for questioners to expect that, the younger the child, the shorter the sentences she will comprehend and produce and the more she will depend on familiar contextual cues to glean meaning.

PRAGMATICS

Children's pragmatic skill, that is, their functional use of language in social interaction (Irwin, 1982), is another important factor in their ability to testify. The procedures of the courtroom can resemble a foreign culture (Flin et al., 1989; Goodman, Taub, et al., 1992; Melton et al., 1992; Saywitz, 1989). The rules of sociolinguistic interaction are governed by intangible rules of evidence, case precedent, and judicial discretion. Young children rely on everyday rules of communication, even in the unique forensic context, and can fail to appreciate that adults are operating under a different set of sociolinguistic principles. Studies are needed to discover the ways in which immature pragmatic skills influence memory performance in questioning about past events. Below, two conversational postulates are introduced as examples with speculation regarding potential implications for children's testimony.

One implicit postulate of conversation is that listeners expect speakers to be sincere (Grice, 1975). Developmental studies suggest that children under 9 years of age may expect a degree of sincerity that is not present in the adversarial process because they have not yet developed an appreciation for the conditions that violate the sincerity postulate (Demorest, Meyer, Phelps, Gardner, & Winner, 1984). Failure to completely understand the speaker's

Table 6.1 Considerations for Talking to Young Children

Avoid	Use
Long compound sentences	Short sentences
Embedded clauses	Simple constructions
3- to 4-syllable words *(identify)*	1- to 2-syllable words *(point to)*
Multiword verbs *(might have been)*	Simple tenses *(-ed, was)*
Uncommon usage	Common terms
Pronouns *(them, their)*	Proper names *(Mary and Jill)*
Referents *(here/there, yesterday/tomorrow)*	Stable terms *(in the back of the room)*
Relational terms *(more, less)*	Concrete visualizable terms *(a lot, a little)*
Failure to introduce new topics	Introduce new topics *("Now, let's talk about school.")*
Passive voice *("Was she hit by him?")*	Active voice *("Did he hit her?")*
Uncommon negatives *("Is that not true?")*	Positive constructions *("Is that true?")*
Nominalization *(when the hitting occurred)*	Subject-verb-object *(when Tom hit Mary)*
Double negatives *("Didn't Mom tell you not to go?")*	Single negatives *("Did Mom tell you not to go?")*
Hypotheticals *("If you want a break, then let me know.")*	Direct approach *("Are you tired?" "Do you want a break?")*

intent could influence how readily children acquiesce to misleading questions. Such uses of everyday conversational rules in the forensic context might impair not only perceptions of children's credibility but the quality of evidence children provide.

Another postulate of conversation is that grammatical conventions are used to introduce, maintain, or change topics. Comments that link a discussion with the next topic of conversation are common in typical conversations. These are often omitted in the formal courtroom questioning (Brennan & Brennan, 1988). Questions often jump from one topic to another without the necessary introduction for children to switch frames of reference. Studies of the manner in which mothers talk to children (e.g., Newhoff & Launer, 1984) suggest that young children rely heavily on adults to structure the conversation and to elaborate on children's responses. Children require transitional comments to signal a change of topic, which are rare in the forensic context. For example, "Before, we were talking about school. Now I want to ask you some questions about your mother." The cumulative effect of rapid switching of topics without proper introduction leaves children disoriented, with little understanding of how and why the questions are being asked. The conventions of courtroom discourse are often poorly matched to the child's level of pragmatic development.

Sensitivity to immature understanding of the rules of social discourse should improve the quality of children's testimony. The question-answering behavior of children as young as 2 years of age has been empirically investigated (Ervin-Tripp & Michell-Kerman, 1977; Parnell & Amerman, 1983). The development of variables that are especially salient in the forensic context have been studied, such as turn taking, topic introduction-maintenance-change, organization and coherency of conversation, interpretation of vocal intensity, intonation, fluency, facial expression, gesture, and speaker's intent. This literature is rich with information from which guidelines could be culled to close the gap between the discourse of the courtroom and children's knowledge of the rules for exchanging information.

CONTENT

To evaluate a suspect's alibi, a witness may be asked to pinpoint the time or duration of an event in minutes and hours; to determine jurisdiction, a witness may be asked to pinpoint a location in terms of miles, city, or state; to identify a perpetrator, a witness may be asked to describe someone's height in feet and inches, and weight in pounds. To do so, a witness should have mastered conventional systems for measuring time, distance, or weight (i.e., in minutes, hours, years, inches, feet, or pounds). These skills are learned gradually over the course of the elementary school years. Many are not fully mastered until adolescence (Brigham, Vanverst, & Bothwell, 1986; Friedman, 1982; Saywitz et al., 1991). Table 6.2 lists a number of skills commonly required of child witnesses.

Questions become problematic when they require skills children have not yet developed. The degree to which the content of the question matches the child's stage of cognitive development affects the accuracy of children's responses. Children may try to answer a question even when they lack the necessary skill, resulting in adults misinterpreting their answers as indications of incompetence. Consider the following illustrations.

Table 6.2   Skills Commonly Required of Child Witnesses in Forensic Interviewing

---

Measurement
  Height (feet and inches)
  Distance (miles)
  Weight (pounds)
  Age (years)
  Time (hours, minutes, days of week, seasons, months)
Body Parts
  Names and functions
Basic Concepts
  First, last, never, always, ever, before, after
Colors
  Basic and uncommon (e.g., tan, mauve)
Locations
  City, state, street
Kinship Terms
Number Skills
Perspective Taking
  Ability to infer others' intentions, perspectives, feelings, thoughts

---

Number. Witnesses are frequently asked how many times something happened; to answer, a witness must be able to count. One 4-year-old witness provided contradictory responses when asked, "How many times did your daddy do this to you?" She held up 10 fingers, and then said "two times" aloud. The judge asked her to count to 10 and she did so proudly. However, many preschoolers may be able to recite the numbers from 1 to 10, but this does not mean they understand the underlying number concepts or that they can count events in time. For them, counting can be a rote skill, like reciting words to a song. Even counting predesignated objects does not ensure that children can count events that do not have discrete boundaries. For preschoolers who reason on the basis of what they see, adults may need to specify the unit to be counted (i.e., describing it in pictures, not concepts) and to define the beginning and end of the event for the child.

Time. Young children are often asked the time and date of an occurrence. Yet, children do not learn to tell clock time fully until 7 years of age, and they will still have some trouble with calendar dates and questions about something that happened before or after something else (Friedman, 1982; Saywitz et al., 1991). By 8 years of age, children can use the names of the days of the week and the seasons accurately (Friedman, 1982). They can reason that, if it was hot out and they were dressed in their bathing suits, then the event probably occurred during the summer. They can describe when two events happened together, such as the abuse occurring while they were on vacation. However, under the age of 10, they may have difficulty reporting events in exact chronological order (A. Brown, 1976). Yet this failing has little bearing on the accuracy of the events they do report, even if reported out of order. This type of normative information is necessary for molding questions to children's levels of functioning.

Perspective. Witnesses are often asked questions that require an inference regarding the intentions, thoughts, feelings, or perceptions of others ("Why didn't you try to run when he began to close the windows and lock the doors?"). Although 3- and 4-year-olds can sometimes see another person's point of view quite accurately, it is not until around 6 to 7 years of age that most children have a fully developed ability to consistently view the world from other perspectives (Selman & Byrne, 1974). Consequently, young children have difficulty answering questions about what another person might have been intending. Children may contradict themselves because they are stretching to try to explain something they do not understand.

Logic. Forensic questions often require advanced hypothetico-deductive reasoning of preschoolers who typically reason on the basis of what they see in a trial-and-error fashion. Children's unbelievable responses can be a function of limited logic rather than of dishonesty or contamination. Preschoolers may appear to engage in magical thinking, creating or accepting illogical explanations (Piaget, 1954). For example, they may believe that inanimate objects possess animate characteristics (e.g., if you cut thread, the thread experiences pain). Such illogical reasoning does not necessarily render the rest of testimony inaccurate or irrelevant.

Preschoolers generalize in ways that seem illogical as they go about creating explanations for what they observe (Piaget, 1954). For example, a child might say, "The train went by because the dog barked" (Singer & Revenson, 1978), a reverse explanation of the dog barking because the train went by. The child is unsure of the causal relations, not about the existence of the train or the dog. Studies show that children can report facts accurately even when they misinterpret other aspects of the event or draw implausible inferences (Goodman & Clarke-Stewart, 1991). However, studies also suggest that, when 3- to 4-year-olds are repeatedly exposed to incriminating comments about someone over many weeks, it may affect even reports of factual information regarding the person's activities (Ceci, Leichtman, & White, in press). In research studies, incriminating comments and highly leading questions do not necessarily lead to false accusations of abuse (Tobey & Goodman, 1992), but findings suggest that the potential for such distortions exists. Interviewers would be wise to keep biases in check, maintain an objective atmosphere, and explore alternative explanations for very young children's statements.

Inconsistencies and misunderstandings result when children are compelled to answer questions requiring skills beyond their stage of cognitive development. One productive avenue for future research will be the development of alternate methods for eliciting forensically relevant information. In one such study, seventy-two 5- and 7-year-olds participated in a physical examination. A week or a month later, they were asked about the doctor's age, height, and the timing of the exam in a variety of ways (Saywitz et al., 1991). The traditional questions required estimation of height in feet and inches, age in years, timing in terms of the date, and duration in terms of minutes. Alternate questions concerned information from which the time and date could be reconstructed (e.g., "Was the doctor old enough to drive a car?" "Did it happen during the week or on the weekend?"). The alternate question about height allowed children to indicate height by pointing to colored bars on a wall.

When collapsed across question content, children's responses were significantly more accurate when asked with the alternate rather than the traditional methods, except for height. Errors on the height task suggest that clinical intuitions may not be validated when subjected to experimental scrutiny. These results underscore the need for empirical investigation to identify the best methods of eliciting accurate content.

Past studies can be germane. Even the clinical method developed by Piaget (1928, 1954) can offer guidance in the pursuit of methods to improve testimony. Piaget questioned children to uncover the reasons behind their responses and to understand their conception of how the world operates. Questions that ask children to elaborate and justify their answers can avoid a great deal of misunderstanding that otherwise goes unnoticed. For example, preschoolers may think the tallest person in the room is the oldest, focusing on height as the only indicator of age. Thus, when they say someone was old, follow-up questions asking children to justify or elaborate on their responses may be necessary to fully understand their answer (e.g., "What makes you think he was old?" "Did he have any hair?" "What color was his hair?").

COMPREHENSION

As it is impossible for legal professionals to become child development experts, questions will never be perfectly matched to children's level of comprehension. Thus studies of comprehension monitoring, the ability to know whether or not one understands a question, and the use of strategies for coping with noncomprehension are pertinent. These skills develop gradually with age (Dickson, 1981; Flavell, 1981; Singer & Flavell, 1981). While preschoolers have been shown to recognize comprehension difficulties and implement strategies for resolving them, they are able to do so only in naturalistic settings when tasks and stimuli are simple, familiar, and require nonverbal responses to physically present referents (Gallagher, 1981; Garvey, 1977; Revelle, Wellman, & Karabenik, 1985). In contrast, in experimental studies with unfamiliar settings, where tasks and stimuli tend to be complex and verbal, young children have difficulty detecting when they have failed to understand. They rarely question ambiguous messages or request clarification from adults (Asher, 1976; Cosgrove & Patterson, 1978; Ironsmith & Whitehurst, 1978; Markman, 1977; Patterson, Massad, & Cosgrove, 1978). In one seminal study, puppets taught 6- and 8-year-olds a magic trick but omitted information vital to completing the trick (Markman, 1977, 1979). Younger children failed to recognize the omission and tried to do the trick without success. They failed to process the message or to evaluate whether it made sense, assuming there was something wrong with the listener, not the message. Older children asked for clarification. Children are likely to demonstrate difficulties in the forensic context that are similar to those seen in the laboratory because of the unfamiliar setting, the lack of physically present referents, and the added burden on memory.

Past studies of methods for improving children's comprehension have come from disparate fields, focusing on reading comprehension (Capelli & Markman, 1982), referential communication games (Cosgrove & Patterson, 1978), and language impaired children (Dollaghan & Kaston, 1986). Such studies have not involved memory or question-answer tasks relevant for child witnesses. To begin to evaluate the applicability of laboratory results to child witnesses, a recent study tested effects of comprehension monitoring training on memory for a past event. The results suggested that, when children do not comprehend lengthy, complex questions about past autobiographical events, they often try to answer these questions anyway; however, they can be taught to identify noncomprehension and to ask for rephrasing (Saywitz & Snyder, 1991; Saywitz et al., 1993, Experiment 4).

In one study, 186 children, aged 6 and 8 years, were interviewed regarding a past event with short-answer questions that varied in linguistic complexity from easy to difficult, but the questions were comparable in memory difficulty as determined by a preliminary study of 66 additional children (Saywitz & Snyder, 1991; Saywitz et al., 1993, Experiment 4). Children were assigned to one of three treatment conditions: (a) comprehension monitoring strategy training, (b) instructions to ask for incomprehensible questions to be rephrased, and (c) control group given motivating instructions to do their best. Groups interacted with similar materials and for equivalent training and testing times. The school activity was videotaped for later comparison with children's recall. Screening tests established that groups were comparable on tests of language comprehension, receptive vocabulary, and intelligence. Children were trained and tested individually. Whenever children indicated they did not understand a question, it was rephrased in simpler grammar.

For children who received no intervention, strategies for responding ranged from requests for repetition to answering a part of the question that they thought they understood, typically the beginning or ending of questions. Requests for the question to be rephrased were rare. They were as likely to respond inaccurately as accurately to difficult questions. A second group was instructed to tell the questioner when they did not understand, and questions were rephrased at the request of the children. The accuracy of their responses was significantly higher. A third group received strategy instructional training in which they watched a videotaped vignette and were asked questions about it, varying in comprehensibility. When answering these questions, they practiced, with feedback, identifying incomprehensible questions and asking for rephrasing. When questioned about the staged event, this group was the most likely to indicate they did not understand, to ask for rephrasing, and to respond accurately to the rephrases. These findings suggest that children's communicative competencies depend heavily on their ability to detect and cope with noncomprehension, a skill that may be enhanced through instruction and preparation.

The studies of courtroom communication and normative language acquisition discussed above suggest that often questions are asked in language too complex for children to comprehend about concepts too abstract for them to understand. When the discrepancy between the language of the courtroom and the language of the child is great, children's responses can appear inconsistent and unreliable due to misunderstandings and communication breakdown. Age-appropriate questioning and preparation overcome many developmental barriers to communicating with child witnesses, allowing children to tell what they know at their optimal level of performance.

Maximizing Memory: The Answers

MEMORY DEVELOPMENT RESEARCH

The literature on children's memories of personally experienced events suggests that child witnesses show both strengths and weaknesses in memory performance. On the one hand, information elicited through free recall ("What happened?") is highly accurate (Fivush, 1993). However, the amount of information provided in free recall is typically modest, necessitating further questions and cues to stimulate retrieval of additional information. Much of this information is elicited piecemeal in response to specific questions that drive the organization of the material. Some of the added information is accurate even several years after an experience (Fivush, 1993; Gold & Neisser, 1980). On the other hand, misleading information can be embedded in specific questions to which young children, like adults, are susceptible. While children over 10 or 11 years of age show adult levels of resistance to misleading questions, children under 5 years of age acquiesce more frequently, especially when questions are highly leading, detailed, incriminating, and repeated over multiple interviews (Ceci et al., in press).

As children grow, they develop strategies for organizing information and retrieving it from memory, reducing the need for aid from questioners. They learn what questions to ask themselves to retrieve facts independently. Their narrative accounts of who, what, and where become more detailed, coherent, and organized. Their increasing knowledge of how narratives are structured guides retrieval, triggering recall of certain types of information, such as setting, participants, actions, conversations, affective states, and consequences (Stein & Glenn, 1978). By 5 years of age, children have learned to give a fairly coherent narrative of a personal experience (Hudson & Shapiro, 1991). As children gain experience, world knowledge, and greater awareness of the investigative and judicial process, they become more aware of forensic relevance and of the types of information and the level of detail expected in the forensic context (Saywitz, 1989). With greater ability to generate strategies and metacognitive knowledge of how and when to apply strategies, retrieval becomes more and more self-controlled. There is less need for leading questions and more resistance to the guidance provided by adult questioners who were not present at the event in question.

While the developmental trends above are relevant, studies of children's eyewitness memory have been essentially descriptive and have not addressed methods of improvement. Laboratory studies of strategy instructional training have demonstrated memory improvement but have not addressed factors salient for generalization to the forensic context (Pressley, Forrest-Pressley, & Elliott-Faust, 1988). Techniques often were designed for educational purposes and limited to strategies like clustering or rehearsal with pictures and word lists—artificial, mundane laboratory tasks. Techniques have not been tested in interviews regarding long-term memory for autobiographical events. Despite their limitations, laboratory studies of strategy instruction have provided insights that can be springboards for current studies related to the needs of child witnesses.

Past studies have demonstrated that, when children are made aware of a retrieval strategy, given a rationale for its utility, and practice using the strategy with feedback and prompting (reinstruction immediately before testing), then strategy use and memory performance improve. Because real-world tasks, like testifying, require the application of more than a single strategy on a single task, researchers have begun to study training packages. These typically add metacognitive knowledge about how and when to apply the strategy to the training package. Strategies such as summarizing, self-questioning, and inferring are taught in this manner to improve memory for prose. Additionally, packages include monitoring strategies, such as self-checking, to determine if a strategy is working, to evaluate reasons for failure, and to generate alternative approaches. These more comprehensive packages are beginning to focus on variables that are highly salient for the forensic context. Attributional and motivational factors are beginning to be studied in the form of self-reinforcement and self-statements ("I can do it"). Unfortunately, many studies fail to test the effectiveness of each component of the package separately. Thus it is difficult to know which components of training are responsible for improvement and worthy of further investment. Moreover, durability of strategy use and transfer to different settings and tasks have been more difficult to demonstrate, but not impossible. The testing of methods to promote generalization is ongoing. The relevance of these studies for improving children's testimony is clear. Future studies are needed that extend both the eyewitness memory literature and the strategy training literature by testing theoretically driven, innovative methods of improvement in paradigms that are sensitive to issues of ecological validity for application to child witnesses.

INNOVATIVE METHODS

Given the high accuracy but modest quantity of young children's free recall and their tendencies to acquiesce to misleading questions, procedures are needed that enhance completeness of initial narratives, reduce the need for leading questions, and strengthen resistance to suggestive questions. In response to these needs, three innovative procedures have been tested. The first is narrative elaboration, a procedure that seeks to maximize children's free recall by using pictorial cues and organizational strategies to trigger a specific memory (Saywitz, Snyder, & Lamphear, 1990). Another technique designed to strengthen unaided recall is a modification of the cognitive interview—a collection of memory jogging techniques successful with adult witnesses (Saywitz et al., 1992). Readers are referred to the chapter by Fisher and McCauley in this volume for a review of this literature. A third approach addresses children's suggestibility directly by teaching them techniques for resisting acquiescence (Saywitz & Moan-Hardie, 1994).

Narrative elaboration. The purpose of narrative elaboration is to enable a child to narrate past events without compromising accuracy and with less need for leading questions, thereby reducing the risk of contamination. A procedure that expands children's initial retelling allows follow-up questions to focus on clarifying information from the initial narrative, not adult supposition. Narrative elaboration draws heavily on studies demonstrating the benefits of practice, feedback, and reinstruction. Also consulted were studies of retrieval strategies—in particular, studies showing that external cues, categorization, and metamemory strategies, when accompanied by a rationale for their use, aid children's recall (e.g., Bartlett, 1932; Kobasigawa, 1974; Kurtz & Borkowski, 1984; Lodico, Ghatala, Levin, Pressley, & Bell, 1983; Pressley, Ross, Levin, & Ghatala, 1984; Pressley et al., 1988; Ryan, Hegion, & Flavell, 1970).

During the narrative elaboration training, children learn to organize the elements of an event into five forensically relevant, theoretically driven categories (participants, setting, actions, conversations/affect, and consequences). Each category is represented by a simple drawing on a card. Children are taught to use the categories and cards as mnemonic devices during questioning. The choice of categorical cues was based both on forensic relevance and on studies of the development of scripts (Nelson & Hudson, 1988), in particular from the work of Stein and Glenn (1978) that suggests children develop a script for mental representation of episodes that is organized according to the five schema-based categories listed above. Also consulted were studies showing that story grammar strategies improve the reading comprehension of poor readers (Short & Ryan, 1984).

Prior to questioning, children practice using this procedure to recall videotaped vignettes, using the cards to remind themselves to report as much as possible about each category. When children are questioned about the event under investigation, they are first asked for free recall ("What happened?"). Then, they are given the cards and told to elaborate on their initial narrative by using the cards to trigger retrieval of any additional information ("Does this picture remind you to tell anything else?").

Three studies were conducted to test the efficacy of the narrative elaboration procedure (Saywitz et al., 1993, Experiments 1-3). In each study, children's memories were tested for a scripted classroom event that involved a clash of adults and in the process involved the children. It was videotaped for later comparison with children's memories. Actors depicted student teachers who came into the classroom to teach a 30-minute history lesson. Midway through the lesson, a confederate teacher entered, accusing one teacher of taking his materials without asking. The first teacher had already distributed the materials to the class, who then became involved in the problem and its resolution. The event was designed to be rich in detail and emotionally compelling. Some children hid the materials in question under their desks and later clapped when the disagreement was resolved.

Despite obvious differences between the experimental paradigm and child abuse, the staged event contained some elements and complexity of the events recalled by child witnesses, increasing its ecological validity. Children's memories were tested after 2 weeks. The memory test questions resembled those asked in child abuse evaluations—narration of interpersonal interactions with follow-up questions (e.g., who was there, what they looked like, and so forth).

In one study, participants included 132 children (sixty-five 7- to 8-year-olds; sixty-seven 10- to 11-year-olds) randomly assigned, within age group, to one of the three treatment conditions: (a) narrative elaboration training, (b) instructions to be complete and accurate, and (c) control—no instructions and no training. Groups interacted with similar materials and were equated on training and testing time.

The group who received the training package reported significantly more correct information in free recall and when cued with the category cards than children in the other two groups, who did not differ from each other. This represented a 53% improvement over the control group. There were no group differences in errors. Thus children's eyewitness accounts were substantially improved without the use of leading questions and without compromising accuracy. In fact, younger children who received the training performed comparably to older children in the control group.

A follow-up study was conducted to test generalization of the benefit to subsequent interviews with unfamiliar authority figures: 33 new subjects (8- to 9-year-olds) were assigned to either training or control conditions. The memory test was conducted by an unfamiliar person posing as a college professor who needed the information to grade the student teachers who conducted the scripted school activity. Results replicated previous findings with the exception that improvement in free recall alone (without category cards) did not reach significance.

Increasing resistance to suggestive questions. Another recent study tested an innovative procedure that was developed to inoculate children against the effects of misleading information and to increase their resistance (Saywitz & Moan-Hardie, 1994). The technique also is based on studies of strategy training demonstrating the benefits of practice, feedback, monitoring, and self-statements. In this study, fifty-five 7-year-olds participated in the school activity described above. They were randomly assigned to one of two treatment conditions: (a) training group—strategy training to resist misleading questions, including practice, feedback, self-monitoring—or (b) control group—motivating instructions to do their best. Groups spent the same amount of time in training and testing, interacting with similar materials. Training and testing were conducted individually. The interviewers posed as college professors in the manner described above.

The intervention did not require discussion of the event under investigation, thus eliminating any possibility or accusation of coaching. First, children in the training group listened to a story about a child who went along with the suggestions of people who put their hopes or guesses into their questions. The unanticipated negative consequences were highlighted. Eventually, the character learned the benefits of telling the truth even in the face of suggestive questions by authority figures. After discussing a variety of reasons children might want to go along with a suggestive question, children were taught a new response strategy that involved (a) stopping and thinking before answering; (b) mentally replaying the event and comparing memory with the guess put into the question; (c) telling the answer if they know the answer but answering "I don't know" or "I don't remember" if there is not a match; (d) using attributional-motivational self-statements to promote confidence and assertiveness ("I knew there would be questions like this." "I can do it." "I won't go along." "I'll tell her she's wrong.") and to inhibit inappropriate responses like guessing ("I won't hurry into a wrong answer."). This response strategy was practiced with feedback in mock questioning about previously viewed videos.

In subsequent interviews about the staged school activity, the training group showed 26% fewer errors in response to misleading questions than the control group, without generating an increase in errors to other types of questions. One unanticipated result occurred. On nonleading questions, the training group responded with "I don't know" more frequently than the control group, who responded correctly more often. Overgeneralization of the "I don't know" strategy demonstrates the need for rigorous testing of interventions used with child witnesses. Unintended side effects must be identified and eliminated through revision and retesting. In a follow-up study of 47 additional children, manipulation of reinforcement patterns and group training eliminated the unintended side effect of lowered correct responses on nontarget questions (Saywitz & Moan-Hardie, 1994). In addition, there was an added benefit: Children made fewer errors on both leading and nonleading questions.

Environmental Concerns

EFFECTS OF ENVIRONMENT ON CHILDREN'S MEMORY

To accommodate child witnesses, modifications of the courtroom environment have been proposed, such as testimony via closed-circuit television (*Maryland v. Craig,* 1990) and closing the courtroom to spectators (*Globe Newspaper Co. v. Superior Court,* 1982). Such legal reforms are thought to facilitate reliable testimony and reduce system-related stress. However, there is little empirical research to guide reform efforts. Until recently, guidance from traditional investigations of children's memory has been limited because researchers strove to study memory in its purest form, uninfluenced by

Next pg...

environmental and emotional factors. Recently, researchers have begun to investigate the notion that environment is not simply the place in which remembering occurs but is a constituent of the remembering process (Ceci, Bronfenbrenner, & Baker, 1988). The physical, social, and psychological setting in which remembering transpires influences ability to recall. For example, researchers found that children's uses of prospective memory strategies were far less efficient in an unfamiliar laboratory than in the child's home (Ceci et al., 1988). They speculated that the laboratory setting induced anxiety incompatible with the deployment of the memory strategy under study.

Other studies have highlighted the significance of the social environment for remembering. In one study, 3-year-olds' autobiographical memory was better in a supportive social atmosphere than in a neutral one. In fact, 3-year-olds in the supportive environment performed as well as 5-year-olds in a neutral environment (Goodman, Bottoms, Schwartz-Kenney, & Rudy, 1991). Further, two studies have found impaired ability to identify an unfamiliar adult when the adult was present during questioning (Dent, 1977; Peters, 1991, Experiment 4). One researcher coined the term *confrontational stress* to explain the results and commented on some children's fear of angering the adult or of recrimination (Peters, 1991). When applied to the child witness, studies imply that the quality of evidence children provide will be, in part, a function of the physical and social setting in which remembering occurs.

HOW ENVIRONMENT AFFECTS TESTIMONY

For the purpose of this discussion, *environment* is broadly defined as the physical, social, and emotional atmosphere in which testimony transpires, governed by the rules of legal process and procedure. Memory performance is thought to be influenced by children's cognitive understanding of the legal system as well as their emotional reactions to it. Cognitive factors include children's limited knowledge and faulty expectations of the environment. Emotional factors include anxiety associated with the fear of the unknown and feelings of inadequacy to cope with the necessities of the system. Traditional theories of memory have failed to address these types of issues, focusing primarily on the development of strategies, metacognition, and the knowledge base. Recent theories of motivated remembering (Paris, 1988), however, have postulated an important role for expectations and emotions as mediators of the discrepancy between memory capability and memory performance.

Within a social-motivational (Paris, 1988; Verdonik, 1988) framework, deliberate attempts to remember, such as testifying, are determined by the selection of a response strategy among alternatives and the belief that it will produce a specific outcome. This can involve a metacognitive appraisal of the task (consequences for error, amount of effort required) and of strategy effectiveness as well as the anticipation of outcomes and consequences (rewards, penalties) and a cost-benefit analysis to determine if the expected outcome is worth the effort required. Judgments about strategy utility are thought to differ across tasks, environments, and people. Tasks can be viewed as interesting and challenging or stressful and unpleasant. Environments can provide either support (cues, feedback, encouragement) or interference (time pressure, discouragement). People's perceptions of self-efficacy (insecurity, grandiosity), their coping patterns (denial, avoidance, hypervigilance, mastery), and their emotions (indifference, ambivalence, fear, joy) can affect the memory product.

A social-motivational framework is well suited to understanding children's testimony because it explains situations of inadequate information processing when children do not perform at their highest level of functioning. Within this framework, there are many reasons children might not apply the most effective strategy known to them. For example, less effective, but familiar and well-practiced, strategies may be chosen because they are easier to implement with less risk of failure. This may be especially true when consequences for failure are perceived to be high, incentives for investing effort are perceived as few, and the environment is perceived to be unfamiliar and unsupportive. Within this framework, transient emotional states can be induced by children's perceptions of the environment and their appraisal of their ability to cope with the situation. For example, anxiety can be triggered when children perceive the situation as frightening vis-à-vis their perception of their own ability to succeed and to overcome their fears. High levels of anxiety could divert attentional resources and disorganize operations, or reduce effort and motivation. A child's personal frame of reference could distort the value and utility of a strategy choice or the probability of a particular outcome. For example, low self-esteem, common among abuse victims, could inflate the perceived probability of memory failure and minimize the perceived value of success, reducing effort and motivation. A theory of motivated remembering suggests that expectations, beliefs, emotional states, and coping patterns will play a prominent role in determining the quality of evidence child witnesses provide.

Cognitive factors. As of yet there is little empirical evidence for a definitive link between familiarity with the legal system and better memory in the courtroom; however, studies have documented misconceptions and limited knowledge of the legal system in children under 10 years of age (Flin et al., 1989; Melton et al., 1992; Saywitz, 1989; Warren-Leubecker et al., 1989). In one representative study, 48 children from 4 to 14 years of age (half child witnesses and half matched age-mates with no legal experience) were interviewed regarding their knowledge of the investigative and judicial process (Saywitz, 1989). In the 4- to 7-year age range, many children did not know that the judge is in charge of the courtroom and assumed the unfamiliar faces in the jury box were friends of the defendant rather than impartial decision makers. Some children viewed court as a "room you pass by on your way to jail" and had no concept of a trial; some believed that a child witness went to jail if he made a mistake on the stand. They assumed that witnesses would be believed and that judges were omniscient, knowing when witnesses were not telling the truth. Child witnesses with personal experience as parties in legal cases showed no better understanding of the process than age-mates without direct experience. In fact, there is some evidence to suggest that they were more confused (Melton et al., 1992; Saywitz, 1989). Findings such as these suggest that children have a limited context for understanding the needs of the various people, their functions, or the rules by which people interact in the legal setting. Given this situation, it could be difficult to formulate an accurate appraisal of task demands and consequences for retrieval.

Thus it is not unreasonable to hypothesize that the quality of children's testimony is affected by their misconceptions about the legal system. For example, expectations that the judge is omniscient could lower the motivation and effort applied to retrieval. Failure to recognize the significance of testimony for the fact-finding and decision-making process could affect the cost-benefit analysis of whether a particular retrieval strategy is worth the effort required for the outcome expected. Some misconceptions could have the opposite effect. The belief that mistakes could cause one to go to jail might increase motivation and effort because the cost of memory error is so high. This belief might also raise the threshold for confidence in one's own memory before responding. Such an inflated threshold might increase suggestibility. Limited metacognitive knowledge of the task demands of recall during testimony could affect decisions about what is relevant to report and how and when to apply retrieval strategies. Misconceptions also could result in heightened or unrealistic fears and failure to use the "big picture" to put feelings in perspective in order to cope with the stress of testifying. Generalized anxiety associated with fear of the unknown could lead to such strategies as avoidance, reducing effort and motivation to the point that the event under investigation might not be retrieved in free recall at all. We have all experienced a situation when our mind goes blank under pressure. Generalized anxiety also could disorganize retrieval efforts even when effort and motivation are high, resulting in a frantic, illogical search.

Preparing child witnesses with a tour of the courtroom and education about the legal system has been suggested frequently as a potential method of improving their testimony. Two recent studies have shown that children can be taught to understand relevant aspects of the investigative and judicial process, but these studies did not demonstrate a link between legal knowledge and memory performance (Sas, 1991; Saywitz et al., 1993, Experiment 7). In one study, alleged victims of child abuse demonstrated more legal knowledge after receiving individual preparation than those who received status quo services. Preparation included education to demystify the process, among other interventions, such as anxiety reduction techniques (Sas, 1991). However, components of the preparation package were not tested individually so that fear reductions could not be attributed to improved legal knowledge. Because abuse is rarely recorded objectively, examination of the effects of preparation on accuracy of memory was not possible. Another study examined effects of court education on mock testimony in a simulated trial environment. Children were questioned about a past staged event that was videotaped for comparison with children's memory (Saywitz et al., 1993, Experiment 7). However, preparation was not associated with memory benefit. The experiment did not re-create the complexities of actual trials or the feelings of actual witnesses. Expanded theories and new methods are going to be needed to address theoretical questions about the role of environmental expectations in the retrieval process as well as practical questions regarding the best methods of preparing child witnesses.

Emotional factors. The bulk of past studies have focused on children's memories for stressful events rather than the effects of stressful recall environments. However, different mental processes may be operative when the locus of stress is the retrieval environment as opposed to the event to be remembered (Davies & Thomson, 1988). There has been much speculation that high levels of stress disrupt attention, disorganize memory operations, reduce motivation, and decrease effort (Paris, 1988; Saywitz & Snyder, 1993). Studies of child witnesses have found that some children express fears of court and experience testifying as traumatic, but others do not (Goodman, Taub, et al., 1992). Prominent fears expressed by children are of public speaking and scrutiny; facing the accused, who might lie in court; losing control; embarrassment; rejection by peers; being screamed at in court; not being believed; and angering family members, especially in intrafamilial cases (Sas, 1991; Saywitz & Nathanson, 1993; Spencer & Flin, 1990). Potential system-related stressors have been identified in the literature, including multiple interviews, multiple unfamiliar interviewers, postponements, and removal from home (Goodman, Taub, et al., 1992; Runyan, Everson, Edelsohn, Hunter, & Coulter, 1988; Spencer & Flin, 1990; Tedesco & Schnell, 1987). However, the underlying mechanisms responsible for heightened stress and impoverished memory are poorly understood. Until more is known, both legal reforms to modify trial procedures and efforts to prepare child witnesses are stymied.

Two recent studies begin to test the hypothesis that anxiety associated with the forensic environment impairs memory performance (Saywitz & Nathanson, 1993; Saywitz et al., 1993, Experiment 9). In the first study, thirty-four 8- to 10-year-olds participated in an activity in their school library, and 2 weeks later their memory for the activity was tested. In groups of four, children learned about the human body with a male research assistant in the library. The event included activities involving touch, such as listening to lungs with a stethoscope, measuring heart rate, and visual inspection of esophagus, so later questioning could resemble some questions typically asked in abuse evaluations (e.g., "Where did he touch you? Did he put anything in your mouth?"). Two weeks later, half the children were questioned at a university law school courtroom in a simulated trial environment with confederate spectators and courtroom personnel. The other half were questioned in a vacant classroom at their school, both by the same interviewer. Children were aware that they were not participating in an actual trial.

Results revealed promising directions for future research. Children questioned at court showed impaired memory performance when compared with age-mates questioned at school.[1] Self-report measures of court-related stress suggested that children interviewed at court rated certain court-related experiences as more stressful than peers interviewed at school (e.g., crying on the stand, fear of speaking in front of strangers). Informal debriefing of children indicated that these items were interpreted as fears of public scrutiny, embarrassment, personal inadequacies, and inability to cope with overwhelming emotions. These factors suggest that self-image may play a powerful role in creating anxiety that interferes with information processing. Some children believed that they would be unable to cope with specific characteristics of the legal environment that they perceived to be threatening. Fearing they were not up to the challenge, motivation, effort, and ability to generate and employ retrieval strategies may have been compromised. Furthermore, children's perceptions of courtroom stress were negatively correlated with correct free recall, suggesting a relation between court-related stress and memory performance worthy of further study. Results suggested that preparation might be more successful if there was greater focus on self-image and specific fears rather than on legal knowledge and a generalized fear of the unknown.

In a follow-up study, more sensitive measures of stress (heart rate, standardized tests of anticipatory and trait anxiety) and self-image (standardized self-report of self-concept and social support) were used with a larger sample (Saywitz et al., 1993, Experiment 9). This time, care was taken to ensure that the encoding and retrieval environments shared no cues in common. In this second study, eighty 8- to 10-year-olds were randomly assigned to mock testimony in the simulated courtroom setting or in a private room at the law school. These children participated in the same staged school activity described above—the physiology lesson.

Impaired free recall and more reactive heart rate patterns, indicative of a stress response, were associated with the courtroom setting in comparison with the private room. For children who were questioned at court, correlations suggested that, the stronger the children believed their social support network to be, the less stressful they perceived the courtroom to be, and the higher children perceived themselves and their social support, the less anticipatory anxiety they reported. In the second study, responses to direct questions did not differ across settings as they did in the first experiment. This could be due to two facts. First, both groups were questioned in unfamiliar environments, creating a more difficult memory task for all. Second, direct questions offer ample retrieval cues, making them less vulnerable than free recall to effects of stress.

In this sample, there were discrepancies between physiological data and self-report data that are not uncommon in this literature as both children and adults may not admit to feelings they are experiencing if they perceive the feelings to be socially undesirable. Anecdotally, some children were observed to be anxious (stuttering, fidgety) and showed erratic heart rate patterns but, after testifying, said the experience was not stressful, even fun. The co-occurrence of recall and heart rate differences between the two environments is a finding worthy of further investigation. Given the reliability problems inherent in children's self-report of emotional state, physiological correlates of anxiety may provide a more sensitive measure of the influence of stressful environments on children's memory. Given that the legal environment is not experienced (consciously or unconsciously) as stressful by all children, it also will be important to pursue studying the specific characteristics of this environment that children perceive as stressful (e.g., public speaking).

These findings highlight the need for further study of methods to create an optimal environment for testifying that maximizes memory function and minimizes stress. Reforms that modify the environment (closed-circuit television, presence of spectators or support persons) should be further studied. Studies that vary separate components of the courtroom experience (e.g., familiarity, formality, presence of support persons or spectators) could guide reform efforts. For example, if the quality of children's evidence varies with the presence of spectators or support persons, in interaction with individual differences among children, then guidelines for closing of the courtroom to spectators or allowing support persons during testimony could be developed.

Future Directions

To improve the quality of children's testimony, we will need to continue to devise new theories and methods to attain a better understanding of the relation between environment, emotion, and testimony. Memory researchers will need to turn their creative energies to elusive variables that are difficult to measure. Beyond the study of stressful retrieval environments, the effects of variables such as self-image, coping patterns, and social support will need to be explored. For example, in our laboratory we have found child witnesses to vary markedly in their approach to preparation. Some are resistant. They want to avoid thinking about testimony until the court date. Others strive for mastery. They want to learn as much as possible about the legal system. Individual differences in strategies for coping with stress will likely be a fruitful avenue for exploration.

Additionally, researchers will need to focus on moments of inadequate information processing under less than optimal conditions by children who have delays, disorders, and maladaptive coping patterns. There is ample reason to believe that child victim witnesses may not always process information similarly to "normal" age-mates in research studies. Two diagnoses common among abuse victims are depression and post-traumatic stress disorder (PTSD; Beitchman, Zucker, Hood, LaCosta, & Akman, 1991). Symptoms of depression include fatigue, poor concentration, delayed response times, anhedonia (lack of motivation, interest, or pleasure), and feelings of hopelessness, helplessness, and despair. Given a theory of motivated remembering, it is not difficult to hypothesize how such symptomatology could dramatically reduce both motivation and effort applied to the retrieval process. Symptoms of post-traumatic stress disorder include recurrent, intrusive, distressing recollections; flashbacks that accompany deliberate recall attempts (reliving, not merely retelling); psychogenic amnesia; and difficulty concentrating. These symptoms might derail a logical appraisal of strategy utility, task demands, outcomes, and consequences, resulting instead in a disoriented, inefficient search or even complete failure to recall. Children suffering from PTSD also show behaviors—such as avoidance of thoughts, feelings, or situations associated with the traumatic event; diminished interest in goal-directed activities; a sense of a foreshortened future; and feelings of detachment—that could affect motivation, effort, and strategy selection.

The goal of this chapter was to present a comprehensive picture of children's testimony as a function of the question, the answer, and the environment rather than of the child alone. Such a framework suggests that practical improvements can come from (a) changing adult behaviors to increase the developmental sensitivity of questions, promoting more effective communication; (b) preparing child witnesses with strategy instructional training, court education on the legal process, and anxiety reduction techniques; and (c) modifying the physical, social, and emotional environment of testifying. Researchers will need to turn their attention to expanded theories, involving variables that traditionally have been difficult to measure. New methods of measurement, such as physiological correlates of emotional states, will need to be created. Innovative methods of improving children's testimony are on the horizon but require further testing of both positive and negative effects to ensure that improvements in one area are not offset by side effects that contaminate testimony in unanticipated ways. Past studies have revealed considerable information about child witnesses' limitations and needs. Devoting similar resources to improving the quality of children's testimony should be rewarded with a greater understanding of memory development and greater protection of both children and adults.

future;
conc.

Note

1. It could be argued that, because both the staged event and the interview were on the school campus, cues in the school environment improved recall of children interviewed at school rather than the courtroom, interfering with memory at court (Davies & Thomson, 1988; Tulving & Thomson, 1973). However, care was taken to ensure that the interviews were conducted in a different setting from the activity (library versus classroom).

7

Improving Eyewitness Testimony
With the Cognitive Interview

RONALD P. FISHER

MICHELLE R. McCAULEY

Surveys of the criminal justice system indicate that the primary determinant of whether or not a case will be solved is the completeness and accuracy of the eyewitness's (EW's) account (RAND, 1975; Sanders, 1986). Despite the importance of EW information, police detectives receive only minimal—and often no—training in effective methods to interview cooperative EWs (Cahill & Mingay, 1986; George & Clifford, 1992; RAND, 1975). More typically, police learn to conduct interviews by trial and error or by emulating the style of a senior officer. Often they are simply given a checklist of evidence to be

AUTHORS' NOTE: Much of the research reported here was supported by grants from the National Institute of Justice (USDJ-83-IJ-CX-0025 and USDJ-85-IJ-CX-0053) and the National Science Foundation (SES8911146). We would like to thank the police officers who participated in the field studies and a crew of devoted research assistants who spent many hours coding data: Denise Chin, Kathy Quigley, Petra Brock, Iris Alhassid, Alisa Simon, Robyn Berliner, and Michael Amador. Many of the ideas stated here overlap with those presented in Fisher, McCauley, and Geiselman (1994).

gathered and are left on their own, without guidance, to elicit the information. Given this lack of training, it should not be surprising that police investigators (and others equally untrained, including defense and prosecuting attorneys) frequently make avoidable mistakes and fail to elicit potentially valuable information.

In response to the need to improve police interview procedures, Fisher and Geiselman developed a new procedure based on the scientific literature of cognitive psychology (hence the name "cognitive interview": CI). This chapter reviews the work done to develop the CI, and it is presented in six sections: (a) principles of the CI, (b) empirical evaluation, (c) extensions and current research, (d) children as witnesses, (e) methodological and legal challenges, and (f) limitations of the CI.

Our approach to enhancing children's recollection was initially to develop a working procedure for adults and then to modify it for children. We did this, in part, because of the great wealth of empirical literature and formal modeling of cognition in adults. The extension from adults to children appears justified as (a) theoretically, there is good reason to believe that many underlying cognitive processes are used by both adults and children (Lindberg, 1980), and (b) empirically, several mnemonics and other cognitive interventions that are effective for adults are also effective for children (Pressley, Borkowski, & Johnson, 1987). The proof of the pudding, as shown in this chapter, is that children's testimony can be enhanced by applying techniques based on adults—albeit with appropriate modifications.

Principles of the CI

The CI has evolved in two distinct phases over the past 10 years. The original version of the CI was made up of a limited set of interviewing principles designed to enhance memory retrieval under the ideal conditions established in our first set of laboratory studies: interviewing college students who were uninvolved bystander witnesses to a simulated event. Since then, we have revised the technique considerably to address the wide range of information-processing problems found in the world of police investigations, with real victims of crime. Here, the interviewer's task is infinitely more complex, as EWs may be frightened, inarticulate, and unwilling to participate in an extensive investigation.

We shall focus here on the revised CI, as it is substantially more effective than the original version (Fisher, Geiselman, Raymond, Jurkevich, & Warhaftig,

1987) and because of its utility in realistic situations. Most of the principles of the CI fall into one of two categories: memory and general cognition, and social dynamics and communication between the interviewer and the EW. Because of space limitations, only thumbnail descriptions of the underlying psychological principles and a sampling of the most important interviewing techniques are included here. A more thorough description of the CI, written in the style of a user's manual, is available in Fisher and Geiselman (1992).

MEMORY AND GENERAL COGNITION

The principles of memory and cognition reflect generally accepted beliefs about mental representation, memory retrieval, and information processing. These principles are derived primarily from the scientific literature in cognition.

Re-create original context. The effectiveness of a retrieval cue is related to the amount of overlap with the originally encoded event (Flexser & Tulving, 1978; Tulving & Thomson, 1973). Therefore EWs are instructed to mentally re-create the environmental, cognitive, physiological, and affective states that existed at the time of the original event.

Partial information. The memory code representing a complex event is made up of several component features (Bower, 1967; Wickens, 1970). Because of this, EWs are encouraged to describe individual features of an event even when the holistic label is not available. For example, if EWs cannot think of a name that was mentioned, they are instructed to recall partial information, such as the number of syllables in the name.

Varied retrieval. There may be several retrieval paths to a stored event, so that information not accessible with one retrieval cue may be accessible with a different cue. Therefore witnesses are asked to think of the event from many different approaches, such as in chronological order and reverse order. (Although these suggestions work effectively with adults, they should not be used with children; Geiselman & Padilla, 1988.) To minimize the possibility that these techniques might encourage fabrication, and as a general safeguard against guessing, EWs are explicitly cautioned not to fabricate answers.

Limited mental resources. People have only limited mental resources to process information (Baddeley, 1986). Therefore any sources of distraction may interfere with the EW's retrieving or describing information from memory. Some of the specific interviewing techniques suggested to minimize distractions are asking open-ended questions and not interrupting in the middle of the EW's response.

Guided imagery. Each EW may have several mental representations of an event (Fisher & Chandler, 1991). Some representations are highly detailed and reflect minute, sensory properties; other representations are more generic and reflect a more abstract, meaningful interpretation of the event (see Paivio's, 1971, dual-coding hypothesis). To induce recall based on the more detailed, sensory representations, EWs are encouraged to close their eyes and use mental imagery (including nonvisual images) to guide their responses.

Witness-compatible questioning. Each EW's mental representation of an event is unique. The interviewer must therefore tailor the questions to the unique mental representation of the particular EW instead of asking all EWs the same set of questions. This rule is violated when interviewers use a standardized checklist to guide their questions.

SOCIAL DYNAMICS AND COMMUNICATION
BETWEEN THE INTERVIEWER AND THE EYEWITNESS

The following principles largely reflect the social nature of the interview and the difference between the interviewer's and the EW's knowledge. Some of our recommendations stem from the scientific literature in communication and small groups; others are based on a task analysis of investigative interviewing and a careful perusal of dozens of taped interviews.

Knowledge of event-specific content. By definition, the EW has firsthand knowledge of the crime not available to the interviewer. Therefore the EW, not the interviewer, should be doing most of the mental activity during the interview. In practice, these roles often are reversed and the EW sits passively waiting for the interviewer to ask questions. Interviewers can induce EWs to take more active roles by explicitly conveying this expectation, asking open-ended questions, and permitting EWs to engage in tangential narration.

Knowledge of crime-relevant information. Although the EW knows more about the details of the specific event, the interviewer knows more about which dimensions of the crime are important for the investigation. The interviewer must therefore direct the EW's report to relevant dimensions, but without dominating the interview. This may be accomplished by framing questions to address informative content and asking closed questions strategically (to complete responses to open-ended questions).

Promoting extensive and detailed responses. Witnesses may provide incomplete and imprecise responses even though they possess extensive, detailed knowledge. This may occur because (a) they edit information they believe is forensically irrelevant or inappropriate, or (b) they are unaccustomed to describing events in detail. These limitations may be overcome by explicitly requesting EWs (a) not to edit any of their thoughts but to describe everything that comes to mind and (b) to describe objects and events in minute detail. Interviewers also may unwittingly prevent extensive responses by interrupting prematurely during a pause in the EW's narration. Speakers frequently pause during narrative descriptions to organize the remainder of their responses (Ford & Holmes, 1978). Any interruption during this pause, even to ask a follow-up question, may cut short additional information that would have been forthcoming.

Using nonverbal responding. Traditionally, interviews are conducted as verbal exchanges. By relying so heavily on the verbal medium, the quality of the interview is limited by the EW's vocabulary. This is particularly so for children, whose verbal skills are often impoverished. Even articulate respondents are limited, as some events or objects are difficult to describe verbally (Leibowitz & Guzy, 1990). To overcome this limitation, EWs should be encouraged to use nonverbal means to replace or supplement their verbal responses. For instance, EWs might be asked to draw a sketch of an object or act out a movement.

In addition to the above, the CI addresses some of the social skills that are critical when interviewing victims of crime: developing rapport, maintaining the EW's confidence, and controlling the EW's anxiety. Finally, the CI follows an orderly sequence. The general strategy is to guide the EW to those memory codes that are richest in relevant information and to facilitate communication when these memory codes have been activated. Each of the five major sections of the CI makes a unique contribution to the overall goal. (a) The introduction and rapport-building phase establishes the essential interpersonal dynamics necessary to promote effective memory and communication during the remainder of the interview. (b) Beginning with an open-ended narrative is crucial for inferring the EW's mental representation of the crime. This then becomes the basis for developing an efficient strategy to probe the EW's memory codes. (c) The probing stage is the primary information-gathering phase. During this phase, the interviewer guides the EW to the richest sources of knowledge and thoroughly exhausts them of their contents. (d) In the review stage, the interviewer reviews the information obtained from the EW to ensure its accuracy. This also provides the EW with an additional opportunity to recall. (e) Finally, the interviewer closes the interview by offering a suggestion to extend the functional life of the interview should the EW later recall additional facts. (See Bull's chapter in this volume for a similar recommendation about the sequence of the interview.)

TRAINING TO CONDUCT THE CI

Learning to conduct the CI properly requires substantial training, as there are many skills to learn, some of which are diametrically opposed to the techniques currently used by many experienced police (see Fisher, Geiselman, & Raymond, 1987, and George, 1991, for descriptions of typical police interviewing procedures). For example, whereas police typically ask a preponderance of closed-ended questions, the CI recommends asking primarily open-ended questions. Police often ask questions in a predetermined order, whereas the CI requires that the interviewer be flexible and make the question sequence compatible with the EW's unique mental representation. Our experience has been that several sessions are required to train investigators properly, and that feedback is an essential component of the training (see Fisher & Geiselman, 1992, chap. 13, for a description of the recommended training program).

Empirical Evaluation

The CI should not be thought of as a formula or recipe for conducting an interview. Rather, it should be regarded as a toolbox of techniques that are selected according to the specific needs of the interview, much as a carpenter's tools are selected according to the specific task. It is unlikely that any interviewer will use all of the recommended techniques in any one interview (George, 1991). We should expect that the technique as it is actually used will vary considerably across interviewers and across specific situations. Evaluation of the CI is not so much a test of the mnemonic value of individual techniques but whether exposure to the *range* of techniques is valuable (although see Geiselman, Fisher, MacKinnon, & Holland, 1986; George, 1991; and Memon, Cronin, Eaves, & Bull, 1992, for tests of specific mnemonic components).

At the time of this writing, more than 25 experiments have been conducted comparing the CI with standard police methods of interviewing. Most of these studies were based on the original version of the CI, which contained only a small subset of the techniques described here (the revised CI). Specifically, the original CI only instructed the EW to (a) re-create the context of the original event, (b) not edit any responses, (c) recall the information in different orders and from different perspectives, and (d) recall partial information. The results of these studies have been reviewed thoroughly in recent articles by Fisher, McCauley, and Geiselman (1994), Memon and Köhnken (1992), Bekerian and Dennett (1993), and Memon and Bull (1991). We shall briefly summarize this body of research and focus primarily on the revised CI.

Original CI. Most of the studies on the original CI conformed to the following paradigm. Volunteer witnesses (typically college students) observed either a live, nonthreatening event or a videotape of a simulated crime. Several hours or a few days later, the EWs participated in a face-to-face interview that resembled a standard police interview or that used the principles of the (original) CI. The interviewers were experienced police detectives or research assistants trained to conduct a police-style interview or the CI. The interviews were tape-recorded, transcribed, and then scored for the number of correct and incorrect bits of information recalled.

The bulk of the earlier studies were conducted in our labs in the United States; however, recently, Köhnken, Memon, and their colleagues have conducted studies in Germany and England. The results from the various labs are highly similar and converge on a common finding. Across 26 studies, the original CI elicited approximately 35% extra correct information than the standard interview. Equally important, there was no increase in the amount of incorrect information (see Köhnken, 1992, for a meta-analysis of the results).

Revised CI. Evaluating the revised CI is difficult because of the limited number of studies. Only four studies meet our criteria as proper tests of the revised

CI. Some studies were not included because they incorporated only a few of the principles of the revised CI; others did not provide extensive enough training—in our judgment—for the interviewers to learn the technique properly. The four studies to be described include two laboratory studies and two field studies, with real victims and witnesses of crime.

In the first laboratory test of the revised CI (Fisher, Geiselman, Raymond, Jurkevich, & Warhaftig, 1987), college students were interviewed 2 days after viewing a videotape of a simulated crime (bank robbery or liquor store robbery). Half of the EWs received the original version of the CI and half received the revised version. The interviews were conducted by high school or undergraduate students who were trained to conduct both versions of the CI.

As in the earlier studies, the interviews were tape-recorded and scored by comparing the transcripts with the videotaped crimes. The revised CI yielded approximately 45% more correct information than did the original version (mean number of facts = 57.5 and 39.6) with no significant loss of accuracy (12.0 versus 9.4 incorrect facts). Compared with a standard police interview (from similar conditions in Geiselman, Fisher, MacKinnon, & Holland, 1985), the revised CI elicited almost twice as much information (96%). This almost twofold increase in information is even more startling when one considers that the standard interview (from Geiselman et al.) was conducted by experienced detectives, whereas the revised CI was conducted by students with approximately 10 hours of training.

A second laboratory study was conducted by George (1991) in England to compare the CI with standard (British) police techniques. In this study, college students observed two actors interrupt a lecture. Two weeks later, the EWs returned to the laboratory where they were interviewed by experienced police officers. As in the earlier study, the total amount of correct information elicited by the CI (67.5 facts) was considerably greater than the standard procedure (49.8 facts). This 35% advantage for the CI was approximately the same for describing events as for describing people (intruders). Again, the mean number of errors elicited was approximately the same for the CI (7.25) as the standard procedure (7.75).

One might argue that laboratory studies are biased against police interviewing techniques, as they have evolved to meet the realistic conditions found in the field, not the artificial conditions found in the laboratory. In response to this objection, two studies were conducted in the field.

In one of these studies (Fisher, Geiselman, & Amador, 1989), 16 experienced detectives from the Robbery Division of the Metro-Dade Police Department

Table 7.1   Number of Facts Elicited by Trained and Untrained Detectives

	Training Phase	
Training Group	Before	After
CI-trained	26.8	39.6
Untrained	23.8	24.2

served as the interviewers. In the initial phase of the study, the detectives tape-recorded four to six interviews, typically from victims or witnesses of purse snatching or commercial robbery. Based on the detectives' performance in these interviews and on their supervisors' ratings, the detectives were divided into two equivalent groups. One group of seven detectives received training on the CI; the other group did not receive this additional training. The training consisted of four 2-hour sessions of lecture and demonstrations of good and poor interviewing techniques. Following training, the detectives conducted a "practice" interview in the field and then received feedback on their technique. In the months following this feedback, detectives tape-recorded several additional field interviews with other victims and witnesses. The taped interviews were then transcribed and scored blind for the number of crime-relevant facts.

As a group, the detectives who received training in the CI collected 48% more information after training than before (Table 7.1). Of the seven trained detectives, six improved dramatically (34%-115%). The one detective who did not change his interviewing style was the only one who failed to improve. A second analysis reflects the Phase × Training interaction, in which the trained and untrained detectives were equivalent before training, but the trained group collected 63% more information after training.

In comparison with laboratory research, field studies do not permit us to determine the accuracy of the elicited information. We therefore estimated accuracy by determining the degree to which EWs' statements were corroborated by other EWs to the crimes. In 22 cases, there was another victim or witness whose descriptions were recorded on the police crime report. In all, there were 325 potentially corroborable statements. Overall, the corroboration rates (percentage of elicited facts corroborated by other EWs) were extremely high and were similar for the pretrained (93.0%) and posttrained interviews (94.5). Although not equivalent to accuracy, these corroboration scores lead us to believe that training in the CI did not promote inaccuracy.

An independent field study of the CI was conducted by George (1991; see also George & Clifford, 1992) with 32 British police investigators from different police departments. Each of the investigators initially tape-recorded three interviews with victims and witnesses of street crimes or serious traffic accidents. The investigators then were assigned randomly to CI training or no additional training. Following training, each investigator tape-recorded another three interviews with victims and witnesses. The tapes were then transcribed and scored for questioning style (kinds of question asked) and amount of information elicited.

The questioning style changed dramatically from before training to after training, but only in the CI group. Compared with their interviewing style before training, the CI group after training (a) asked fewer questions, (b) asked a higher proportion of open-ended questions, (c) injected more pauses, and (d) asked fewer leading questions. This change in questioning style was accompanied by an increase in the amount of information elicited. The CI group elicited more information than did the standard police interview, whether comparing trained with untrained interviewers (14% advantage) or comparing the trained detectives after versus before training (55% advantage). This advantage of the CI held for a variety of types of information (e.g., object, person, location).

The revised CI has now been found to be effective in four independently conducted studies with different pools of interviewers and EWs in each study. In all four studies, the pattern was the same: The CI elicited more correct information than did a standard police interview (or than the original version of the CI, which had earlier been shown to be more effective than a police interview) and without eliciting additional incorrect (or uncorroborated) information.

Extensions and Current Research

Given the past success of the CI to elicit more complete EW descriptions, we are currently examining its use in a related EW task: identifying suspects from lineups. In addition, we are exploring the CI for use in noncriminal investigations.

Identifying suspects. There are some suggestions that the cognitive processes mediating recall and recognition may differ (e.g., Pigott & Brigham, 1985;

Wells, 1985), so we were initially uncertain about the CI's success in a person-identification task. In the first experiment (Fisher, Quigley, Brock, Chin, & Cutler, 1990), EWs observed a staged theft; 2 days later they tried to describe the suspect and identify him from a four-person lineup. Half of the EWs were given the CI before attempting identification and half were given a standard (description) interview before identification. Although the EWs provided better descriptions of the thief with the CI than with the standard interview, they were no more successful in the identification task. Those receiving the CI were correct on 61% of the lineups; those receiving the standard interview were correct on 64%.

Given this failure of the CI, we modified it in light of recent suggestions that face recognition (a) may be interfered with by verbal coding (Schooler & Engstler-Schooler, 1990) and (b) relies primarily on interfeatural (holistic) information (Wells & Turtle, 1987). The modified (for recognition) CI encouraged EWs to (a) concentrate more on developing pictorial information and suppressing verbal descriptions and (b) think in terms of holistic properties of the face rather than specific features. In a test of this modified-for-recognition CI, 2 days after viewing a videotape of a robbery EWs attempted to identify the suspect from a five-person lineup. Again there were no differences: Subjects in the CI and unaided conditions were correct on the same percentage of trials (63% versus 65%). Two additional studies were conducted and the results remained unchanged: The CI did not improve identification from lineups or photo arrays. It is not clear to us why the CI was ineffective with the identification task, especially given the success of other researchers who have used components of the CI (context reinstatement) to enhance person recognition (Krafka & Penrod, 1985; Malpass & Devine, 1981). Nevertheless, the fact remains that the CI did not enhance recognition.

Noncriminal investigations. Although the legal ramifications of a criminal investigation may be more serious than for a civil investigation, we might expect that the EW's task, and hence the cognitive mechanisms employed, is similar. If so, the CI ought to extend to a wide variety of investigative interviews. We describe one such situation: witnessing a car accident (see Fisher & Quigley, 1991, for a public health investigation of ill persons recalling the foods eaten at an earlier meal).

In a study recently completed in our laboratory, college students watched a short videotape including a 15-second excerpt of a car accident. The EWs were then interviewed either with the CI or with a standard protocol modeled after that used by investigators from the National Transportation Safety Board. All of the EWs were interviewed twice: 5 minutes after viewing the accident and again 2 weeks later. Half of the EWs received the same type of interview on the two occasions (either both CI or both standard) and half received different types of interview (standard on one and CI on the other).

The results showed that, for both the initial interview and second interview, almost twice as many facts were elicited with the CI than with the standard interview. On the initial interview, the CI elicited a mean of 25.9 correct facts compared with the standard interview's 14.9 facts. The scores were almost identical on the second interview: CI = 24.6 and standard = 14.8.

Of interest, there was almost no forgetting from the first to the second interview, despite the 2-week delay, perhaps reflecting the memory-enhancing effects of the initial retrieval attempt (Fisher & Chandler, 1991).

As opposed to the findings in all of our prior studies, we observed here that significantly more errors were elicited by the CI (10.4 and 10.5 on the first and second interviews, respectively) than with the standard interview (6.1 and 6.8). Note that, although the CI elicited more total errors than did the standard interview, the *rate* of inaccuracy (number of errors divided by total number of responses) was approximately the same for the CI (.29) and the standard interview (.30).

Although the CI elicited more information than did the standard on the first interview, there was no carryover effect to the second interview. The CI-CI group did not recall more correct information on the second interview (mean = 24.0) than did the standard-CI group (22.9). Similarly, the additional errors elicited by the CI on the first interview did not carry over to the second interview. This lack of carryover effects can be interpreted either positively or negatively. On the positive side, having conducted a standard interview immediately after an event does not mitigate the effects of a later CI (versus a later standard interview). On the negative side, having done an initial CI does not increase the amount of information that will be elicited by a later interview. The advantage conferred by conducting a CI is restricted to that particular interview.

One insight into the effectiveness of the CI comes from analyzing the information recalled into those facts elicited by open-ended requests (e.g., "Describe the driver of the car at fault.") and those elicited by specific, closed requests (e.g., "What color was the car at fault?"). In the present experiment, the CI elicited considerably more correct information than did the standard for open-ended requests (mean number of facts recalled = 21.9 versus 9.9, respectively). However, there was almost no difference between the CI and the standard when specific, closed questions were asked (19.0 versus 16.7). This trend mirrors the results found in George's (1991) field study, where the advantage of the CI was very large when open-ended questions were asked (24.1 bits of information for the CI, but only 6.4 bits for the standard). There was only a small advantage, however, when specific, closed questions were asked (4.6 versus 2.7). One possible implication of this finding is that the CI will be most effective in those cases where the investigator has the least amount of prior knowledge—and hence should ask more open-ended questions. Conversely, if the investigator is interested in ascertaining only a limited pool of facts, and can formulate all of the requisite closed questions, then the CI will have less value.

Children as Witnesses

In recent years, an increasing number of children have been asked to testify, especially about events in which they were alleged to be victims. In response to this public concern, there has been a marked increase in research on children's eyewitness testimony. Much of this research is directed toward describing children's and adults' normative performance, specifically in terms of their relative accuracy and suggestibility (see Ceci & Bruck, 1993a, for a review). An alternative approach, which we believe to be more valuable, is to develop intervention programs to enhance children's recollection. As Fivush and Shukat (this volume) suggest: "Research needs to focus on finding better ways to elicit what we now know young children are able to recall" (p. 22).

Three studies previously evaluated the original CI's effectiveness with children (Geiselman & Padilla, 1988; Geiselman, Saywitz, & Bornstein, 1990; Memon et al., 1992). In Geiselman and Padilla, 15 children between the ages of 7 and 12 viewed a videotaped robbery. Three days later the children were interviewed about the robbery using either a standard interview or CI. Compared with the standard interview, the CI elicited 21% more accurate items reported without an increase in errors. Geiselman et al. (1990) tested 38 children between 7 and 11 years old after they played games involving actions and touching with an adult experimenter ("Simon Says"). After 2 days, the children were given either a standard interview or a CI. In comparison with the standard, the CI increased the number of correct facts by 26% across both age groups without increasing the amount of incorrect information reported.

Memon et al. (1992) assessed thirty-one 7-year-old children's memory for an annual school-sponsored vision test. Two days after the vision test, the children were interviewed either with a standard interview or with the CI. They described adults present during the vision test, the actions involved in the test, and also the location. Memon et al. did not find any beneficial effect of the CI in terms of the overall amount of correct information elicited. However, the CI did elicit more information about the location of objects and the people involved in the activity.

In light of the original CI's success with children, we examined whether the revised CI, modified to accommodate the processing styles of children, could improve recall to a greater extent. The primary modification of the CI was geared toward overcoming children's tendency to provide very brief responses when speaking to unfamiliar adults. Toward that aim, we primed children to provide extensive and elaborate responses in a preliminary phase of the interview by asking them to describe an action that they were familiar with (brushing their teeth in Experiment 1, a popular computer game in Experiment 2). During this activity, the adult interviewer conveyed the need to generate detailed responses either by probing extensively (Experiment 1) or by pretending not to know how to play the game (Experiment 2). We hypothesized that the children would carry over the style of detailed descriptions elicited in the preliminary phase to the experimental event.

In the first experiment (McCauley & Fisher, 1992), 7-year-old children interacted with an adult experimenter by going through a series of actions in the form of a Simon Says game. Two weeks later the children were interviewed about the Simon Says activities either in the standard format used by investigative interviewers (see Geiselman & Padilla, 1988, for a description) or by the CI as revised for children. The children who received the CI correctly recalled almost twice as many actions (15.6) as those who received the standard interview (8.4). The number of incorrect activities recalled was surprisingly small and similar for the two groups (mean = 0.55).

One potential criticism of the first experiment is that our definition of a "standard investigative interview" may have been incorrect and that real-world investigative interviews are actually better than our experimental version. We addressed this problem in a second experiment by asking professional social workers who interview children for the legal system to construct an interview protocol for us modeling their own procedures (as modified for the Simon Says format). Our research assistants followed this protocol as the standard interview. As an additional control condition, two of the professional children's interviewers also served as interviewers in the experiment. The procedure was similar to that of Experiment 1, with the exception that the children were interviewed twice after the Simon Says game: either 1 to 4 hours later or after 2 weeks. The results mimicked those of Experiment 1 for both interviews. On the first interview, the CI (19.9 correct facts) elicited approximately 65% more information than both standard interviews, with virtually no difference between the interviews conducted by our research assistants (12.1) and those conducted by professionals (11.8). The same pattern of results was found for the second interview: CI = 18.5 facts; research assistant standard = 12.8; professional standard = 12.8. The number of incorrect facts elicited was again extremely low and equivalent for the CI and the two standard interviews. Similar to the traffic accident study with adults, there was no drop in amount or accuracy of information recalled from a first interview (few hours' delay) to a 2-week delay interview.

Methodological and Legal Challenges

As with other new techniques, we expect use of the CI to be challenged by the legal system. This reflects a healthy skepticism and should be encouraged. We shall try to anticipate the kinds of objections opponents of the CI may raise and examine them in light of empirical evidence. First, we shall examine some potential methodological problems and then explore possible legal concerns.

Methodological problems. The effectiveness of the CI may reflect an artifact in the design of the experiments. Perhaps some other factor correlated with implementing the CI was responsible for its effects. Four such alternative interpretations are that (a) the CI does not enhance recollection but simply lowers the EW's threshold to say anything, whether correct or not; (b) the CI takes longer than does a standard interview, and it is the additional time that is responsible for the extra information; (c) the CI-trained interviewers may be more motivated than their standard counterparts to conduct good interviews (Hawthorne effect) and may even subtly convey the correct answers to the EWs; and (d) the information elicited by the CI is not relevant for police investigations.

   a. In more than 20 published experiments conducted on the CI, there were
       no reliable differences between the number of errors elicited in the CI

and standard conditions—although recently we have seen two unpublished studies with increased errors. Furthermore, the error *rates* (proportion of responses that were incorrect) in these studies typically were lower in the CI than in the standard condition. The overall evidence then suggests that the CI does not lower recall accuracy.

b. In some of the laboratory studies, the CI took longer to conduct than the standard interview. However, there is no reason to believe that time itself was responsible for the better recall. Roediger and Thorpe (1978) found that increasing the amount of time allotted for recall led to more correct responses; however, this was at the expense of increased intrusions. This suggests that increased time does not enhance recall as much as it lowers the threshold for responding. In one early study of the (original) CI, interview time was covaried out, yet the CI still elicited more correct information than did the standard interview (Geiselman et al., 1985). Finally, in the two field studies conducted on the CI, the amount of time to conduct the CI and standard interviews did not differ reliably. In fact, in George's (1991) study, the CI-trained interviewers took less time to conduct the interview after training than before training.

c. The CI interviewers probably realized that they were the "experimental group" in our studies. However, there is no evidence that they tried any harder to conduct effective interviews. If they did, one might have expected them to ask more questions. On the contrary, the CI-trained interviewers asked fewer questions than did the standard interviewers (Geiselman et al., 1985; George, 1991). Second, it may have been possible for the interviewers to subtly convey the correct answers to the EWs in the laboratory studies—as they interviewed several EWs about the same event. Our analysis of the taped interviews did not reveal any such practice. If this did occur, the superiority of the CI should have increased across blocks of trials, that is, as the interviewer became more familiar with the crime. We found, however, that the superiority of the CI was as great on the first interview conducted by an interviewer—when he had no prior knowledge of the crime—as on later interviews about the crime (Geiselman et al., 1985).

d. One might reasonably argue that academic psychologists do not know what information is relevant for police investigations. Hence the "additional information" elicited by the CI may be of little practical import. This argument may be true in part, especially for those laboratory studies in which the interviewers were research assistants. However, the same pattern of results was found in the two field studies in which the interviewers were experienced detectives trying to solve a real crime. Furthermore, the second field study (George, 1991) was conducted by an experienced police officer (Detective Sergeant Richard George of the City of London Police Department). We are confident in assuming that he correctly evaluated the relevance of the information elicited.

Legal challenges. We expect that legal challenges of the CI will follow along the same lines as those applied to hypnosis: (a) it is unreliable as a memory enhancer, (b) it leads to increased error or confabulation, and (c) it renders EWs hypersuggestible to leading questions (Gudjonsson, 1992; Wrightsman, 1991). As far as we know, none of these problems has been found with the CI.

a. In 23 of the 24 experiments that we are aware of, the CI has led to more information than has a standard interview. Note that this holds only when EWs are describing people or events, not when they are identifying people from lineups or photo arrays.
b. As mentioned earlier, all of the published studies show no differences in the numbers of errors (fabrications) elicited by the CI and standard interviews. When error *rate* is used as the index of fabrication, the CI generally promotes more accurate responding.
c. When tested in the field, CI-trained interviewers asked *fewer*, not more, leading questions than did standard interviewers (George, 1991). This should not be surprising given that, in comparison with standard interviewers, CI interviewers (a) asked proportionally more open-ended questions, which lend themselves easily to neutral wording, and (b) asked fewer questions overall. In the one laboratory study where (mis)leading questions were introduced intentionally, those EWs given the (original) CI were less influenced by the (mis)leading information than those who were given the standard interview (Geiselman, Fisher, Cohen, Holland, & Surtes, 1986). Thus the concern about suggestibility to leading questions argues in favor of, not in opposition to, using the CI.

Limitations of the CI

Although the CI has been demonstrated to be an effective investigative procedure under some circumstances, there are restrictions on its utility. The technique is geared to assisting EWs to overcome the cognitive limitations of average citizens. In many police investigations, however, the major stumbling block is that potential EWs do not want to participate. They may be suspects; they may not want to take the time; they may not want to "get involved." The CI is not intended to overcome these motivational barriers and is not at all useful in such situations. In a similar vein, the CI's effectiveness will be restricted to those cases that depend heavily on EW evidence, such as robbery or assault. Cases that depend primarily on physical evidence (e.g., fingerprints) or on documentation will be unaffected.

Despite some of our findings that the CI did not take reliably longer to conduct than did a standard interview, we expect that it should take somewhat longer. That should limit the CI's use to those cases in which there is adequate time to conduct a thorough interview. Given the workload of many investigators, the CI will likely be used only in major crimes, where more resources can be applied. Often, a preliminary interview will be conducted by a uniformed police officer shortly after a crime has been committed. This interview has limited scope (often to elicit a cursory description of the getaway vehicle and the assailant) and must be completed quickly. Given these constraints, we expect the CI to be less practical here.

The CI requires considerable mental concentration on the part of the interviewer. He or she must make more on-line decisions and show greater flexibility than is typically demonstrated in police interviews. In that sense, it is more difficult to conduct the CI than the standard interview.

Finally, we expect that the CI will be most valuable in the earlier phases of the investigation, before the EW has had ample time to rehearse the event repeatedly and to prepare a set account to be staged in the courtroom. Attorneys may find the technique most useful when first meeting with clients to elicit a more complete description of the event in question. In the courtroom, where much of the EW's testimony is scripted, the CI should be of less value.

Conclusion

Thus far, the CI has been found effective within limited parameters: eliciting descriptions of events from motivated child or adult EWs shortly after the event has occurred (within 2 weeks). Clearly, this covers only a restricted subset of the kinds of investigative interviews that actually take place. Victims are often the elderly, who have unique information-processing deficits; several months or even years may pass before an EW is interviewed; innocent suspects must be interviewed to elicit exculpatory evidence; and so on. For the CI to be of greatest value to the legal system, (a) it must be modified to meet the information-processing demands of these unexplored areas, and (b) its limitations must be clearly recognized. This is especially the case with children who have been physically or sexually abused, as their ability or willingness to testify may not be limited primarily by problems of memory or communication. In such instances, the CI's effectiveness likely will be enhanced if it is used in concert with other psychological techniques that are better suited to deal with the child's emotional distress or confusion (Westcott, 1992a).

The potential of the CI to improve the quality of forensic investigations has been demonstrated. Converting that potential into practice requires modifying the training that police (and attorneys) receive. Many current training programs focus on the *content* of the information to be elicited without addressing the *process* of acquiring information. We are encouraged to see that, recently, suggestions have been made to rectify this situation by providing training in CI techniques (George & Clifford, 1992). If such a policy decision is made, then one direction for future research is to develop improved methods of training novices (and retraining experienced investigators) to learn the CI.

8

The Use of Dolls in Interviewing Young Children

JUDY S. DeLOACHE

In today's increasingly circuslike atmosphere in which fears of widespread but undiscovered child abuse compete for attention with fears of false allegations of abuse, there is no more crucial agenda than the development of better techniques for interviewing children. The goal is to avoid tragedy on either side—either by failing to detect real instances of abuse or by mistakenly identifying abuse where none exists. As is becoming all too apparent, it is dismayingly easy to err in either direction.

Many of the other chapters in this volume attest to the energy and effort being devoted to developing improved procedures for interviewing children and to validating those new techniques. It is encouraging that many of these new techniques have been informed by our current research base on basic memory processes in children and that serious attention is being given to evaluating objectively the worth of the proposed improvements. We are seeing a healthy interchange of basic and applied research, both in terms of the rationale for the innovations and in terms of assessing their efficacy.

AUTHOR'S NOTE: This chapter was presented at the 1993 Kent Psychology Forum. The research discussed in the chapter was supported by a grant (HD25271) from the National Institutes of Health.

This chapter focuses on a particular interview technique—the use of anatomically correct dolls—that has become commonplace in interviewing children when sexual abuse is suspected. Based on my research in a very different domain—the early development of symbolization—I question the appropriateness of using dolls to interview very young children, that is, children 3 years of age and younger.

Anatomically correct (detailed, explicit, and so on) is a euphemism for dolls that include some representation of external genitalia (penis, vagina). Many have, in addition, penetrable orifices (vagina, anus, mouth), breasts, and a tongue. Further embellishments to some dolls include body hair, moustaches on male dolls, and even detachable, interchangeable circumcised and uncircumcised penises.

The use of such dolls has become standard practice for a wide variety of professionals associated with investigations of abuse, including social workers, psychologists, psychiatrists, pediatricians, police, and other legal professionals. According to Boat and Everson's (1988b) survey of the use of anatomically correct dolls by various professional groups in North Carolina, dolls were used by 68% of child protective workers, 35% of law enforcement officers, 28% of mental health professionals, and 13% of physicians. A minority of those who reported using the dolls had received training. Although most endorsed the use of a structured protocol, few actually employed one. A more recent survey of mental health and legal professionals in the Boston area reported that 73% of the respondents used dolls at least some of the time (Kendall-Tackett & Watson, 1992). Almost all had received training in the use of dolls, and most followed a protocol.

The basic motivation for using such dolls is the belief that their presence will facilitate the discovery of truth—that children will give better, more accurate, more complete information when interviewed with dolls than when interviewed without them. What assumptions underlie this belief? Is the belief justified?

Assumptions About the Use of Anatomically Correct Dolls

The basic idea underlying the use of dolls is that they will elicit information from children that they are unable or unwilling to give verbally. There are three groups of children whose limited verbal abilities make them obvious targets for the use of dolls—young children, retarded children, and children who do not speak the same language as the interviewer.

Age is the factor that is most often relevant: "It is primarily the 2-, 3-, and 4-year-old child for whom sexually anatomically correct doll interviews are geared" (Terr in Yates & Terr, 1988, p. 256), and "the dolls are especially useful with children who are younger than age 3" (Yates in Yates & Terr, 1988, p. 255).

Very young children have generally limited verbal skills that can compromise their ability to describe their experiences completely and coherently. In addition, young children may lack specific vocabulary, such as names for body parts and sexual actions. With respect to generally limited language abilities, it is assumed that children might be able to demonstrate with dolls what they are unable to describe with words. With respect to deficient knowledge of particular names and terms, dolls can be used to elicit a child's idiosyncratic names for body parts, which the interviewer can then use. Alternatively, the child can be taught appropriate names. In either case, the goal is for the child and interviewer to share a common vocabulary to minimize the chance for miscommunication.

Dolls are also considered useful for interviewing children of any age who are unwilling or unable to describe their experience for reasons other than basic verbal abilities. Children may be too embarrassed to talk about experiences they view as painful, frightening, or humiliating. It is assumed that children may reveal information with dolls that emotional factors prevent their talking about. Yates notes that the presence of genitalia on the dolls "gives the child tacit permission to explore sexual topics" (Yates & Terr, 1988, p. 255).

Finally, it has also been suggested that dolls may serve a mnemonic function, such as "stimulus support" for memory (Goodman & Aman, 1990). According to Westcott, Davies, and Clifford (1989),

> dolls may act as stimuli to aid the child's memory: this could be through a "cuing" action, or through a "guiding" action. The sight of the anatomical doll with its deliberately sexual body parts may "cue" memories associated with the events that have taken place. (p. 12)

One assumption that is implicit in this passage is that seeing the doll would cause the child to think of his or her own body.

In summary, numerous benefits—linguistic, emotional, and cognitive—are assumed to result from the use of anatomical dolls in interviewing children.

Issues Concerning the Use of Dolls

Although, as noted above, dolls are commonly used by a variety of different professionals, there is great controversy concerning their use. One major concern is whether dolls actually elicit sexualized play by children who have been abused. Here, the issue is false negatives; children who have been victims of sexual abuse might, for a variety of reasons, provide no evidence of such abuse when presented with anatomical dolls.

The second and most hotly debated issue has to do with the extent to which anatomically explicit dolls, by their very nature, might lead to improper inferences of sexual abuse. Suggestibility, a very thorny issue in interviewing young children in general, is especially worrisome with respect to the use of dolls. One concern is that perfectly innocent exploration of the novel body parts on these dolls could be erroneously taken as evidence of abuse. Or children might enact sexual activities they have learned about in some way other than by being abused (e.g., from television or from being questioned about suspected abuse). The very real fear is of false positives—concluding that a nonabused child has been a victim of abuse because of how he or she interacts with the dolls. These issues can be resolved only through research.

Research on the Use of Anatomically Correct Dolls

In spite of the fact that anatomical dolls have been in widespread use for several years, there is still a very small base of published empirical investigations directly concerned with evaluating their use. The majority of that research has addressed the two issues described above.

1. Do anatomical dolls elicit differential behavior by abused and nonabused children? In the first published study comparing the behavior of a group of 2- to 6-year-old children who had been referred for suspicion of sexual abuse and a group of nonreferred children, White, Strom, Santilli, and Halpin (1986) reported more "suspicious" behavior with the dolls for the referred group. Jampole and Weber (1987) and August and Forman (1989) found similar results for the free doll play of small groups of abused and nonreferred children. Leventhal, Hamilton, Rekedal, Tebano-Micci, and Eyster (1989) reported that 66% of a group of children who were "strongly suspected" to have been abused provided a "detailed description and demonstration of abuse" using anatomical dolls, whereas only 24% of children for whom there was a lower level of suspicion of abuse gave such detailed accounts. Cohn (1991), however, observed very similar behaviors with dolls by groups of referred and nonreferred 2- to 6-year-old children.

2. Do anatomical dolls elicit sexual behavior from nonabused children? The second issue has been addressed by studies done with reasonably large samples of presumably nonabused children. The preponderance of evidence seems to be that anatomically explicit dolls do not elicit substantial amounts of sexual behavior from 2- to 8-year-old children (Cohn, 1991; Glaser & Collins, 1989; Sivan, Schor, Koeppl, & Noble, 1988). These investigators all reported that the children they observed playing with dolls were not unusually interested in them. Although some children inspected the dolls' genitals, they did not appear to be either fascinated or repulsed by them. In their study of over 200 presumably nonabused children between 2 and 5 years of age, Everson and Boat (1990b) reported that only 6% of their sample enacted clear sexual intercourse with the dolls. They concluded that "anatomical dolls are not overly suggestive to young, sexually naive children" (p. 736).

The same conclusion was reached by Goodman and Aman (1990) in the most systematic and carefully controlled study to date investigating the use of dolls. All the 3- and 5-year-old children in the study experienced a structured play session with a male experimenter. In a subsequent session, they were interviewed about their experience during the previous session by a female experimenter who either did or did not use dolls to conduct the interview. There were four different interview conditions for each age group: anatomically detailed dolls, regular dolls (identical to the anatomical ones, minus sexual characteristics), dolls in view (visible in the room but out of reach), and no dolls.

During the interview, the children were asked both open-ended recall questions and more specific probes. Also included were several misleading questions, including some specific abuse-related questions (e.g., "Show me where he touched you." "Did he touch your private parts?").

As expected, there were significant age differences on nearly every measure recorded: The 5-year-olds communicated more correct information overall; they gave more accurate answers to the misleading questions; and they gave fewer incorrect answers (commission errors). The use of dolls had no effect on the extent to which the children gave incorrect information. The children in the doll conditions were no more likely than those in the other conditions to answer incorrectly when misleading, suggestive questions were asked. "The use of anatomically detailed dolls in and of itself did not increase the chances of obtaining a false report of abuse" (Goodman, Rudy, Bottoms, & Aman, 1990, p. 271).

The published research thus lends little support to the two concerns that have been raised most vociferously and frequently about the use of anatomical dolls in interviewing young children. Children's behavior with the dolls seems to differ as a function of their abuse status, as it must if the dolls are to be of any value at all, and the dolls do not seem to elicit high rates of misleading sexual behavior by nonabused children. Thus neither false negatives nor false positives seem to occur with great regularity.

One caveat must be made here, however. These data were probably collected in relatively ideal conditions; that is, the interviewers were probably for the most part well trained, skillful, and supervised and the interviews done under relatively well-controlled conditions. We do not know whether similar results would be obtained from less skillful and experienced interviewers working with children under the variety of stressful conditions associated with child abuse investigations.

3. A neglected issue: Does the use of anatomical dolls aid in the identification of abused children? With all the concern that has been voiced about the variety of problems with respect to the use of anatomical dolls, there seems to have been remarkably little attention paid to the absolutely fundamental question of whether dolls actually help in the identification of child abuse. Saying that abused and nonabused children's behavior with the dolls differs is not tantamount to saying that the dolls help in making the diagnosis of abuse.

Only two published studies have addressed this issue, and they hardly resolve it. Leventhal et al. (1989) reviewed the records of 83 children younger than 7 years of age who had been evaluated at the Yale-New Haven Hospital due to suspicion of child abuse. Anatomically correct dolls were used in interviews with 60 of the children. For the 43 children who were over 36 months of age, more information was obtained when the dolls were used: 8 of the 43 children provided detailed descriptions about what had happened to them without the dolls, but 29 furnished details when the dolls were used. The authors note that many of these children had originally given vague accounts or had denied the occurrence of any abuse. They report the following impressive example:

> A 66-month-old child repeatedly said that nothing had happened when interviewed by the social worker. When the dolls were shown to him, however, he immediately took the two male dolls, said that the little one was him and big one was J., put the little doll on his stomach, and then showed and explained how J.'s penis had touched his anus. (Leventhal et al., 1989, p. 903)

The authors concluded that the doll interviews markedly improved the overall accuracy of the identification of abuse.

There are some problems with this study, however, that mitigate this strong conclusion. First, the diagnostic interview typically began with a social worker simply asking the child (without the dolls present) to describe what had happened. Later the dolls were introduced, and the child was again asked what had happened as well as both open-ended and more directed questions. It appears then that the comparison made in this study between information obtained with and without dolls was confounded with the timing of the dolls' use in the interview. Would the results have been the same if the children had been questioned with the dolls before being questioned verbally? It also appears that more probing questions may have been asked while the dolls were being used than before they were introduced. What if no dolls had been introduced but the interviewer had continued talking with the child and asking more pointed questions? These factors make it difficult to disentangle the use of dolls from other aspects of the interviews.

A second problem concerns the way the data were reported. Ratings of "overall likelihood of sexual abuse" were compared based on whatever noninterview information existed from physical evidence, witnesses, and so forth versus the noninterview plus the interview information. The fact that judgments based on both sources of information were deemed to be more accurate than those based on only one does not mean that the use of dolls was the deciding factor. Perhaps verbal-only interviews would have improved judgment accuracy almost as much.

Finally, the conclusion of this study may not apply to children younger than 36 months. None of the 13 children under that age was able to give an adequately "detailed description and demonstration," although the authors do note that 8 of these 13 did provide "some information" with the dolls.

The Goodman and Aman (1990) study described earlier also involved a direct comparison of 3- and 5-year-olds' memory performance with and without dolls as stimulus support. They reported no significant differences as a function of doll condition for either age group. In terms of the overall amount of information that the children communicated correctly (either verbally or through reenactment), the 5-year-old children did somewhat but not significantly better in the doll conditions (anatomical and regular dolls) than in the no-doll condition. The performance of the 3-year-olds was almost identical with and without dolls. It is worth noting that, for the two doll conditions, performance was somewhat lower with the anatomically detailed dolls than with the regular dolls for both age groups.

As was mentioned earlier, whether dolls were used in interviewing the children failed to influence the performance of either age group in terms of incorrect responses and their responses to the misleading "abuse" questions. The Goodman and Aman (1990) study thus provides little support for the use of dolls with very young children—the group that is considered the prime target for doll use (Yates & Terr, 1988).

Even less support for the use of dolls when questioning very young children comes from recent research by Gordon et al. (1993) in which 3- and 5-year-old children were interviewed about a routine physical examination. There were two interview conditions of interest here: Verbal—a standard verbal protocol was followed with no dolls present—and Representational—the child was instructed to use the doll as a model for him- or herself and to show what happened during the examination.

The expected age difference in performance was found, with the overall recall performance of the 5-year-olds being significantly better than that of the 3-year-olds. More important, an interaction of doll condition and age was found. As Goodman and Aman also reported (1990), the use of dolls provided some benefit to the older children's performance: The total recall score for the 5-year-olds was 73% in the Verbal (no-doll) condition, but 87% in the Representational (doll) condition. There was, however, no difference in the two conditions for the 3-year-olds (69% and 65%, respectively).

In an attempt to provide a direct and generous assessment of any benefit conferred by the presence of the doll, these investigators examined the total amount of elaborative detail, including verbal elaborations, nonverbal elaborations not using the doll, and nonverbal elaborations using the doll. Nonverbal elaborations with the doll contributed only a 3% increment to the total amount of elaborative detail provided by the children. Gordon et al. (1993) concluded that the presence of a doll "did not increase substantially the production of elaborations, at either age. Although the children generated some nonverbal elaboration about their check-ups, very little of this detail involved the use of the doll (i.e., the majority was simply gestural), and most, in fact, was redundant with that provided verbally" (pp. 471-472).

Summary of Research

Research on the use of anatomical dolls to interview young children should allay the worst fears of high rates of false negatives and false positives. However, the research offers meager support for the supposition that dolls enhance children's reports. I have summarized three studies in which direct comparisons were made. One, which had a sample of presumably abused children, found some benefit from the presence of dolls, even for 3-year-olds. However, various methodological problems cast doubt on this conclusion. In two very well-controlled studies with nonabused samples, some benefits of doll use were found for 5-year-old children, but not for 3-year-olds. Given that these younger children are more often the target population for doll use, these results provide very little encouragement for the practice.

Why has the use of anatomically correct dolls become so widespread in the absence of empirical support for its efficacy? One reason is probably the fact that this practice accords with our naive intuitions, our "folk theory," about children's cognition. Even very young children enjoy playing with dolls, and they do so in ways that are comprehensible and meaningful to adults. From this, adults assume that children understand dolls in the same way that adults do. It is further assumed that, because dolls are the province of young children, the presence of a doll will put them at ease, and they will project their own knowledge and feelings onto it. Hence dolls will serve as effective stimulus support for memory retrieval about the children's own experiences.

Implicit in this view is the assumption that young children can and will readily identify with a doll and treat it as a representation for themselves and that they will be able to use the doll to enact their own experience. My research on the early development of symbolic functioning suggests that this assumption is probably false.

When young children are asked to use a doll to demonstrate something they experienced (e.g., where they were touched), they are in effect being asked to use an object—the doll—as a symbol for something other than itself. My research suggests that the general failure of dolls to improve the reports of very young (i.e., 3-year-old) children may be attributable to their general deficits in symbolization. I submit that there are no transparent symbolic relations—not even one so apparently straightforward and natural as a doll standing for a young child. Thus, contrary to the naive assumption of most adults, young children may have difficulty understanding the basic self-doll relation. Obviously, if a child fails to interpret the doll used in an interview as a representation of him- or herself, then there is little likelihood that the use of the doll will improve the child's report.

In the following section, I will review several studies of young children's use and understanding of external symbols, emphasizing the counterintuitive nature of many of the findings. These studies reveal that symbolic relations that appear obvious to adults and older children are remarkably nonobvious to younger and less experienced symbol users. I will discuss this research in some detail even though it is not directly concerned with eyewitness testimony, because it illustrates how poor our adult intuitions are when it comes to young children and symbols.

Studies of Symbol Use and Understanding by Very Young Children

I have for several years been investigating early symbolic functioning. My colleagues and I have primarily examined 2- to 3-year-old children's understanding of external symbols such as pictures, maps, and scale models. In most of this research, one of these symbolic media is used to give young children information about the location of an attractive toy that is hidden somewhere in a room. The children are then asked to retrieve the toy. If they understand the representational relation between the symbol and what it stands for, then they should know where to find the hidden toy. If, however, the children do not appreciate what the symbol represents, they have no way of knowing where to find the hidden toy.

Our research with scale models is most relevant to the topic of using dolls to interview young children. Scale models are somewhat unusual symbols, in that they are also real objects that are interesting in their own right. This dual nature of scale models is also true of dolls.

In our scale model task, the child watches as the experimenter hides a small toy somewhere (behind a chair, under a pillow) in the scale model of a room. The child is told that a larger version of the toy will be hidden in the same place in the room.

The performance of $2\frac{1}{2}$- and 3-year-old children differs dramatically in this task. In the original study (DeLoache, 1987), the errorless retrieval rate was 77% for the 3-year-old children, but only 15% for the $2\frac{1}{2}$-year-olds. The 3-year-olds successfully exploited the information from the model to find the larger toy in the room. In contrast, the $2\frac{1}{2}$-year-olds gave no evidence of realizing that the model and room were related. This difference was not due to memory or motivational differences, because both groups could find the miniature toy they had observed being hidden in the model.

These $2\frac{1}{2}$-year-olds understood everything about the task except the critical fact that the room and the model were related. They willingly searched for the toy hidden in the room, but they apparently failed to realize they had information that told them the correct location.

Why is it so difficult for young children to understand the model-room relation? I have proposed the dual representation hypothesis (DeLoache, 1987, 1991), which emphasizes the inherent double nature of models: Although they serve as representations of a larger space, they are also objects themselves. A child, in performing the model task, must deal with this dual nature and respond to the model both as an object (a miniature room in which things can be hidden and found) and at the same time as a symbol that represents something other than itself (the larger room and its hiding places).

Achieving a dual representation of a single object is difficult: The fact that the model is a highly attractive and salient object makes it hard for very young children to simultaneously appreciate it as a representation of the room. Their attention is directed to the model as object, and they are typically very interested in it. That focus makes it very difficult for them to see it in relation to something else. Hence the $2\frac{1}{2}$-year-olds in the original and subsequent model studies failed to exploit the model as a source of information about the room.

The dual representation hypothesis generated the following counterintuitive prediction: $2\frac{1}{2}$-year-olds should more successfully retrieve an object hidden in a room when given information about the location of the object via pictures of the room than via a scale model of the room. This prediction is contrary to a large amount of research showing better cognitive performance with real objects than with pictures (e.g., Daehler, Lonardo, & Bukatko, 1979; DeLoache, 1986; Sigel, 1953; Sigel, Anderson, & Shapiro, 1966). However, the reasoning is that pictures constitute a medium that does not require a dual representation. Even though they are real objects, they are very simple as objects and are not themselves attractive and interesting. Furthermore, even $2\frac{1}{2}$-year-old children know that pictures serve primarily to represent something else (DeLoache & Burns, 1994). Because children are used to thinking only of what a picture depicts, they do not have to suppress a strong response to it as an object.

The performance of $2\frac{1}{2}$-year-old children was compared in the standard model task versus a picture task in which the experimenter simply pointed at the appropriate place on a picture of the room to indicate to the child where the toy was hidden. Different kinds of pictures were used in different studies, including various color photographs and line drawings. In all these studies, the $2\frac{1}{2}$-year-old subjects performed very successfully in the picture tasks (70%-85%), but very unsuccessfully in the model task (15%-20%). The results thus supported the dual representation hypothesis: These young children could use information presented in a symbolic medium, when the symbol itself was not salient and interesting to them, but they failed to use the information available in an inherently interesting object symbol.

Two studies tested predictions that, although they follow directly from the dual representation hypothesis, are otherwise counterintuitive. In the first, we attempted to decrease the salience of the model as an object by placing it behind a window. Our reasoning was that, if the children never touched the model or retrieved the miniature toy from it, the model would be less salient as an object. Hence it would be easier for them to detect its relation to its referent. The results confirmed the prediction. Our subjects were significantly more successful when they had no access to the model as an object (window condition) than when they did have access to it (standard model task).

In a second direct test of the dual representation hypothesis, we did the opposite: We attempted to increase the salience of the model as an object, predicting poorer performance as a result. The subjects were 3-year-olds, an age group that typically succeeds in the standard model task. To increase salience, we simply gave the children extra experience with the model—5 to 10 minutes of play with the model and its contents before we began the standard model task (a manipulation that, except for the dual representation hypothesis, one might assume would increase performance).

The predicted results were again obtained. The children who had extra time physically manipulating the model were less successful at using it as a source of information for the room than were children who did not have this extra experience.

I now describe the most stringent test of the dual representation hypothesis to date. This study (DeLoache, 1993; DeLoache, Miller, Rosengren, & Bryant, 1993) clearly demonstrates that it is specifically the representational feature of a scale model that makes the model task difficult for very young children.

We convinced 2½-year-old children that we were shrinking a room. This rather peculiar experimental manipulation was done with the goal of removing the representational nature of the task. Our reasoning was that, if the children believed that the model actually was the room, then no dual representation would be required. Thinking that the model and room are one and the same thing, they should be able to apply what they know about one space to the other.

We used an artificial room (a 1.9 × 2.6 × 1.9 m room constructed of white fabric walls) and a scale model of that room, both of which have been used in several previous model studies. In the orientation phase of the study, 2½-year-old children were introduced to a troll doll, to the troll's room (the portable room), and to a "shrinking machine." The child was told that the machine could "shrink toys." To demonstrate, the experimenter pointed the machine at the doll and "turned it on." The child and experimenter then waited in an adjoining room, listening to the sounds of the shrinking machine (a tape recording of computer-generated tones). Upon reentering the lab room, the child discovered a miniature troll in place of the larger toy that had been there before. Next, the doll was "enlarged" by the machine. Finally, the artificial room was shrunk and then enlarged again.

On the first experimental trial, the child watched as the troll was hidden in the artificial room, the shrinking machine was aimed at the room, and the child and experimenter again waited in the adjoining room. Upon entering the lab, the child found the scale model situated in the middle of the space that had been occupied by the artificial room. The child was encouraged to find the troll, which was, of course, hidden in the model in the place that corresponded to where the larger doll had been hidden in the room. On the next trial, the child watched as the miniature troll was hidden in the model, waited while the room was "blown up" by the machine, and then searched in the room. Subsequent trials alternated between shrinking and enlarging events. All the experimenters and parents judged that the children firmly believed that we really were shrinking and enlarging the troll and the room.

The results were as predicted. The $2\frac{1}{2}$-year-olds in the shrinking room condition performed 76% errorless retrievals, a rate significantly better than that of two different control groups in the standard task using the same artificial room and model.

The typical failure of $2\frac{1}{2}$-year-old children in the standard model task is thus due to its representational nature and specifically to the need for dual representation. When there is an identity relation between the room and model, these children are successful at applying what they know about one space to the other. When there is a symbolic relation between the two so that dual representation is required, they fail.

The dual representation hypothesis has thus received strong empirical support. Four highly counterintuitive predictions were made and confirmed: (a) Two-dimensional pictures are a more useful source of information for $2\frac{1}{2}$-year-old children than three-dimensional models; (b) restricting young children's access to a model makes them better able to exploit its symbolic content; (c) providing extra experience with a model renders its symbolic content less accessible to 3-year-olds; and (d) removing the symbolic nature of the model task (via the "incredible shrinking room" manipulation) makes it easier for $2\frac{1}{2}$-year-olds to apply information gained from the model to the room. This research reveals that symbolic relationships in which an object (or set of objects) stands for something other than itself are difficult for very young children to appreciate, even when the symbol is highly iconic.

I have emphasized the counterintuitive nature of these results to highlight two things: (a) the strength of the support that has been adduced for the dual representation hypothesis and (b) the fact that adult intuitions about the symbolic functioning of young children are very poor. Adults are so steeped in symbols that they frequently fail to realize that the symbol-referent relations that are so obvious to them are not at all obvious to someone with less experience using symbols. In the following section, I consider the implications of my research on scale models for a different type of object symbol—dolls. Dual representation is a barrier to very young children's success in the model task. Might it also make it difficult for them to interpret a doll as a representation of themselves and to use it to enact their own experience?

Dolls and Dual Representation

My colleagues and I have completed one study directly addressing this issue (DeLoache & Marzolf, in press), and a second is currently under way. A total of 72 children participated in the first experiment, with 24 children in each of three age groups—$2\frac{1}{2}$-, 3-, and 4- year-olds.

Each child individually participated in a 20- to 30-minute play session with an adult male experimenter. A "Simon Says" game (similar to the one used by Goodman & Aman, 1990) involved the child and experimenter touching each other. The experimenter would announce that "Simon says, Don [the experimenter], touch [subject's name] on the [hand, foot]." In a joint book-reading activity, the experimenter peeled stickers off a simple book and placed them on the child (e.g., on the wrist or knee). These games were designed to ensure that, during the course of the play session, the experimenter touched the child several times.

Immediately following the play session, an adult female experimenter interviewed each child. She introduced a doll of the sort commonly used in abuse investigations. The doll matched the subject's own gender and race. The experimenter instructed the child, "Let's pretend that this doll is you," and she pointed out similarities between the doll and the child (eyes, nose, hair color, and so on).

The experimenter asked the child whether he or she had been touched by the male experimenter. If the child responded affirmatively (as almost all subjects did), the experimenter then asked, "Where did Don touch you?" If the child did not use the doll in responding to the question, the experimenter further requested, "Show me on the doll where Don touched you."

Each child was also given, one at a time, a set of miniature stickers corresponding to the larger ones that the experimenter had placed on him or her. The subject was asked to "put the little [duck] sticker on the doll in the same place where Don put the [duck] sticker on you." At the time that the children were asked to do the sticker placement, most of them were still wearing their own stickers. Thus, if they equated the doll with themselves, there was no memory load—they could easily check their own body as a guide to where to position the stickers on the doll.

Several aspects of the children's behavior supported the hypothesis that they would have difficulty using the doll as a representation of themselves. Some of our subjects (especially the younger ones) were reluctant to accept the self-doll relation at all. The most obvious evidence of this came from comments like the following (quite similar to those reported by Goodman & Aman, 1990): "No, that not the Evan doll! You think I'm a doll or what? . . . Doll not me!" "It's scary." "Not the Elizabeth doll!"

As Figure 8.1 shows, our youngest subjects also had difficulty with the simplest action we asked them to carry out on the doll. When asked to use the doll to show where stickers had been put on them, the $2\frac{1}{2}$-year-olds succeeded in doing so less than half the time. (This poor performance was in spite of the fact that our criteria for a correct placement were very liberal—for example, anywhere on either arm from the elbow down would be counted as correct for a sticker that had been placed on the child's left wrist.) Only a quarter of the $2\frac{1}{2}$-year-old children managed to place more than half of the stickers correctly.

The older children were much more successful in their sticker placements, but the 3-year-olds still made a number of errors. Only 63% of them placed more than half of their stickers correctly.

Possibly the most indisputable evidence that a child was relating his or her own body to the doll was self-referencing, that is, looking for the relevant sticker on the child's own body before placing the smaller one on the doll. Of the children who were still wearing the stickers during the interview, the proportion who self-referenced at least once was 78%, 72%, and 40% of the 4-, 3-, and $2\frac{1}{2}$-year-olds, respectively. This suggests that some of the children's

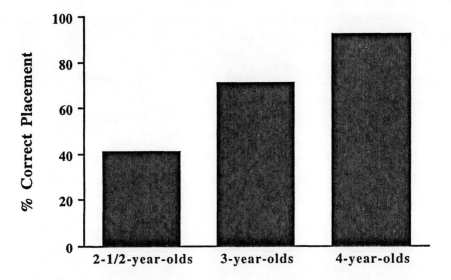

Figure 8.1. Percentage of correct sticker placements on the doll as a function of age.

placements of the stickers on the doll were not based on their own experience. Like the younger children in the model task who understand that they are supposed to search for a toy in the room but do not realize it has anything to do with their experience in the model, some of these children knew they were supposed to put the stickers on the doll but did so independently of the stickers on their own bodies.

The children's behavior in the sticker placement task thus suggests that these children had difficulty using a doll as a representation of themselves. Our youngest subjects were very poor at reproducing with the doll their own very recent experience, even though there was no memory load and all that was required was mapping from one's own body to the doll.

The second and most important measure of children's ability to use the doll to report their experience was their response to the experimenter's questions about where they had been touched. Table 8.1 shows the proportion of all touches that the children actually experienced that they reported correctly. Any kind of response—verbal or nonverbal—was counted, and we were again liberal in what counted as correct response. Nevertheless, our younger subjects did not give very complete reports; indeed, the 2½- and 3-year-olds mentioned fewer than half of the places they had actually been touched.

Table 8.1   Proportion of Actual Touches Reported and Shown as a Function of Age

| | Age | | |
Actual Touches	$2\frac{1}{2}$-year-olds	3-year-olds	4-year-olds
Proportion reported	.34	.38	.61
Proportion shown on doll	.18	.25	.50

The most important data for our purposes here come from the assessment of how accurate the children were in showing on the doll where they had been touched. Recall that whenever children reported, either verbally or nonverbally on themselves, that they had been touched, they were requested to demonstrate on the doll where they had been touched. The bottom line of Table 8.1 shows the proportion of all the touches they experienced that they accurately showed on the doll.

The results were clear: The children reported less information using the doll than they did through verbal statements or gestures to their own bodies. Thus one could get a better picture of where and how often these children had been touched by simply asking them directly for that information than by trying to get them to demonstrate it with a doll. Comparison of the first and second lines of Table 8.1 reveals that the $2\frac{1}{2}$-year-olds showed on the doll only slightly more than half of the places they had just indicated they had been touched. The 3-year-olds were somewhat better, but it is clear that their "testimony" was better without than with the doll.

Our young subjects thus had serious difficulty using a doll to indicate what part of their own body had been touched. These data cannot tell us whether the children simply failed to appreciate the self-doll relation in the first place (as is often the case in our model task) or whether they just had trouble mapping from their own bodies to the doll's body. In either case, the data call into question the assumption that young children will readily identify with a doll and use it as a representation of themselves. Our subjects never spontaneously used the doll in response to our questions, not even to support or elaborate their verbal reports. They used the doll only at the behest of the experimenter, and they were not very competent at doing so.

Our results thus agree with those of Goodman and Aman (1990) and Gordon et al. (1993) in showing no advantage of using a doll to question very young children. This was true in the present study, even though all children were strongly encouraged to use the doll. The use of dolls to question children of 3 and below is thus questionable on both empirical and theoretical (dual representation) grounds.

Although these results are highly consistent, they are limited with respect to the kinds of events involved. None was upsetting or intense, and both our study and Goodman and Aman's (1990) took place in a laboratory setting. Accordingly, we are currently conducting a second study in which we are interviewing young children, either with or without dolls, about a real-life event that is intense and emotionally upsetting to them. We have enlisted the cooperation of some local preschools. When an incident occurs in which a child gets upset, a teacher fills out a report describing what happened. The next day we interview the child about the incident.

This research is still in a very preliminary stage, but one phenomenon that we and others have previously noted has occurred again. Some children are highly reluctant to accept the self-doll relation when it is proposed to them. We have a dramatic videotape of one young boy who wants nothing to do with the interviewer's suggestion that he should "pretend this doll is you." The child visibly shrinks away from her and, as she persists in trying to get him to accept the doll, he eventually disappears off the side of the screen. When the interviewer finally puts the dolls away, he sits down and tells her what happened to him the day before.

This phenomenon is important, because avoidance of anatomically correct dolls in clinical settings is sometimes taken as evidence suggestive of abuse. Our results indicate this is highly questionable at best; if some presumably nonabused children shrink away from a clothed doll in a relatively nonthreatening situation, how can we have any confidence that such a response has anything to do with abuse?

Summary and Conclusions

Although anatomically correct dolls are widely believed to facilitate the investigation of child abuse, there is extremely meager empirical or theoretical support for using dolls to interview very young children, that is, children of 3 years of age or less. Most of the surprisingly small number of studies that have investigated this issue have been directed toward answering two commonly voiced fears about the use of dolls.

As my literature review indicated, supporters of doll use can take comfort that groups of children referred for suspicion of child abuse usually show more sexual play with anatomical dolls than do groups of nonreferred children and that such dolls do not elicit high rates of sexual play by nonabused children. However, it is still the case that not all abused children play in a suspicious manner with the dolls, and some presumably nonabused children exhibit quite sexualized behaviors with them. Is the glass half empty, or is it half full?

To my mind, the most important research finding about the use of dolls with very young children is that there is no good evidence that the dolls help. In three recent, carefully designed, and well-controlled studies of nonabused children (DeLoache & Marzolf, in press; Goodman & Aman, 1990; Gordon et al., 1993), interviews using dolls elicited no more or better information than interviews done without them. My study (DeLoache & Marzolf, in press) suggested that the presence of the doll might even interfere with the memory reports of the youngest children, a possibility that Melton and Limber (1989) have raised. The idea that very young children might actually provide less information in the presence of dolls is consistent with my prior research demonstrating the great fragility of symbolic understanding and use in this age group. Our current study, in which young children are questioned either with or without dolls present, should provide a clear answer to this question.

9

Innovative Techniques for the Questioning of Child Witnesses, Especially Those Who Are Young and Those With Learning Disability

RAY BULL

In the introduction to their excellent edited book *Knowing and Remembering in Young Children,* Judith Hudson and Robyn Fivush (1990) made the important point that "younger children have not yet learned the conventional framework for recounting the past, and therefore depend more on the adult's questions to guide their recall than do older children." The present chapter examines some ways in which young child witnesses can be interviewed so as to provide as valid and full accounts as possible of what has happened to them.

The first part of this chapter provides an abbreviated account of some aspects of the recently published (by Her Majesty's Stationery Office, produced in consultation with the Department of Health) *Memorandum of Good Practice on Video Recorded Interviews with Child Witnesses for Criminal Proceedings* for the interviewing of child witnesses (Home Office, 1992) and my involvement in this. The final section of the chapter looks at the interviewing of children with learning difficulty/disability (which in some countries is still referred to as mental "handicap"/"retardation").

Recent Developments in Britain and the Government's *Memorandum of Good Practice* for Interviewing Children

The *Memorandum of Good Practice* covers a very wide range of issues. Advice on the legal conditions about which a criminal court may wish to be satisfied before admitting a video recording is included, as is guidance on the legal rules to be observed in producing an evidential recording acceptable to criminal courts (see also Birch, 1992). It gives guidance on what to do prior to an interview, including when and where to conduct the video recording and the equipment to use. An essential component gives advice on conducting the interviews so that children can give as full an account as possible without undue influence taking place. The *Memorandum* also provides recommendations about postinterview issues such as storage, custody, and disposal of such video recordings.

I will here give a fairly brief overview of what the *Memorandum* says about the actual conducting of interviews, especially questioning techniques. The views expressed here are based on research literature, professional publications, and other information made available to me by many helpful people in various countries; they do not necessarily represent the views of any organization. A fuller account is available in Bull (1992, 1994).

White (1990) argued that, "until relatively recently, suspected victims of child sexual abuse did not receive much special consideration with reference as to how they should be interviewed" (p. 368). She suggested that "techniques for interviewing these young children have been based on practical experiences and are now only beginning to receive any research attention" (p. 369). She pointed out that, "while a number of authors have made detailed suggestions of how best to interact with a child suspected of being a victim of child abuse . . . interviewers have been forced to discover . . . techniques which work best in their particular situation" (p. 369).

The main purpose of the Home Office *Memorandum of Good Practice* is to help those making video recordings of interviews with child witnesses where it is intended that the result should be acceptable in criminal proceedings. Following the *Memorandum* is voluntary, but it may become widely accepted to do so. In U.K. courts, questions are likely to be asked about whether an interview followed the *Memorandum*.

The purpose of the video-recorded interview with a child witness is to obtain as full and reliable an account as possible. Current and past criticisms of some interviews with child witnesses (for example, by the Irish Law Reform

Commission, 1989, 1990) have focused on the questioning techniques employed (Flin, Bull, Boon, & Knox, 1992, 1993). These criticisms have been concerned with the possibility that interviewers have (probably unwittingly) contaminated the child's account by virtue of the use of suggestive, leading, biasing, or pressurizing questions (Loftus & Davies, 1984).

In 1988 David Jones, a respected British child psychiatrist experienced in interviewing children who may have been abused, made the sensible recommendation (Jones & McQuiston, 1988) of dividing interviews with such children into four phases, which I describe as (a) rapport, (b) free narrative, (c) questioning, and (d) closure.

In 1991 another very experienced British psychiatrist (Eileen Vizard) made a similar recommendation. In the first working draft of the *Memorandum* that I produced for the Home Office, I adopted such a phased approach. However, within the questioning phase, my draft (and the published *Memorandum*) was much more specific about the various types of questioning and the most appropriate order in which these various forms of questions should be put within the questioning phase (my specificity concerning various question types was particularly assisted by a paper published by the American Professional Society on the Abuse of Children).

John Yuille (1988) has similarly recommended that, to obtain as full a statement as possible from the child that is uncontaminated by the interviewer, a "step-wise" procedure be adopted. This step-wise procedure was developed in Germany over a number of decades (Steller & Köhnken, 1989; Undeutsch, 1982) by psychologists with substantial experience in interviewing children who may have been sexually abused. It was developed to obtain an appropriate statement from the child that could then be analyzed to determine whether it demonstrated the criteria thought to be associated with genuinely experienced events (Köhnken, 1990; Steller & Boychuk, 1992).

In July 1992 at a seminar held in London, Yuille presented some preliminary findings from his Canadian field study designed to evaluate the effects of training interviewers in the step-wise approach. In British Columbia, a joint training program for police, social workers, and prosecutors was set up. All the participants received several days' training in step-wise interviewing. With the permission of the "real life" witnesses interviewed before and after these interviewers had received the training, the tape recordings of nearly 200 interviews were passed to researchers for evaluation. The research team developed a rating technique concerning the effectiveness of the interviews. Interviews were classified as "useless," first, if no conclusion could be drawn about whether the child had been abused and, second, if the interviewer conducted a poor interview. Yuille reported that, whereas 35% of the pretraining interviews were classified as "useless" (and this is a large percentage), only 14% of the posttraining interviews were classified as "useless." This is an important finding. In addition, of the 156 people who received the training, only 1 made a negative remark about it. Most described it as easy to follow.

The Home Office *Memorandum of Good Practice* (1992) makes the following points:

> The basic aim of the interview is to obtain a truthful account from the child, in a way which is fair and in the child's interests and acceptable to the courts. What follows is a recommended protocol for interviewing based on a phased approach. This treats the interview as a process in which a variety of interviewing techniques are deployed in relatively discrete phases, proceeding from general to open to specific and closed forms of question. It is suggested that this approach is likely to achieve the basic aim of listening to what the child has to say, if anything, about the alleged offence. However, inclusion of the phased approach in this Memorandum should not be taken to imply that all other techniques are necessarily unacceptable or to preclude their development. Neither should what follows be regarded as a check-list to be rigidly worked through. Nevertheless, the sound legal framework it provides should not be departed from by members of investigating teams unless they have fully discussed and agreed the reasons for doing so and have consulted their senior managers. (p. 15)

PHASE 1: RAPPORT

As Boggs and Eyberg (1990) and Myers (1987), among others, have pointed out, the essential first phase of the interview is the establishing of rapport between the child and the interviewer. Questioning of the child about the alleged incident(s) should never occur without adequate rapport having been established first. The child should be helped to relax and to feel as comfortable as possible. Children, especially young ones, may not be used to speaking to strangers. Indeed, many are advised not to do so.

PHASE 2: FREE NARRATIVE ACCOUNT

If it is deemed appropriate, after having established rapport, to continue with the interview, the child should first be asked to provide *in her own words* an account of the relevant event(s). Research has confirmed that in their free narrative accounts younger children usually provide less information than do older children and adults. (Nevertheless, this information is typically no less accurate.) However, it is younger children whose accounts are probably most tainted by inappropriate questioning. Therefore, in the free narrative phase, younger children especially should be encouraged to provide an account in their own words by the use of appropriate open-ended prompts (such as "What happened next?"). In his review of "wait time," Tobin (1987) reported that teachers obtained fuller replies from pupils if they were able to wait longer than 3 seconds (which they found difficult) before speaking, once pupils appeared to stop speaking. The interviewer should resist the temptation to speak as soon as the child appears to stop doing so. The interviewer must be patient and tolerant of pauses (including long ones) and silences.

With young children, it should be communicated to them that the interviewer genuinely has no idea what has happened to them. Fielding and Conroy (1992) and McGurk and Glachan (1988) have noted that younger children often are reluctant to believe that they know anything useful that adults do not already know. Also, young children often assume that, because one adult knows what happened to them (e.g., the perpetrator), other adults may somehow be privy to this knowledge (Toglia, Ross, Ceci, & Hembrooke, 1992). In addition, in the interview, children may not realize that they are in a situation in which their usual rules of conversation with adults, in which adults already know the answers, are *reversed* or altered. Similarly, interviewers must be aware that expecting a witness to speak in a frank and open manner about personal/sexual matters reverses the usual convention of normal conversation in which many people talk about such matters only in an allusive way (Wattam, 1992), though very young children may not yet have learned this convention.

One benefit of obtaining from the child an uncontaminated free narrative account may be (as Shuy, 1986, suggests) that jurors may be more impressed by a free narrative account than "the more courtroom style of highly controlled, brief answer, fragmented testimony" that is occasioned by questioning. Research on interviewing adults has found that police officers often interrupt cooperative witnesses while they are speaking, even on relevant matters (Fisher, Geiselman, & Raymond, 1987). However, the child's free narrative account may be judged by the interviewer not to have provided sufficient information and it might therefore be decided to move into a phase in which questions are put to the child.

Research has been conducted in which children witness complex events either live or via a video recording. This research showed that, when simply asked to describe what happened in their own words, children most often produce reliable accounts. That is, the vast majority of what most of them say in these (often ingenious) studies (e.g., Price & Goodman, 1990) is an accurate account of what happened, but rarely is a full account given by anyone (Ceci, Ross, & Toglia, 1989; Ceci, Toglia, & Ross, 1987; Dent & Flin, 1992; Irish Law Reform Commission, 1990; Oates, 1990; Perry & Wrightsman, 1991; Spencer, Nicholson, Flin, & Bull, 1990). However, young children usually report less than do older children or adults (Flin, Boon, Knox, & Bull, 1992; List, 1986). Therefore, especially with young children, some form of questioning is often needed.

Gabarino and Stott (1991), among others, have noted that skill in questioning is a key issue in conducting interviews with children (see Toglia, Ross, Ceci, & Hembrooke, 1992). Research has demonstrated that inappropriate questioning can bias the replies of adults as well as of children and that questions vary in the extent to which they can influence replies to them.

PHASE 3: QUESTIONING

Open-ended questions. In deciding whether or not to proceed on to a subsequent phase of the interview, the needs of the child (and those of criminal justice) must be considered. If the child seems distressed, the interviewer should make a judgment as to whether this is caused by the child giving her account or by the interviewing. If the latter, pressing ahead with more interviewing is inappropriate. When the child has finished the free narrative account (the length of which may vary as a function of a host of factors, including the child's age), questions can be asked. However, it is most important that interviewers appreciate that there are *different types* of questions, some of which will be less likely to bias the child's account than others. In asking any questions, the interviewer must take account of the child's stage of development (which should have been noted during the rapport and free narrative phases as well as from preinterview information).

Open-ended questions ask the child to provide more information but in a way that does not lead or pressurize the child. As Moston (1990) has argued, like all questions used in the interview, these questions must be phrased in a manner that implies that an inability to remember (or not knowing the answer) is acceptable.

Some questions employing the word *why* may be interpreted by children as attributing blame/guilt to them. Such questions should be avoided. Also to be avoided is the repeating of a question soon after a child has answered it, because this can be interpreted by children as a criticism of their original response. Siegal, Waters, and Dinwiddy (1988) have pointed out that close repetition of a question may cause the child to change his answer to one he thinks the interviewer wants to hear. Poole and White (1991; see also Moston, 1987) reported that when a question is repeated children tend to assume that their original answer must have been incorrect, and so they may therefore change their answer when the question is posed again.

For a child who provided little relevant information in the free narrative phase, a focused yet open-ended question could be in the following form: "Is there anything worrying you?" or "Are there some things you are not happy about?" Only one question should be asked per utterance. For children whose free narrative account provided rather more relevant information, the questions asked could be more focused yet still open ended. For example, "Could you please tell me more about the man by the railway bridge?" (given that the child has mentioned a man by the bridge).

Specific yet nonleading questions. Such questions allow for extension and clarification of previously provided information from both the free narrative and the subsequent phase. They also provide an opportunity for the child who has said very little in connection with the purpose of the interview to be reminded of what the focus of the interview is without the child being asked leading questions. For a child who has already provided information that a man by the railway bridge hurt her and that he was wearing a jacket, a specific yet nonleading question could be as follows: "What color was the man's jacket?"

Adults sometimes falsely assume that children, even young ones, must know what is relevant. Understanding what is relevant assists a witness to focus his or her account, and specific yet nonleading questions allow the interviewer to guide the witness in an evidentially sound manner. Questions must not be leading in the sense that the interviewer implies the answer (even though in some cases it may be inevitable that questions will refer to disputed facts). In addition, the interviewer should be aware that most people, and especially young children, may give a reply to a question merely to meet the perceived needs of the interviewer (Gudjonsson, 1992). Thus, during this subphase, questions that require a "yes" or "no" answer, or ones that allow only one of two possible responses, should not be asked (Choi, 1991).

Closed questions. If specific yet nonleading questions have not been sufficiently productive, then closed questions could be asked. Closed questions are ones that give the interviewee a limited number of alternative responses, but preferably more than two. For example, "Was the man's jacket you mentioned, green or red or blue, or another color? Or can't you remember?" Such a question would not normally be deemed a leading question. If a closed question permits only one of two responses, then the response of both children and adults may not necessarily be a good indication of what is in their memory, especially if their are unwilling to give a "don't know" response and/or the interview setting has not emphasized this as an acceptable reply. Such a limited closed question may not be leading, but one has to consider how truly informative a reply to it is (Choi, 1991).

Sue White (1990) pointed out some of the possible problems in using multiple-choice closed questions. As an example, White suggested that

> a listing of possible perpetrators might include only one name that the child knows. When the child selects it due to familiarity, the interviewer may assume that the selection is directly related to the allegation. For example, if the child is asked by the interviewer, "Has anyone ever touched you?" and she responds, "Yes," the interviewer might then introduce a multiple-choice question: "Was it someone named Dave, Russell, or Gerald?" Having a father named Gerald and never having known anyone with any of the other names, the child replies "Gerald." The interviewer then may inappropriately conclude that the person identified is the perpetrator.

If at the end of this phase the interviewer is of the opinion that further questioning is still necessary, then it could be decided to move into a phase of leading questions. However, there must be a *clear* appreciation that a leading style of questioning may have limited evidential value in criminal proceedings.

Leading questions. A leading question is one that implies the answer. Such questions would usually not be permitted as part of the child witness's live "evidence-in-chief" in a criminal trial. (In court, counsel can object to the use of a leading question before a witness giving evidence-in-chief responds to it.) The greatest care must be taken when questioning the witness about central matters that are likely to be disputed in court. Leading questions, especially about such matters, are best left to the very final questioning phase, especially because the definition of a leading question depends in part on what the respondent has already said.

Both adult and child interviewees' responses to leading questions can be more the result of the questioning than of valid remembering. Stone and Lemanek (1990) have argued that some witnesses, and in particular young children, may be more willing to respond to "yes/no" questions with a "yes" response. If leading questions permitting only a "yes/no" response are asked, then it is imperative that these should be phrased so that questions on the same issue sometimes produce a "yes" response and sometimes a "no" response. Given that, when asking a leading question, one cannot know whether the answer will provide more information than that suggested by the question, leading questions should only be asked about evidentially relevant matters when all the above phases have been passed through.

If a leading question is used because the child seems to need to be led, and it produces an evidentially related response (particularly one that contains relevant information not led by the question), then the interviewer should *immediately* refrain from asking further leading questions but revert to one of the nonleading phases described above. In this way, the interview can avoid being one composed largely of leading questions. Responses to leading questions relating to central facts of a case that have not already been described by the child in an earlier phase of the interview will probably be of limited evidential value in criminal courts, especially if the interviewer fails to offer the child the opportunity to expand (without being led) on her response to such leading questions.

The use of dolls and other props. There are a number of quite different purposes that dolls and props may serve but space limitations preclude further mention of these here (see Everson & Boat, 1990a; Goodman & Aman, 1990; Maan, 1991; Vizard, 1991).

New interviewing procedures with props and dolls. Mel Pipe's ongoing research in New Zealand (Pipe, 1992; Pipe, Gee, & Wilson, 1993; Pipe & Wilson, 1994; Wilson & Pipe, 1989) and recent work in Germany by Dahmen-Zimmer and Loohs (1992) does suggest that props/toys may assist children in an evidentially sound way (but see DeLoache, 1990, and this volume). Therefore I am not sure that I agree with the recent claim by Raskin and Esplin (1991) that "puppets, drawings, good touch/bad touch games, and toys are generally unnecessary and should be avoided whenever possible" (p. 270). Clearly, such procedures can be used inappropriately, but much more research is necessary to develop adequate procedures. Raskin and Esplin have claimed that "they frequently distract the child from the task of providing complete and accurate descriptions, and they can be suggestive, provoke fantasy and lack a scientific basis" (p. 270). Researchers need to develop scientifically based recommendations for the use of props and toys based on proper research. This is an urgent need.

PHASE 4: CLOSING THE INTERVIEW

Recapitulation. During this aspect of closing the interview, the interviewer should check with the child that the interviewer has correctly understood the evidentially important parts (if any) of the child's account. This should be done (like the questioning) using the child's own language, not as a summary provided by the interviewer in adult language (which could be mistaken but with which the child may nevertheless agree). If the child has described acts of sexual or physical abuse, the interviewer could ask (in a skillful manner) if the child has seen films, videos, magazines, or books of this nature.

It has sometimes been suggested that at the end of the interview a "suggestibility check" be conducted on the child (e.g., Yuille, 1988). I do not recommend this unless there is a very good reason to do so (see Raskin & Esplin, 1991, for some good points on this issue).

Closure. The interviewer should always try to ensure that the interview ends appropriately. Although it may not always be necessary to pass through each of the above phases before going on to the next, there should be a good reason for not doing so. Every interview must have a closing phase conducted in the interest of the child. In this phase, it may be a useful idea to discuss again some of the "neutral" topics mentioned by the child in the rapport phase.

In this phase, regardless of the outcome of the interview, every effort should be made to ensure that the child is not distressed but is in a positive frame of mind. Even if the appropriate, professional decision has been to terminate the interview before sufficient information has been gathered from the witness for criminal proceedings, the child must not be made to feel that she has failed.

This ends my brief overview of a major part of the *Memorandum of Good Practice.* My working draft of the *Memorandum* also made mention of new interviewing techniques being developed for children, but this does not appear in the published version because it was felt that not enough research had by then been published on these techniques to justify their recommendation.

Children With "Learning Difficulty"

In 1991 Ann Craft pointed out that people who work with those who have a learning disability are becoming increasingly aware of their lack of expertise in assisting such people to give accounts of what has happened to them. Some authors have persuasively argued (e.g, Turk & Brown, 1992; Westcott, 1991) that children with learning difficulty may well be those most at risk of sexual abuse, yet those most denied access to the justice system.

In 1992 Westcott noted in her survey of teams from the National Society for the Prevention of Cruelty to Children (NSPCC),

> who worked with one or more disabled children, several workers specifically referred to feeling unsure of how to respond to the child, and how to work with him or her. For example, workers mentioned being unable to gauge how much the child had actually understood, and described their initial "panic" reaction on working with a child with disabilities. This "deskilling" effect needs to be recognised, and acted upon, to prevent it becoming a barrier to effective communication. (Westcott, 1992b, p. 7)

To assist interviewers, Bull and Cullen (1992, 1993) recently produced (at the request of the Crown Office in Scotland) a booklet to help prosecutors interview adult "witnesses who may have a mental handicap."

Walter Coles (1990), who is a member of the Royal Canadian Mounted Police, has reported that "investigating cases of sexual abuse of persons with disabilities is extremely difficult" (p. 35), yet "disabled persons have the right to be protected, and they have the right to live a life free of sexual abuse" (p. 43). The *Memorandum of Good Practice* states that, when a child has a disability of any kind, particular care should be taken to "develop effective strategies for the interview to minimise the effect of such disabilities" (p. 10). However, Westcott (1992b) has pointed out that in the *Memorandum* "the real problems facing children with disabilities is not acknowledged" (p. 10). I agree with this. The *Memorandum* says very little on the extra procedures and skills that might assist children with special needs to give an account because so little is known on this topic, particularly in terms of procedures whose effectiveness have been researched and evaluated.

Westcott (1992b), among others, has emphasized how rarely evidence from children with special needs has been used in court, even though they may well be at greater risk of abuse. She made the point that "existing child protection services need to be revised to become accessible to all children (irrespective of disability) who may need to use them. Special training is essential for all professionals involved" (p. 13). But what should this "special training" consist of? Let us turn to the relevant (though meager) research.

More than 10 years ago, Sigelman, Budd, Spanhel, and Schoenrock (1981) pointed out that

> recent emphasis on the rights of handicapped persons and legislation requiring their involvement in decisions affecting them have heightened interest in giving mentally retarded persons opportunities to speak for themselves. Yet there has been virtually no attention given to establishing the reliability and validity of answers given by mentally retarded persons. (p. 348)

Have the circumstances changed very much in the last decade? Certainly the terminology used to describe people has changed, but have interviewers of people with learning difficulty been provided with much research-based information that would enable them to assist the interviewees to give a reliable and valid account? I believe the answer is no.

Sigelman et al. (1981) stated that their own previous "research program designed to assess the reliability and validity of answers given by mentally retarded children and adults in interviews leaves no doubts about the ruinous effects of acquiescence" (by which they meant "yeasaying in response to yes-no questions") (p. 348). They further stated (a) that "not only were rates of acquiescence alarmingly high, but acquiescence was negatively correlated with IQ" and (b) that "mentally retarded people may be especially likely to give biased answers that are influenced by question structure and wording" (p. 348).

Sigelman et al. then posed the crucial question: "If there is reason to avoid yes/no questions . . . how then *can* one obtain valid answers from mentally retarded people?" (p. 348). This is especially so because "very young children sometimes prefer the last of two options" (Siegel & Goldstein, 1969, cited in Sigelman et al., 1981, p. 348). Though not directly concerned with witnessing, the aim of Sigelman et al.'s (1981) study was to evaluate "either-or questions as an alternative to yes-no questions in interviewing mentally retarded persons." They asked children (aged 11 to 17 years, mean IQ = 42 in one group, IQ = 48 in another) and adults (mean IQ = 32) questions about their daily lives (the answers to which could be checked for accuracy). They compared the accuracy of the answers to yes/no questions with those to either/or questions. Sometimes questions were asked that, if both were answered "yes," would indicate inconsistency in the accuracy of responding (e.g., "Are you usually happy?" followed later by "Are you usually sad?").

Sigelman et al. found that the consistency of response was higher for the opposite-worded either/or questions (e.g., "Are you usually happy or sad?" followed later by "Are you usually sad or happy?") than for opposing yes/no questions (as explained in the previous paragraph). They found that "an average of fully 43.9% of the respondents contradicted themselves by responding 'yes' to both of the oppositely worded yes-no questions." In comparison, only 13% of the adult respondents contradicted themselves by twice choosing the second alternative in response to opposite-worded either/or questions, and only 2% did so by twice choosing the first option. When the respondents' answers were checked for accuracy, if the correct answer to a yes/no question was no, such responses occurred much less often than (a) correct yes answers to yes/no questions and (b) correct answers to either/or questions.

Sigelman et al. also examined the extra usefulness of replacing "verbal either-or questions" with "pictorial either-or questions." They found that more interviewees answered the pictorial questions (89%) than the verbal questions (72%), that such answers were more consistent with each other than those with verbal questions, and that such answers were correct slightly more often. In particular, "the picture questions yielded no sign of response bias."

Sigelman et al. concluded by pointing out that "the present study is limited by small samples and by the restriction of test questions to a few highly subjective topic areas . . . [C]onclusions . . . need to be replicated . . . [T]he use of pictures in interviewing mentally retarded persons warrants further evaluation." Part of our own proposed research will involve replications and refinements of Sigelman et al.'s work, noting that pictorial questions (see Saywitz, Snyder, & Lamphear, 1990) may possibly reduce the need for interviewees to rely on their own short-term memory to retain in mind the alternatives contained in verbally presented "either/or" questions.

Much more recently, Geoffrey Fisher (1990), who has considerable experience interviewing children with learning difficulty, pointed out that the preliminary findings in the early 1980s by Sigelman and colleagues sat well with his experience. Fisher, however, did not present much to the reader other than specific advice about the act of interviewing children with a learning difficulty, noting that "interviewing retarded children follows essentially the same format as that for children with normal intelligence" (p. 88).

In 1986 Dent carried out a small-scale study designed "to investigate the usefulness of different interviewing techniques with mildly mentally handicapped children" (p. 13). She stated that

> two studies (Pear & Wyatt, 1914; Gudjonsson & Gunn, 1982) have directly investigated the reliability of testimony from mentally handicapped persons. Pear and Wyatt found that mentally handicapped children's unprompted recall was as reliable, and prompted recall much less reliable, than recall from children of normal intelligence. Gudjonsson and Gunn, in a single case investigation, found that their mentally handicapped subject was only suggestible about facts of which she was unsure. (p. 13)

She noted: "These studies indicate that the testimony of mentally handicapped persons can be reliable, but little practical information is available concerning optimal interviewing techniques" (p. 13).

While children's unprompted recall is usually very accurate, it is frequently the case that such recall is not as complete as that of adults, and therefore some questioning of children may often be necessary. However, such questioning should not bias the children's accounts (see Bull, 1992). Dent (1986) noted that "the problem is that of a cleft stick. On the one hand mentally handicapped persons are in need of prompts to access their memory, on the other hand, their recall may be adversely influenced by the nature of the prompts used" (p. 14). She examined the effects on children (aged 8 to 11 years, "from an ESN (M) school . . . mean IQ = 62") of "free recall, general questions and specific questions" about a staged incident at school. "Free narration consisted of unprompted free recall except for the cues contained in the instructions given in all conditions. General questions were of the form, 'What did the man look like?,' and specific questions were of the form, 'What color was the man's hair?' " (p. 15). Dent found that children asked specific questions produced the most information, followed by those asked general questions; those asked for free recall produced the least information. *However*, in terms of how accurate this information was, that produced in response to specific questions was the *least* accurate, with more than 30% of it being incorrect. The information provided in free recall was more accurate (around 20% of it being incorrect), and that produced in response to general questions was the most accurate (at around 90% correct).

Dent noted that "these data give support to the hypothesis that general questions would be the optimal technique for use with mentally handicapped children" (p. 16). There is, however, a fault in Dent's reasoning, and this relates to the nature of the specific questions used. Specific questions need not necessarily involve more suggestion and response bias than open-ended questions. Dent's pioneering study is in need of replication with far greater emphasis placed on the *various* types of specific questions that exist (see Bull, 1992). It may be the case that certain types of specific questions can be found that do not bias the information provided by children with learning difficulty.

Dent (1986) argued that her findings lead to the recommendation that "general open-ended questions would appear to be optimal for use with mildly handicapped children" (p. 17). She suggested that a partial explanation of her findings could come from the work of Glidden and Mar (1978), "who found that, for retarded subjects, accessibility of information stored in memory was a greater deficit than the availability of the information" (p. 16).

Dent raised the question of suggestibility in children who have learning difficulty. The review by Ceci and Bruck (1993a) on the suggestibility of child witnesses says little on this topic (as does Doris, 1991), presumably because so little is known. Gudjonsson's (1992) seminal overview of the role of suggestibility in adults, and Clare and Gudjonsson's (1993) paper on the implications for police questioning of the interrogative suggestibility and acquiescence of adults with learning disability, clearly indicate that such factors are very relevant to testimony. Gudjonsson (1992) has developed reliable methods of quantifying these factors in adults, and it now seems time to attempt to do so in children (noting Baxter, 1990, who points out that robust individual differences between children in suggestibility may not exist).

Summary

In this chapter, I described recent legal developments in Britain relating to child witnesses. I then presented a summary of the main points on interviewing contained in the government's *Memorandum of Good Practice* and reviewed the very limited research literature on the interviewing of children with learning difficulty/mental handicap.

This is a very exciting time for research on assisting children to provide valid accounts. As Ornstein and his colleagues (Ornstein, Gordon, & Larus, 1992) have recently pointed out: "The development and use of interview procedures that are informed by *research* on memory will permit the generation of questions to which children will be most likely to respond effectively" (italics added). However, proper interviewing/questioning procedures with child witnesses/victims must be used not only in precourt settings but *in court* as well (Flin & Bull, 1990; Flin, Bull, Boon, & Knox, 1992, 1993). Jean Mandler (1990) has pointed out that young children may well be able to recall as much as can older children, but it will take the interviewer (and the child) a lot more work to extract the information. I hope that this chapter will make such extraction a little easier.

PART III

Social Policy Implications

One of our goals as psychologists is to "apply and make public . . . knowledge . . . in order to contribute to human welfare . . . and work to mitigate the causes of human suffering" (APA, 1993, Principle F, p. xxxi). The final part of this book focuses on this concern by emphasizing social policy issues. The chapter by Davies and Westcott as well as that by Tobey et al. discuss research that deals directly with one of the newest and most controversial legal reforms, namely, the use of closed-circuit television (CCTV). The chapter by Flin provides a brief overview of psychological research on child witnesses with particular attention to the impact that such research has had on legal reforms for accommodating the special needs of child witnesses.

Children experience a great deal of stress as a consequence of testifying in criminal court. Of particular concern is the possibility that the stress experienced by children who testify about sexual assault is so great it might interfere with their cognitive and emotional development (Goodman, Levine, Melton, & Ogden, 1991). One of the greatest sources of perceived stress for the child eyewitness is the fear of seeing the accused during testimony (Flin, Davies, & Tarrant, 1988; Goodman, Levine, Melton, & Ogden, 1991; Goodman, Taub, et al., 1992; Whitcomb, Shapiro, & Stellwagen, 1985). An innovative procedure that circumvents the need for children to face the accused is to have them testify via CCTV. In Britain the need for protective measures is assumed (see

195

Bull, and Davies & Westcott, this volume), and consequently children often testify via CCTV. In contrast, in the United States the Sixth Amendment right to confrontation takes precedence in most cases and therefore children rarely testify via CCTV.

The widespread use of CCTV in England has afforded British psychologists Davies and Westcott a unique opportunity to conduct field research aimed at assessing the effects of CCTV when used in actual court trials. Specifically, they were able to examine how the use of CCTV affected court officials' perceptions of the child witness and they also were able to assess how CCTV affected the witnesses' demeanor during testimony.

American researchers Tobey et al. have developed an experimental paradigm for assessing the consequences of CCTV that is impressive in its scope and ecological validity. In their paradigm, they stage an extremely realistic mock trial, including a mock jury made up of community participants. One of the great advantages of their procedure is that the accuracy of the child witness can be assessed, because, unlike real court cases, what actually happened to the children is known by the researcher. In addition, Tobey et al. were able to assess how CCTV affects the jurors' perception of the child as well as the influence of CCTV on the final verdict. The effects on the jury are both direct and indirect. Direct effects are those that are caused by the medium itself. For example, the implication may be that the accused is indeed guilty if the court goes to the trouble of shielding the witness from the mere sight of the accused. Indirect effects are those that affect the child's performance. For example, past research has established that children who provide detailed, confident, and consistent testimony are viewed as credible witnesses (Goodman, Bottoms, Herscovici, & Shaver, 1989). It may be that the child witness who has the opportunity to use CCTV may act more confident and give better answers and therefore be perceived as a more reliable witness. The research described in Tobey et al.'s chapter represents a significant step toward a more complete understanding of the effects of CCTV on the quality of children's testimony and jurors' perception of that testimony.

Although the use of CCTV seems to be a promising technique for shielding children from some of the potential stresses of a court trial, it is infrequently used in the United States. However, in *Craig v. Maryland* the Supreme Court concluded that protective measures may be used in cases of severe stress, particularly when direct confrontation of the accused is likely to affect the child's ability to communicate. However, *Craig v. Maryland* did not specify how much trauma justifies the abridgment of the Sixth Amendment (Goodman, Levine, Melton, & Ogden, 1991). The following chapters present some much needed empirical data on some of the positive and negative consequences associated with the use of CCTV.

KAREN L. CHAMBERS

The Child Witness in the Courtroom

Empowerment or Protection?

GRAHAM DAVIES

HELEN WESTCOTT

In Britain, as in the United States, there is a widespread consensus that child witnesses are particularly disadvantaged by the adversarial system of justice (Perry, 1992; Spencer & Flin, 1990; Whitcomb, 1992; Whitcomb, Shapiro, & Stellwagen, 1985). A number of aspects of legal procedure and courtroom practice have been highlighted that provide particular difficulties for child witnesses (Boon, Davies, & Noon, 1992; Jones, 1990). One significant fear is of giving testimony in the physical presence of the accused. Such fears are particularly acute in cases of alleged sexual abuse in which the accused is frequently known to the child (Goodman, Taub, et al., 1992). In a study in Denver, Colorado, which questioned children as to their sources of stress immediately prior to testimony, 34 of the 36 children who addressed the question were either "very unhappy" or "unhappy" about testifying in the presence of the accused (Goodman et al., 1988). Similar concerns were expressed

199

by child witnesses interviewed in Scotland (Flin, Davies, & Tarrant, 1988) and Australia (Cashmore, 1992).

A second cluster of worries surround giving evidence in open court. The courtroom itself is an unfamiliar setting for most children, which is compounded by the formality and conventions of courtroom proceedings. Children in both Britain (Flin, Stevenson, & Davies, 1989) and the United States (Saywitz, 1989; Warren-Leubecker, Tate, Hinton, & Ozbek, 1989) are generally ignorant of the nature and function of the court and its officials. A misbelief common among younger (8 years or less) witnesses is that a summons to court will lead to punishment for the child concerned (Dezwirek-Sas, Hurley, Austin, & Wolfe, 1991; Flin et al., 1988). In the United Kingdom, feelings of alienation are further compounded by the wearing of court dress—a gown and wig—by the judge and barristers. In the Goodman et al. (1988) study, concern over giving evidence in the courtroom ranked second among witnesses' reported fears, whereas a similar study in Ontario, Canada, found "giving evidence in the stand" one of the highest rated concerns among a group of 168 prospective witnesses aged 7 to 14 years (Dezwirek-Sas et al., 1991).

A third set of fears is associated with examination and cross-examination. Adults, let alone children, have difficulties coming to terms with the conventions of the adversarial system, with its emphasis not on the disinterested search for truth but on charge and countercharge (King & Piper, 1990). In child sexual abuse cases, physical evidence is not normally available, and cases will hinge on the plausibility of testimony provided by the child or group of children. A child who is cross-examined in such cases may be told that his testimony is at best a fantasy and at worst a tissue of lies made up to discredit the defendant (Dziech & Schudson, 1991; Spencer & Flin, 1990). Children typically have a much simpler understanding of language and range of vocabulary. Consequently, they are more likely to be confused at trial by the style of questioning adopted by defense counsel (Brennan & Brennan, 1990). A "not guilty" verdict returned in a case where a child is telling the truth is inevitably seen by the victim as invalidating her sense of self (Tedesco & Schnell, 1987). Not a surprise, Canadian research confirms that fears of the defendant being found not guilty also figure among major concerns of child witnesses (Dezwirek-Sas et al., 1991).

While it is a relatively straightforward research problem to establish the concerns of child witnesses, it has proved a much more difficult exercise to unequivocally demonstrate their impact in terms of short- and long-term trauma for the child witness (Davies & Noon, 1991; Goodman, Taub, et al., 1992; Jones, 1990). While there are claims that a minority may welcome the opportunity to testify (Berliner & Barbieri, 1984), fears of the kind described would lead to a prediction that courtroom experience would have a negative impact for the vast majority of children. The best evidence for the adverse effects of court experience is probably the study of Goodman, Taub, et al. (1992), which showed slower rates of recovery among children involved in court proceedings, though there was little measurable impact for the period leading up to court appearance.

In this chapter, we consider what progress has been made in facilitating children's testimony in criminal cases in legal systems that employ the adversarial principles. Two broad streams of reform are discerned: (a) trying to prepare children so that they are better able to cope with the adult demands of the courtroom (the *empowerment* tradition) and (b) seeking to amend and adjust legal procedure to try to take account of the particular difficulties experienced by child witnesses (the *protection* school). In the following section, we seek to demonstrate that legal traditions rather than philosophical differences have dictated which solution court systems have pursued. Recent research findings pertaining to the alternative approaches are then surveyed before discussing the extent to which empowerment and protection represent complementary or distinct methods of assisting the child.

To Confront or Not to Confront?

Although both share common legal roots, British and American law embody a number of interesting differences as well as similarities. One of these concerns the principle of confrontation: the rights of the accused to be confronted with witnesses against them at trial. In the United States this right is enshrined in the Sixth Amendment to the U.S. Constitution, but no such constitutional right exists in Britain.

Criminal law in England and Wales, while seeing confrontation as the defendant's right, has long established that, under some circumstances, the wider goals of justice may demand abrogation of this right (*R. v. Smellie*, 1919). This robust approach to the perceived needs of child witnesses has been upheld in more recent judgments (*R v. X, Y, Z*, 1990) and has opened the way to a range of legislation designed to protect child witnesses from the sight of the accused and the atmosphere of the courtroom while tendering their evidence. The 1988 Criminal Justice Act legalized two-way closed-circuit television to permit children to give evidence from a room outside the courtroom via a live interactive televised link. Provision of the video link was restricted to children aged less than 14 years in cases of sexual or physical assault and this was extended to 17 years in sexual assault cases in 1991.

Further steps to minimize children's appearance in the criminal courts in England and Wales came with the 1991 Criminal Justice Act, in which, following a favorable report by Justice Pigot (1989), the use of prerecorded videotaped evidence was made legal in criminal trials. The act dictates that, while the child must still be available for cross-examination, a videotaped interview may be substituted for the child's live examination in court by the prosecutor.

In the United States, the home of the confrontation clause, there are few signs of the protection philosophy gaining ground, despite widespread concerns over "legal process trauma" (Libai, 1969) among children. In the 1980s many states moved to introduce legislation designed to protect children from the full rigors of courtroom appearance. These included the provision of screens or closed-circuit television and legal exceptions to permit the introduction of videotaped statements or other forms of hearsay (see Montoya, 1992; Myers, 1987, for comprehensive reviews).

The right of the judge routinely to permit children to testify from behind a transparent screen (*Coy v. Iowa*, 1988) or in an adjacent room with proceedings being relayed via closed-circuit television (*Craig v. Maryland*, 1989) were both successfully challenged at appeal (Gordon, 1992). When these issues were raised at the U.S. Supreme Court, the Court narrowly ruled that protection might on occasion take precedence over the Sixth Amendment in the wider interests of justice (Goodman, Levine, & Melton, 1992). Such protection, the Court ruled, could only be offered on a case-by-case basis with due cause being demonstrated for individual witnesses.

This judgment proved insufficient for the Maryland Supreme Court to change its decision in *Craig*, though a later conviction involving a two-way link and prior consultation over use *was* upheld (see *Gilbert v. Maryland*, 1990). In general, the use of screens or televised links remains rare in American trials: In California only 1 video-link trial appears to have taken place in the 3 years to 1988 (California Attorney General's Office, 1988). While minor changes to furnishings or the removal of court dress are tolerated (Perry, 1992), other protectionist measures of the kind that are legal in England and Wales remain rare in the United States. For the great majority of children, precourt preparation and empowerment offer the only course to reduce the stresses on the child witness (Montoya, 1992). But what is the evidence on the impact of such proceedings? We now turn to recent research findings that have examined the impact of empowerment and protection.

– Pretrial prep

Empowerment

As professional interest in the prosecution of child sex abuse grew in the 1980s, so clinicians, particularly in the United States, were quick to recognize the value of preparing children for court appearance. The influential report of Whitcomb et al. (1985) promoted empowerment through preparation and argued that such preparation might obviate the need for protective measures, such as CCTV or taped interviews. A number of empowerment programs were developed, notably in Canada (Dezwirek-Sas, 1992) and the United States (Sisterman Keeney, Amacher, & Kastanakis, 1992), though there continued to be comparatively little interest in the United Kingdom (but see Aldridge & Freshwater, 1993).

Like protection, empowerment has its critics both among prosecution and defense agencies. From the prosecution standpoint, pretrial preparation may run the risk of "frightening the child off" (Morgan & Zedner, 1992), while the defense may use involvement of the child in such programs to claim contamination of evidence (Plotnikoff, 1990). A range of programs are encompassed by the term *empowerment*. Here the emphasis will be on preparatory techniques as opposed to the provision of victim assistants who provide an adult supporter at court (Morgan & Williams, 1992). This review also omits research on specific procedures to improve children's recall, which is described elsewhere (see Saywitz, this volume). Rather, emphasis will be placed on those interagency programs that attempt to ensure, through a mixture of information and support, that the child is mentally and emotionally prepared for the courtroom experience.

Most child witness empowerment programs or "court schools" (Whitcomb, 1992) share similar exercises and components. They may be offered on a group _UK/USA_ or individual basis and include booklets, models, or role-playing in which children are introduced to the major figures in court and learn about their roles. This may involve children trying on judges' clothes and role-playing the different courtroom personnel (Dezwirek-Sas et al., 1991; Sisterman Keeney et al., 1992).

Written exercises and drawing may explore the child's feelings about his or her forthcoming court appearance, and desensitization through clinical methods may be used to reduce anxiety. No details of the particular child's case are discussed to try to avoid any allegations of coaching. Children may, however, be taught the meaning of the oath, the importance of telling the truth, and ways in which to respond to defense tactics under cross-examination.

Central to almost all empowerment packages is a trip to the courtroom. Depending on the particular program, children may take part in a case role-play in court or be asked to point out the positions of different courtroom personnel (Dezwirek-Sas et al., 1991; Sisterman Keeney et al., 1992). The child may also be permitted to view part of an ongoing trial.

Through these different components, programs aim to empower children by educating them about courtroom procedures and personnel, by helping them to tell their story competently during testifying, and by helping the children cope with their stress and anxieties relating to their role as a witness. The programs also offer social support prior to, during, and subsequent to the child taking the stand.

Perhaps the most famous empowerment program was that of the London Family Court Clinic in Ontario, Canada (Dezwirek-Sas, 1992; Dezwirek-Sas et al., 1991). It encompassed all the traditional elements but was notable for its empirical evaluation of the project's outcome. The purpose of the Child Witness Project was "to develop a successful model of intervention for child sexual abuse victims testifying in court, such that their potential for secondary trauma was lessened" (Dezwirek-Sas, 1992, p. 189). The project ran for 3 years and involved 144 consenting child witnesses aged 5 to 17 years (mean age 11.5 years). The great majority of witnesses (91%) were also alleged victims of abuse; most of the allegations (71%) involved inappropriate touching; sexual intercourse figured in one third of all charges.

On acceptance into the project, children were randomly assigned to one of two groups. The first (control) group received only the standard procedure offered to all child witnesses, that is, a tour of the courtroom and one individual discussion on court procedures by the Victim Witness Assistance Program. The second "treatment" group additionally received individual preparation provided by the Child Witness Project.

The effectiveness of the Child Witness Project was evaluated using a variety of outcome measures that were taken prior to intervention on intake, then postintervention, and then at all stages of court proceedings and at follow-up. The measures pertained to the child's general psychosocial adjustment, the child's specific court fears and knowledge of court, the child's performance in the courtroom, and, finally, the child's and parent's perception of the preparation offered to them by the project. In addition, the child's performance in the courtroom was assessed by the project research assistant, police, and crown attorneys.

A more systematic analysis was conducted on a subsample of 120 children, of whom 71 received the treatment program spread over up to eight sessions and 49 were assigned to the control group. While a proper attempt was made to match the samples on relevant variables, the treatment group contained more children who alleged full intercourse and repeated abuse. They also experienced longer pretrial delays, a significant stressor for children (Burgess & Holstrom, 1978), but this did at least result in more extensive preparation.

Comparisons of court knowledge subsequent to trial showed a predictable superiority for the treatment group. However, comparisons of pre- and postcourt fears showed a significant decline over time for both conditions; the trend was greater in the treatment group but failed to reach statistical significance. Direct comparisons of this kind need to be treated with caution, given the differences in the patterns of abuse associated with the two groups. However, when involvement in the treatment program was entered into a multiple regression involving a range of pre- and postcourt adjustment measures, treatment proved a significant predictor of subsequent adjustment.

Courtroom measures showed no significant differences in the rated competency of the treatment and control children, though the scales employed for most of the project lacked sensitivity (Dezwirek-Sas et al., 1991, p. 60). Assessment by police personnel showed no significant difference between the two groups. However, crown attorneys rated the behavior of the prepared children as significantly superior to that of controls, and 60% of the cases involving treatment children resulted in guilty verdicts compared with only 40% of controls. Once again, however, caution is needed in interpreting this latter finding given the differences in the nature of the cases in the two samples. The overall conviction rate, including late guilty pleas, ran at 73% for the total sample of 122 cases. Finally, the vast majority of both parents and children found the program helpful and supportive.

Dezwirek-Sas and colleagues judged the project to have been an overall success. Prepared children presented better in court and displayed lower levels of anxiety on at least some measures of performance. More generally, the advocacy role adopted by project staff went beyond maintaining the rights of individual child witnesses: "Its lobbying led to changes in the attitudes, and in the practices of many police and crown attorneys" (Dezwirek-Sas et al., 1991, p. 118).

Protection

As has been noted earlier, forms of protection can involve shielding the child but may still require their attendance at court, whereas others may exclude the child altogether. In the former tradition is the use of screens or closed-circuit television and, in the latter, the use of pretrial hearings or videotaped testimony.

The use of screens is legal in the United Kingdom both in crown court proceedings before juries and also in magistrates courts, which deal with committal proceedings. Only limited descriptive information is available concerning their use and effectiveness (Morgan & Plotnikoff, 1990). Clearly, children are protected from the defendant when giving evidence but are still very much in court, which is itself a significant stressor (Cashmore, 1992). One of the attractions of the use of closed-circuit television (CCTV) is not only that it can be arranged so as to prevent children from seeing the accused but also that evidence can be tendered without the need to enter the courtroom. Recently, two major evaluations of CCTV have been published in England and Australia, which, through a range of outcome measures, give a comprehensive view of this novel form of testimony.

Davies and Noon (1991) report on evaluation of the first 23 months' usage of the English version of CCTV: the "Livelink." At the time of the evaluation, the equipment was installed in some 14 of the 72 crown court centers in England and Wales. The evaluation covered two main areas. First the views of users of the system, such as judges, lawyers, and court officials, were canvassed (the views of children were explicitly excluded from the research for legal reasons). Second, members of the research team attended 100 trials in which the Livelink was employed and rated the children's quality of testimony and demeanor during the trial, using scales derived from Goodman, Taub, et al. (1992).

Unlike Australia and the United States, it is not necessary for the prosecution to make a special case for the use of the Livelink; there is a presumption of need. In the period January 1989 to December 1990, there were 544 requests to use the Link, all but 3% of which were granted by the presiding judge. Where trials went ahead, the outcome was known in 454 cases. In some 37% of instances, a late guilty plea was entered by the defendant immediately prior to trial. Where trials went ahead, a further 28% resulted in the conviction of the accused, providing an overall conviction rate of 65%.

Information on the types of charges and the nature of the defendants and witnesses can be gleaned from notes and ratings on the 100 cases attended by our observers. These cases involved 154 children (100 females, 54 males) who ranged in age from 4 years 9 months to 13 years 9 months, with a mean age of 10 years 2 months. The sample included 12 children aged less than 8 years, 4 of whom were permitted to give evidence on oath and only 1 of whom was deemed incompetent by the court. The overwhelming proportion (94%) were appearing in sexual assault cases of which indecent assault (66%) formed the largest category. In contrast to the experience in the United States, where the defendant was known to the child in 98% of cases (Goodman, Taub, et al., 1992), around 22% of our sample were total strangers. Only 24% were parents or stepparents, a possible reflection of prosecution policy in England and Wales.

Children's evidence is invariably taken first in trials in England, but children still waited between 5 minutes and over 6 hours to give their testimony—an average of 2 hours 46 minutes. The taking of evidence took anything from 6 minutes to 2 hours 10 minutes, with cross-examination taking rather longer (an average of 25 minutes) than examination in chief (18 minutes). Around half (54%) were required for a brief reexamination by the prosecutor (6 minutes). One of the few concessions observed to the age and vulnerability of the witnesses was the removal of wigs by lawyers during questioning (62% of instances) and, occasionally, gowns (19%).

A canvas of the opinions of law officers revealed a generally positive evaluation of the impact of the Livelink. In all, the researchers were able to sample the views of 50 crown court judges who had presided at Link trials, 86 barristers (of whom 64 had appeared for the prosecution), and 13 of the 14 court clerks who were responsible for running the CCTV courts. The overall reactions of all groups at the end of the pilot period was overwhelmingly favorable. Some 74% of judges and 83% of barristers, as well as 13 of the 14 court clerks, had formed either a "favorable" or a "very favorable" impression of the Link. Of interest, defense barristers were no less favorably inclined than the prosecution, though there was a discrepancy in sample size.

All groups were asked to identify any particular advantages or disadvantages, and the views of the judges may be taken as representative. The first advantage mentioned by 38% reflected the original motives for the scheme's introduction: the protection the Link provided against seeing the accused and the sometimes oppressive atmosphere of the courtroom. However, the major advantage, mentioned by 48% of those questioned, was the reduction in perceived levels of stress for the child, with a further 20% believing that witnesses gave more information on the Link than in conventional courtroom testimony. One judge wrote: "I am sure that the great advantage of the Livelink is that children no longer dry up from stage fright."

These observations on the beneficial impact of the Link were also reflected in the behavioral ratings made by the trained court observers. Ratings of unhappiness while giving testimony indicated that only 26% of children were seen as "unhappy" or "very unhappy" when examined by the prosecution, a figure that rose significantly to 37% under cross-examination. The great majority of children (87%) were judged to have given their evidence effectively when questioned by the prosecution, a figure that fell significantly to 69% under cross-examination. Degree of detail, an important measure of the perceived credibility of child witnesses (Tobey et al., this volume; Westcott, Davies, & Clifford, 1991), was also high during the prosecutor's examination. A total of 71% of children were rated as offering "some" or "a lot" of detail under examination, a figure that fell to 65% when the defense questioned the child.

The view that the Link children were more relaxed and forthcoming than is customary in trials of this type also received some support from a comparison between the Link sample and a group of children testifying in open court in Scotland whose performance and behavior had been assessed by Flin, Bull, Boon, and Knox (1990). While the scales used in the two studies were very similar, differences in the nature of the samples made any comparison somewhat tentative. The Scottish sample was smaller (28 cases) and differed from the Livelink group in having both a preponderance of boys (the sex ratio was almost exactly reversed) and physical as opposed to sexual assaults. Nonetheless, these factors might be expected to favor the Scottish group, whereas all differences in overall ratings favored the Link sample. Consistent with the law officer's observations, the English children testifying on the Link were judged significantly less unhappy, more forthcoming, and more audible than their Scottish counterparts and showed greater resistance to leading questions, both in examination and in cross-examination.

Clearly, differences in the nature of the samples must qualify any interpretation of these latter findings, but they do parallel the recent experimental results of Saywitz and Nathanson (1992). They demonstrated that child volunteers who answered questions about a classroom incident in a moot court manifested higher levels of measurable anxiety than those who answered the same questions in a small, unfamiliar room. Moreover, this heightened anxiety was associated with less information being given by the child and, in one study, reduced resistance to leading questions.

Davies and Noon's generally positive evaluation of the Link is also complemented by the research of Cashmore (1992), who studied CCTV in operation in one center, Canberra, Australia, where it was introduced on an experimental basis as an option in civil and criminal cases involving sexual abuse up to, but not including, the Supreme Court. Thus, unlike Davies and Noon's sample, CCTV was being used for nonjury trials presided over by a magistrate. The Australian court also differed from that in England in that each submission to use CCTV had to be justified before a judge; there was no presumption of use. Half the applications were opposed by the defense.

In this rather different legal climate, Cashmore was able to observe only 18 cases in which use of CCTV was permitted during her 30 months of observation, an appreciably smaller sample than in the English work. On the other hand, her research possessed three major advantages over the English study. First, a direct comparison was made between the Link children and a sample who did *not* give evidence via CCTV but testified in the same court. Second, she was given permission to talk to the children concerned and their parents regarding their experience of CCTV. Third, all interactions on CCTV at court were recorded and made available to the researcher for careful scrutiny. Apart from this, her design followed a pattern similar to Davies and Noon's: a sampling of the views of all those concerned in the preparation and trial of child abuse cases and the use of in-court ratings covering the behavior and performance of the child and legal personnel.

Like the English research, she found a widespread acceptance of the value of CCTV by the end of the pilot period. This positive view extended from social workers and police officers to judges and lawyers. Like Davies and Noon, she also found few differences in attitude between lawyers appearing for the defense and those for the prosecution, though defense lawyers in general seemed more skeptical toward the idea that children might suffer in the witness box (see Leippe, Brigham, Cousins, & Romanczyk, 1989). As in the English work, defense lawyers claimed that a major advantage of CCTV was that the children were generally more composed and could therefore be questioned more rigorously with less risk of the child breaking down and swaying the jury unduly to the prosecution case.

As for the children themselves, not all had been consulted as to whether they wished to use CCTV, but all who did use it seemed pleased with the system. Children opting for CCTV cited the need to be protected from sight of the accused (59%) as their principal reason. A small group of eight children actively rejected CCTV and wished to give evidence in open court, a wish that was respected. Reasons mentioned included a wish to confront the accused and curiosity over the court system. This group provides more substance for the claims that a minority of children, far from being intimidated by the court process, actively seek out the opportunity to testify against defendants in open court (Berliner & Barbieri, 1984).

Cashmore compared her group of CCTV users with two control groups of nonusers on a range of rating scales relating to their performance in court. A first analysis compared CCTV users and nonusers in the Canberra court with a second set of controls who gave conventional open-court testimony in New South Wales. The inclusion of the latter control arose due to concerns about the comparability of the same-court controls who were older in age than the CCTV group (11.8 versus 14.5 years). The New South Wales controls were similar in age to the CCTV group and were involved in cases of similar severity.

Comparison on a range of scales relating to performance and demeanor showed only two main effects: CCTV users were rated as less anxious in giving their testimony than either of the controls, and the New South Wales group were rated as less fluent than the original Canberra controls.

In a further effort to partial out the effects of CCTV as such, Cashmore conducted a second set of analyses with her control subjects partitioned into those who actively chose to give evidence in open court as opposed to via CCTV ("refusers") and those who would like to have but were prevented from doing so ("deprived"). When the rating scale data were analyzed in this way, a much larger number of significant effects emerged, but these were now all contrasts between the "deprived" witnesses on the one hand and the CCTV users and "refusers" on the other; there were no significant differences between "refusers" and CCTV users on any scales. Those scales on which significant overall effects occurred showed striking parallels with the findings of Davies and Noon. The "deprived" group were more unhappy and showed poorer concentration during the prosecutors' examinations and were rated as more unhappy, less cooperative, and providing fewer details during defense cross-examination.

Cashmore concluded that, while CCTV has significant advantages for many children, much of its effect might be mediated more by the sense of power and control it gave to the child than by the medium itself. In support of this, she noted the lack of difference in performance between CCTV users and the "refuser" group. Cashmore also noted two more subtle effects of CCTV on the behavior of the magistrates and the lawyers. Magistrates were found to intervene more frequently when a child was being questioned on television than in open court, and prosecution lawyers were rated as significantly more supportive when questioning children on camera than face-to-face. Cashmore concluded that the presence of CCTV served as a reminder to participants in trials that they were dealing with children who have special needs and problems.

There appear to be few substantial differences in outcome but some differences of interpretation between the studies of Davies and Noon and Cashmore. Davies and Noon attribute more direct effects to the medium, while Cashmore emphasizes indirect effects. Neither set of data is conclusive because of the design problems inherent in research in the courts. Cashmore's CCTV sample was small and differed appreciably in age from her "refusers." Davies and Noon's comparison of users and nonusers is qualified by differences in the size and characteristics of the sample. Both research groups are united in seeing CCTV as a valuable aid but not a total answer to the problems of the child witness.

A second important application of video technology is the prerecorded videotaped interview. Legislation to make such interviews legally admissible in England and Wales came into effect in October 1992 under the provisions of the 1991 Criminal Justice Act. The conduct of interviews will be governed by a special *Memorandum of Good Practice* (see Bull, this volume). Over the next 2 years the impact of the legislation is to be evaluated by the author on behalf of the Home Office. The research program will focus on four main areas. First, the take-up and use of video recordings will be studied by examining the fate of recordings made by investigative teams to see how many lead to successful prosecutions and what proportion are rejected by the courts as unsuitable. Second, the conduct of videotape trials in a sample of 10 jurisdictions will be studied by in-court observation based on the same rating scales used in previous studies. Third, a sample of tapes will be scrutinized to ascertain the degree to which they follow the advisory *Memorandum*. Finally, the views of court officials and police and social work personnel will be sampled both generally and in relation to specific investigations, to establish how far the intentions of the new legislation are borne out in practice.

Empowerment or Protection?

On the basis of the existing research evidence, both protection and empowerment appear to be promising procedures for reducing the trauma of testifying for many vulnerable child witnesses. The protection avenue is essentially a *systems-centered* approach that uses video technology to circumvent the conventions of open court so as to ameliorate the known concerns of children. The empowerment avenue, by contrast, is essentially a *child-centered* strategy that focuses on adapting the young witness to the adult demands of the legal system. Both may be seen as attempts to ameliorate the decision to prosecute sex offenders, which is essentially *offender centered* (Morgan & Zedner, 1992).

Recent court-based research has gone a considerable way in providing an empirical rationale for both empowerment and protection as intervention procedures. Regarding empowerment, children who are individually prepared for court, both emotionally and in terms of information, are perceived by attorneys as more effective witnesses who also show lowered levels of anxiety, on at least some measures, relative to children who receive minimal preparation. Regarding protection, children who use CCTV are perceived to display less anxiety during the tendering of their evidence and to be more forthcoming in their answers than those giving evidence in open court.

Clearly, there is a need for more court-based research to be conducted to buttress these initial findings and address some of the design problems attached to existing research. As Goodman, Taub, et al. (1992) have observed, the use of totally watertight designs in this area is ethically and legally impossible. While the allocation of matched pairs of children to treatment conditions to produce the kind of "high and clear" findings demanded by some critics (Underwager & Wakefield, 1992) is out of the question, there is always room for more and better research.

Such research need not be confined to court-based work; conventional laboratory research has an important supplementary role. Regarding protection, experiments have been employed profitably to explore the impact on juror perception of live as opposed to televised witnesses (see Davies & Noon, in press, for a review) and could be used to explore the question of whether CCTV has more direct (Davies & Noon) as opposed to indirect (Cashmore) effects on witness performance. The work of Tobey, Goodman, et al. reported in this volume represents an excellent example of how methodological rigor may profitably be combined with elements of forensic realism. Likewise, in the empowerment tradition, the recent work of Saywitz (see Saywitz, this volume) demonstrates how careful laboratory research, allied to a regard for developmental variables, can facilitate children's recall on the stand.

From existing research, it is unclear whether the effects of protection and empowerment are mediated by the same or different mechanisms. One plausible hypothesis would link reduced anxiety to increased access to memory and hence the quality of evidence volunteered (Saywitz & Nathanson, 1992). This single mechanism could account for the facilitative effects of both protection and empowerment. However, empowerment goes beyond mere improvements on the stand and also seeks better posttrial adjustment (Dezwirek-Sas et al., 1991). One way of exploring the relative impact of the two procedures would be to conduct a full factorial design in a suitable court system: to contrast the effect of protection *or* empowerment with protection *and* empowerment. If the combined effects of both treatments exceeded the impact of the individual components, then this would be strong evidence for a need for a more complex explanation.

Do existing findings suggest that one approach is likely to be more effective than the other in both securing the child's well-being and leading to better evidence? This seems an unprofitable argument to pursue as long as constitutional constraints place such severe limitations on the use of innovative procedures like CCTV (Goodman, Taub, et al., 1992; Gordon, 1992). In the United States, for instance, empowerment seems the only practical way forward to ease the problems of the child witness (Montoya, 1992; Wilson, 1989). In the United Kingdom, by contrast, protection has been the ruling ethic, and empowerment programs are a relatively recent development (Plotnikoff, 1990).

This growing interest in both empowerment and protection by judicial authorities is a welcome recognition of the vulnerabilities of children caught up in the law. One possible danger is that the very success of such measures may encourage the view that criminal prosecution is the best or only way of dealing with sexual abuse (Morgan & Zedner, 1992). For a child, involvement in the legal process, with its attendant delays, interviews, and courtroom appearances, is likely to continue to be a major source of trauma, irrespective of the availability of protection or empowerment. Perhaps the time has come to look more carefully at mechanisms for dealing fairly and effectively with sexual abuse allegations that do not involve the methods and trappings of our adversarial legal system.

future. radical change necessary?

Balancing the Rights of Children and Defendants

Effects of Closed-Circuit Television on Children's Accuracy and Jurors' Perceptions

ANN E. TOBEY

GAIL S. GOODMAN

JENNIFER M. BATTERMAN-FAUNCE

HOLLY K. ORCUTT

TOBY SACHSENMAIER

In summer 1989 in a suburb of Buffalo, New York, Barbara James, under the impression that her children were possessed by the devil, murdered two of them by slashing their throats and attempted to murder a third. This third

AUTHORS' NOTE: We gratefully acknowledge the substantial assistance of Dave Barringer, Greg Clark, Cheryl Shapiro, Sherry Thomas, and a score of undergraduate research assistants at the State University of New York at Buffalo. The research reported in this chapter was supported in part by a grant to Gail S. Goodman from the National Center on Child Abuse and Neglect and the Baldy Center on Law and Social Policy as well as a Grant in Aid to Ann E. Tobey from Sigma Xi.

rights of D v. rights of v/w.

child, then 9 years old, lived to tell the story. At the age of 10, he took the stand, and seeing his mother for the first time since the incident, was asked to testify against her. The prosecution requested that the boy be permitted to testify via closed-circuit television rather than face-to-face with his mother, but the request was denied. Therefore this child testified in a traditional courtroom setting. Was this child's experience in the courtroom another form of victimization, this time by the legal system? Were his rights served? Would he have been able to give more detailed and accurate testimony in a less stressful setting? Would the use of protective measures imply that Mrs. James was guilty because her child needed to be protected from her? Perhaps another child of weaker constitution would not have been able to endure testifying face-to-face with an assailant. Would justice have been served if this had been the case? When evidence is scanty and the trial depends on a child's testimony, the case may have to be dropped when a child is too frightened to take the stand.

-ve against measures

The issues raised by the James case are similar to issues typically encountered in prosecutions of child sexual abuse. In such cases, it can be traumatic for a child to take the stand to face the accused. Furthermore, due to the private nature of sexual abuse, the word of an adult is pitted against the word of a child often with little or no supporting evidence, posing a difficult dilemma for jurors. The widely publicized McMartin Preschool trial highlights the predicament faced by jurors in cases of child sexual abuse. During the 2½-year trial, 11 children provided testimony. Although a majority of jurors believed that some abuse had taken place, they returned a decision of "not guilty" on 52 counts of lewd and lascivious acts because they could not determine what portion of the children's testimony was accurate and what was the product of fantasy or coaching.

Child V adult

In cases like the McMartin Preschool trial, where there is little corroborating evidence, jurors must struggle to discern accuracies from inaccuracies in children's testimony. Although the accuracy of children's testimony is important (see Spencer & Flin, 1990), it is jurors' perceptions of that testimony that directly affect the outcome of a trial. Thus, from a legal perspective, the accuracy of eyewitness testimony is only as important as the fact finder's ability to reach the truth.

Children's evidence has historically been a point of controversy (Goodman, 1984a; Perry & Wrightsman, 1991). More recently, research has challenged the view that children are necessarily incompetent witnesses, and laws restricting children's testimony have been lifted, leading to more children taking the stand. The increase of child witnesses has fueled concern for those children who must testify. In recent times, a variety of protective measures that remove children from direct exposure to the accused, and in some cases the courtroom as well, have been introduced.

However, the use of protective measures has sparked a heated debate concerning the protection of child witnesses versus the rights of defendants. There has been much speculation but little empirical evidence brought to bear on this debate concerning advantages and disadvantages of protective measures, such as closed-circuit television, when children testify. Those who advocate protective measures reason that, if children do not have to face the defendant, and possibly not enter the courtroom altogether, they will be less traumatized by testifying. Although reducing the stress the child experiences is a goal in itself, reduced stress may have the added effect of aiding the child's testimony by leading to more complete and accurate reports. It is this latter point that has been especially important in legal decisions concerning use of closed-circuit technology. In contrast, those who oppose the use of protective measures argue that such technology violates defendants' rights, eroding the presumption of innocence, and impeding the abilities of fact finders to assess accurately the credibility of child witnesses.

Indeed, it is possible that use of closed-circuit testimony and other protective measures influences the way in which jurors perceive trial proceedings. Such influences may be direct (e.g., the influence of the medium itself on perceptions of the child and defendant) or indirect via their effects on the child witness (e.g., the degree to which the jury can determine the accuracy of the child witness may be based, in part, on the child's performance, which, in turn, may be affected by the closed-circuit technology). An example of a direct effect would be when the use of protective measures biases the jury against the defendant, thereby violating his or her rights. An example of an indirect effect would be a child whose testimony is more confident or consistent as a result of the less stressful closed-circuit context and is consequently seen as more believable by jurors. To protect child witnesses as well as innocent defendants, it is essential to determine the ways in which the use of closed-circuit technology affects children and their testimony as well as the degree to which jurors' duties as fact finders may be inhibited or enhanced by use of closed-circuit testimony.

The introduction of closed-circuit technology into the courtroom when children testify raises important questions. Are children more accurate when they testify via closed-circuit television rather than in open court? Are jurors better able to discern the accuracy of child witnesses in live or closed-circuit trials? How does the use of closed-circuit testimony affect jurors' perceptions of children's confidence and consistency, cues often used by jurors as indices of accuracy? Are jurors' perceptions different for younger versus older children when closed-circuit television is employed? Are jurors biased by use of closed-circuit testimony, leading them to regard the defendant more negatively or view him as guilty when, in fact, he is not guilty? Likewise, does the use of closed-circuit technology bias jurors for or against child witnesses?

In the present chapter, literature pertinent to these questions is reviewed, followed by a summary of our recent research, which attempts to answer the questions posed above. In the review, we discuss the following topics in turn: (a) use of protective measures when children testify, (b) effects of stress on children's reports, (c) effects of protective measures on jurors' abilities to discern accurate from inaccurate testimony, and (d) the degree to which jurors may be biased for or against the defendant by use of closed-circuit technology.

Use of Protective Measures for Children Who Testify

In recent years, the number of children involved in the legal system has increased substantially, corresponding to an increase in reports of child abuse (American Association for Protecting Children, 1988). Along with the higher number of children asked to take the stand is growing awareness that the legal system does not adequately accommodate child witnesses. As a result, many legal restrictions (e.g., corroboration rules, competency hearings) on children's testimony have been retracted or reduced, and special concerns have arisen about how to protect children from stressful court experiences.

One of the most difficult parts of testifying for the child victim witness is facing the accused (Flin, Davies, & Tarrant, 1988; Goodman, Taub, et al., 1992; Whitcomb, Shapiro, & Stellwagen, 1985). Often the offending adult will have bribed or threatened the child to keep the abuse a secret (Bander, Fein, & Bishop, 1981). Clearly, revealing the secret in the presence of the perpetrator in court can be a frightening experience for a young child. Furthermore, seeing the accused may reactivate memories of the negative experiences long after the child has begun to recover. The stress of testifying in front of the accused can have a dual effect on child witnesses. First, the possibility exists that child witnesses may experience psychological trauma as a result of facing the accused. Second, if children are traumatized or intimidated, the accuracy and completeness of their testimony may be compromised. Thus concern lies not only with the psychological well-being of child witnesses but with the integrity of their testimony as well.

To protect children from face-to-face confrontation and help ensure that they can testify successfully, a number of innovative procedures have been introduced. Libai (1969) was one of the first to advocate child-friendly courtrooms. Since then, protective measures such as screens, closed-circuit television, videotaped testimony, or the introduction of hearsay have been employed in a variety of states (Whitcomb, 1992) and a number of countries (Cashmore, 1992; Davies & Noon, 1991). Closed-circuit technology removes children from having to testify in the physical presence of the accused as well as removing them from the sometimes overwhelming context of the courtroom itself. In a typical closed-circuit arrangement, children testify from a room adjacent to the courtroom while their testimony is simultaneously viewed on monitors in the main courtroom. In a two-way closed-circuit arrangement, children have access to a monitor allowing them to view the courtroom proceedings; when one-way closed-circuit technology is employed, children cannot see the courtroom. As of 1985, four states had enacted laws authorizing use of closed-circuit television in child abuse cases, and by the close of 1989, 32 states statutorily authorized judges to allow certain child witnesses to testify via closed-circuit television (Whitcomb, 1992). These states vary widely as to the conditions required for the employment of closed-circuit technology.

Despite apparent openness toward use of protective measures, prosecutors remain hesitant to call a child witness to the stand or to employ protective measures when children testify. As is true for other types of criminal litigation, most child abuse prosecutions do not go forward to trial but are instead resolved through plea bargains, which are often accompanied by admissions of guilt. At times, however, one reason for refraining from going to trial involves insecurities about the child witness. Children's testimony is controversial; stereotypes held about children make it difficult to convict without corroborating evidence; there is no guarantee that a particular child will be able to testify effectively; and fear exists that children will be further victimized by the legal process (Berliner & Barbieri, 1984; Melton, 1984).

When given the choice of having a child witness testify live or over closed-circuit television, most prosecutors prefer to present a live witness (Goodman, Bulkley, Quas, & Shapiro, in preparation). A live witness is thought to have greater influence on the jury, enhancing the immediacy of the testimony and increasing the emotional impact compared with a televised witness (Davies &

Noon, 1991; MacFarlane, 1985). Additionally, when using protective measures in the courtroom, such as a screen or closed-circuit television, the prosecution risks the possibility of the case being overturned on appeal. Protective measures have been challenged as unconstitutional—threatening the defendant's Sixth Amendment right to face-to-face confrontation with the accused and the defendant's Fourteenth Amendment right to due process. Although a number of states authorized the use of protective measures, it was not until relatively recently that the U.S. Supreme Court became involved in determining the constitutionality of such measures.

Coy v. Iowa (1988) highlights the importance of the defendant's rights when using protective measures in child sexual abuse cases. In this case, the defendant was accused of sexually assaulting two 13-year-old girls. To protect the witnesses, a screen was erected to prevent eye contact between the girls and the defendant. Coy was convicted but he then appealed, asserting that the use of the screen violated his Sixth and Fourteenth Amendment rights. Regarding Sixth Amendment rights, use of measures that remove the witness from face-to-face confrontation could interfere with jurors' abilities to reach the truth when a child testifies. For instance, Justice Scalia reasoned that, by observing the child testify in front of the defendant, jurors are given the opportunity to factor nonverbal cues (e.g., eye contact) into their overall impressions. Regarding the Fourteenth Amendment right to due process, the use of a screen or closed-circuit television could be unfair to the defendant. The defense in the *Coy* case reasoned that protective measures would make the defendant appear guilty, hence biasing the jury against the defendant by eroding the presumption of innocence. The jury might infer that, if protection is required for the witness, the defendant must be guilty. The U.S. Supreme Court decided in favor of defendant Coy, and in the process stated that confrontation reduces the temptation for the witness to lie and increases the jury's opportunity to determine if the witness is lying.

A more recent U.S. Supreme Court decision should alleviate some of the reluctance associated with use of protective measures. In *Maryland v. Craig* (1990), the Supreme Court ruled in favor of the use of closed-circuit television in child sexual abuse cases when the child would be so traumatized by face-to-face confrontation with the accused that the child would not be able to reasonably communicate. In effect, the ruling indicated that the use of closed-circuit television does not necessarily violate the defendant's Sixth Amendment right. The *Maryland v. Craig* decision was not without its dissenters (the ruling was made by a slim majority), and concern remains as to the defendant's Fourteenth Amendment rights. Future rulings by the U.S. Supreme Court may add clarity to the *Craig* decision.

A number of countries have now experimented with the use of closed-circuit television in actual child sexual abuse trials. A recent study conducted by Davies and Noon (1991) in England serves to highlight some of the advantages and disadvantages associated with use of closed-circuit technology (see Davies & Westcott, this volume). These researchers followed 154 children as they gave evidence in 100 trials employing closed-circuit technology. One of the main advantages of closed-circuit technology was that it seemed to result in less stress and more complete testimony by child victims/witnesses. One of the main disadvantages was the loss of immediacy and impact of the child's testimony on the jury. A study conducted in Australia by Cashmore (1992) suggests that children should be permitted to choose whether to testify via closed-circuit television or in open court. Some children actually preferred facing the accused in court.

In summary, arguments can be made both for and against the use of protective measures. In general, it is possible, as claimed by those who oppose protective measures, that protective measures such as closed-circuit television cause jurors to become biased against the defendant and interfere with jurors' abilities to discern accurate from inaccurate testimony. It is also possible, as claimed by supporters, that closed-circuit testimony enhances fact finders' abilities to reach the truth and that live testimony actually hinders fact finders in their endeavors to serve justice. Proponents of protective measures base such assertions largely on the belief that children can be easily intimidated by face-to-face confrontation with the accused, thus compromising their testimony and impeding the pursuit of justice. Indeed, there is evidence to support this view, as discussed next.

Stress at the Time of Reporting

If children's testimony is compromised by the courtroom context in which they testify, then jurors' duty as fact finders may be impeded. If children find testifying via closed-circuit television less intimidating than testifying in open court, then they may produce more complete and accurate reports when protective measures are employed, giving jurors firmer ground on which to base their decisions. In his dissenting opinion in *Coy v. Iowa* (1988), Justice Blackmun argued that the fear and trauma associated with testifying in front of the defendant may traumatize the child and undermine the truth finding function of the trial by inhibiting effective testimony. In fact, research indicates that the completeness of children's testimony may be seriously compromised by heightened emotional arousal. When confronted with the accused, children may refuse to testify, be unable to verbalize answers, or be tearful and have difficulty making correct identifications.

At least two studies concerning actual child witnesses indicate that facing the defendant is especially intimidating to children. In a survey of professionals who work with child sexual abuse victims, Whitcomb et al. (1985) found that the fear most frequently reported by children is facing the defendant. Also, in a field study of children's reactions to testifying in court, Goodman, Taub, et al. (1992) questioned children waiting to testify or emerging from the courtroom. For most of these children, facing the defendant was the most negative and frightening aspect of testifying. In fact, fear of the defendant was related to children being less able to answer the prosecutor's questions in court and children expressing postprosecution dissatisfaction with the legal system.

Not only may many children experience emotional distress when facing the defendant, but their reports may be compromised as well. Several experimental studies support the notion that confrontational stress has a negative effect on the accuracy and completeness of children's reports (e.g., Bussey, Lee, & Ross, 1991; Dent, 1977; Peters, 1990). For example, Peters (1990) examined the effects of the physical presence of the perpetrator on the accuracy of children's reports during an interrogation. Eighty children, with a mean age of 7 years, observed a research assistant stealing a student's book. The research assistant then said to the child, "Don't tell anyone about this. It will be our little secret. You know how to keep a secret, don't you?" When the parents and another research assistant returned, the "thief" either remained present in the room (perpetrator present) or left to attend a meeting (perpetrator absent). The student returned and demanded to know what had happened to his book. The parent then questioned the child about the missing book. Results indicated that there was significant reluctance in revealing what happened when the thief was present. Only 5% of the children were immediately truthful when the thief was present as opposed to 28% when he was absent. When left alone with their parents, 68% and 65% of children in the thief-present and -absent conditions, respectively, told their parents about the theft. Finally, almost four times as many children in the thief-present condition never informed on the thief compared with children in the thief-absent condition. The most frequently cited reason for not telling the truth was a desire to keep a secret (when in fact most of the children did not display any overt consent to keep the secret). Clearly, if the request to keep a secret were associated with a threat, it could create a potent motivational force to withhold information, especially when children are asked to tell in the presence of the perpetrator.

Similarly, Bussey et al. (1991) tested the hypothesis that children are less likely to make accusatory statements in the presence of the defendant. Children ages 3 to 9 years were questioned after witnessing a confederate break a glass. Results indicated that younger children (ages 3 to 5 years) were less likely to disclose the incident in the presence of the accused than when he was absent. Although the older children (9-year-olds) were more willing than younger children to report the incident with the defendant present, they also expressed discomfort when making reports in the presence of the accused.

In a study of the effects of fact-to-face confrontation in court, Hill and Hill (1987) examined children's testimony when children were questioned in a small room by only one unfamiliar adult as compared with being questioned in a typical courtroom context. In this study, 37 children aged 7 to 9 years viewed a videotape of a negative interaction between a father and daughter. The next day, half the children testified about what they saw on the videotape in a courtroom setting where the defendant (the father) was present. The other half were questioned in a small room by a sole interviewer. Results indicated that, when children testified from the small room, they testified more completely and accurately. Furthermore, children in the courtroom displayed behaviors indicative of anxiety, such as twisting hair, attempting to leave the courtroom, crying, and shaking. Children in the small room indicated that they would be more willing to participate in a similar study again in the future than children in the courtroom condition, most of whom said they would not ever want to testify again (an important point given that a child may be asked to take the stand multiple times). These results occurred despite the fact that the witnesses were not victims of the defendant and they were not testifying about an actual crime. Saywitz and Nathanson (1993) report similar findings.

In addition, research has shown that a supportive atmosphere can have a positive effect on children's reports. Goodman, Bottoms, Schwartz-Kenney, and Rudy (1991) found that young children committed fewer errors of commission and were less suggestible in response to leading questions when interviewed in a reinforcing and supportive manner. In addition, the presence of a supportive person (e.g., a child's friend) has also been found to lead to more accurate testimony (Moston, 1989; Moston & Engelberg, 1992).

Given this evidence on the effects of stress at the time of report, how will the use of closed-circuit testimony affect jurors' perceptions of child witnesses? Taken together, the studies indicate that it may be very difficult for children to recount events fully and accurately when the perpetrator is physically present. Contrary to arguments put forth by members of the Supreme Court (see *Coy v. Iowa*, 1988), absence of a face-to-face encounter does not seem to increase children's errors of identification or commission errors, at least under the situations studied so far by researchers. If the use of protective measures can decrease the intimidation and stress children feel when facing the defendant, such measures may also increase the veracity and completeness of children's reports, thereby aiding the fact finder's mission. Further research is needed, however, particularly on effects of innovative techniques on the testimony of children who are motivated or coached to lie.

Effects of Protective Measures on Jurors' Perceptions

Jurors may be affected by the employment of closed-circuit technology in a number of ways. Of particular importance, use of closed-circuit technology may impair or enhance jurors' abilities to discern accurate from inaccurate testimony. How well can jurors assess the accuracy of children's testimony and how might use of closed-circuit technology affect their ability to discern children's accuracy? Studies relevant to these two questions are considered next. However, use of protective measures might also affect jurors' perceptions of child witnesses by influencing jurors' stereotypes and biases rather than their discernment per se. Thus studies relevant to jurors' stereotypes and biases concerning child witnesses and defendants are also reviewed, with an eye to how they relate to use of closed-circuit technology.

ABILITY TO DISCERN ACCURATE TESTIMONY

Clearly, when a child provides crucial testimony at a trial, the fact-finding mission may be profoundly affected by jurors' abilities to discern accurate from inaccurate testimony. As previously noted, how the use of closed-circuit television might affect jurors' abilities is a debatable issue. Does the use of protective measures diminish or enhance jurors' abilities to discriminate accurate from inaccurate testimony given by child witnesses? To date, the majority of research related to the discernment question has focused on jurors' perceptions of adult rather than child witnesses. This research indicates that jurors have difficulty correctly assessing the accuracy of adult witnesses (see Wells & Murray, 1984, for a review).

Only a handful of studies have investigated jurors' abilities to discern accurate from inaccurate testimony when children testify. Goodman, Bottoms, Herscovici, and Shaver (1989, Experiment 1) videotaped 3- to 6-year-olds as they underwent direct and cross-examination concerning inoculations they had received approximately 9 months to a year earlier. The videotaped testimony was shown to mock jurors, who rated the accuracy of the children's reports. Overall, jurors were unable to distinguish accurate from inaccurate testimony.

Wells, Turtle, and Luss (1989) videotaped 8-year-olds, 10-year-olds, and college students answering direct- and cross-examination questions about a videotape of a crime. Mock jurors viewed the videotaped testimony and estimated the accuracy of each witness. Although jurors were fairly accurate at estimating witness performance on the direct-examination questions, they seriously overestimated the younger children's performance on cross-examination questions.

Leippe, Manion, and Romanczyk (1992, 1993) asked 5- to 6-year-olds, 9- to 10-year-olds, and college students to participate in a brief, leisurely interaction that involved being touched with brushes by a stranger. Subjects were videotaped while answering free recall and direct questions about the event. Mock jurors viewed the questioning and were asked to make a variety of ratings concerning the accuracy and believability of the witnesses. Younger children were viewed as less believable than adults even when their reports were more accurate. Mock jurors were fairly good at discerning accurate from inaccurate reports given by the older children, but when evaluating the reports of the younger children, mock jurors underbelieved the accurate children and overbelieved the inaccurate children.

From this review, it can be tentatively inferred that jurors have difficulty discerning the accuracy of reports especially when given by younger children. It is likely that fact finders use inappropriate behavioral and verbal cues when attempting to assess witness accuracy. Research with adult witnesses indicates that jurors rely heavily on witness confidence even though confidence has been found to be a weak predictor of accuracy (Deffenbacher, 1980; Wells & Murray, 1984). As indicated below, witness confidence may also influence jurors' perceptions of child witnesses.

The implications of the above findings for use of closed-circuit technology are less clear. Each of the above studies employed videotaped testimony, making it difficult to infer the degree to which jurors might discern accurate from inaccurate testimony differently in a live trial versus a closed-circuit television trial. If, however, children are less stressed and more forthcoming when they testify via closed-circuit television than in open court, closed-circuit technology might aid jurors in discerning the accuracy of children's testimony because jurors would have more information to go on.

SOURCES OF BIAS

Jurors' abilities to discern the veracity of children's reports may be affected by biases they hold about child witnesses and defendants in relation to the use of closed-circuit technology. In their communication/persuasion model of jurors' reactions to child witnesses, Leippe and Romanczyk (1987) propose that jurors may hold stereotypical views of children as witnesses and that these stereotypes have an impact on decisions before any other information is taken into account. In this model, they portray child witnesses as communicators attempting to persuade jurors of the accuracy of their accounts. Source variables, such as the confidence of child witnesses, are thought to play a role in the persuasion process. It is probable that source variables (e.g., confidence and consistency) that have been found to influence jurors' perceptions may be affected by the use of closed-circuit technology.

Recent survey findings are consistent with the postulation that laypersons generally hold negative stereotypes of children compared with adults at least concerning memory abilities; adults may possess more positive stereotypes of children's honesty and sincerity (Leippe & Romanczyk, 1987; Ross, Dunning, Toglia, & Ceci, 1989; Yarmey & Jones, 1983). Trial simulation research has attempted to examine the degree to which jurors perceive child witnesses as less credible than adults and the degree to which jurors are willing to convict based on a child's testimony. Much of this research has focused on witness characteristics such as age. A number of studies have found that, as age increases, perceived credibility also increases (Goodman, Golding, Helgeson, Haith, & Michelli, 1987; Leippe & Romanczyk, 1987, 1989). Nevertheless, other studies have shown that the influence of age on perceptions of credibility is not uniformly negative (Duggan et al., 1989; Goodman et al., 1989, Experiment 2; Leippe & Romanczyk, 1989; Nigro, Buckley, Hill, & Nelson, 1989; Ross et al., 1987).

However, research concerning the effects of stereotypes on social judgments leads to the prediction that jurors may rely on witness behavior (e.g., confidence of presentation) as well as witness age when determining credibility. Research in social psychology, for example, indicates that stereotypes have a strong impact on social judgment but that the specific effects vary with the degree to which the observed behavior fits the stereotype. For example, children may not be expected to be confident and consistent in their testimony; the degree of confidence and consistency they display may confirm or disconfirm jurors' stereotypes of children and thus affect children's perceived credibility (Leippe et al., 1992; Luss & Wells, 1992). Perceptions of children's confidence and consistency may, in turn, be affected by the use of protective measures (Davies & Noon, 1991).

Leippe et al. (1992) examined determinants of believability and accuracy for child and adult witnesses and found that the strongest predictors of mock jurors' perceptions of believability and accuracy were jurors' ratings of witness confidence and consistency. Of interest, confidence and consistency as rated by the mock jurors were not associated with actual accuracy. Actual accuracy, in turn, was associated with longer memory reports, fewer "don't knows," and more powerful speech for the 9- to 10-year-olds and adults but with the opposite characteristics for younger children. In this study, witnesses who appeared confident also appeared to avoid self-contradiction, hedges, and hesitations and to speak in longer, more elaborate sentences. If jurors expect an accurate witness to communicate confidently and consistently, attributes that are not necessarily associated with accurate young child witnesses, then it follows that jurors will have difficulty discerning accurate from inaccurate testimony given by young children. Furthermore, if children appear more confident and consistent, they will seem believable and credible even when they are inaccurate.

Two studies are of particular importance to these issues because they examined perceptions of children's testimony both in and out of traditional courtroom settings. Davies and Noon (1991; see Davies & Westcott, this volume) compared children's open court testimony with the testimony of children testifying over closed-circuit television. Of interest, the children in the latter trials were rated as more resistant to leading questions about peripheral detail, more consistent, more confident, and less unhappy than the children who testified in a traditional courtroom setting. Based on these findings, Davies and Noon conclude that the use of closed-circuit technology facilitates the giving of evidence. When these findings are combined with data that show that witness confidence, consistency, and recall of peripheral detail are positively related to jurors' perceptions of accuracy, then it is possible that witnesses who testify via closed-circuit television may be seen as more accurate.

Swim, Borgida, and McCoy (1992) examined the effects of videotaped depositions on mock jurors' perceptions of a child witness and a defendant as well as on guilty verdicts. In this study, 143 student mock jurors watched either a videotape of a live trial in which a child witness presented testimony or a videotape of a trial in which the child's videotape deposition was used. Jurors were asked to fill out pre- and postdeliberation questionnaires concerning their perceptions of the key trial participants, including evaluation of the witnesses and the defendant, and to indicate pro-prosecution and pro-defense feelings during the course of the trial. Jurors remembered more of the child's testimony when she testified via videotaped deposition than when she testified in court. In contrast to the findings reported by Davies and Noon (1991), jurors did not see the child as more or less believable, confident, consistent, or accurate as a result of medium of presentation. However, use of a videotaped trial to depict the live-trial condition may have led jurors to react differently from how they would react in the actual presence of a child witness. In essence, both conditions in the Swim et al. study were presented on videotape. Thus the expected results may have been stronger had the live-testimony condition involved live rather than videotaped witnesses. Furthermore, reactions to the child witness are qualified by the fact that the child was an actress following a script.

Thus relatively little is known regarding effects of closed-circuit technology on stereotypes of or biases about child witnesses. One might expect based on Davies and Noon's (1991) study that, if facing the defendant limits the amount of detail children are willing to report and inhibits the appearance of confidence and consistency, then children may be viewed as less credible when testifying in the presence of the defendant than when testifying via closed-circuit television. Therefore children who do not have to face the defendant because they testify via closed-circuit television may appear more confident and consistent, may provide more detail, and may be perceived as more accurate and believable to jurors. This pattern would be expected to benefit justice when child witnesses are accurate but to hinder justice when child witnesses are inaccurate.

When closed-circuit television is employed, concerns have also been voiced about the possibility that biases will adversely affect perceptions of defendants, as opposed to child witnesses. Specifically, considerable concern has been raised that a negative bias may be imposed on the defendant through the use of protective measures. As previously noted, the possibility exists that protective measures will violate the defendant's Fourteenth Amendment right to due process. There may be an assumption of guilt if protective measures such as closed-circuit testimony are employed. If this is indeed the case, it would likely result in jurors developing more negative impressions of the defendant and a presumption of guilt as evidenced in more guilty verdicts.

In the study by Swim et al. (1992) in which testimony presented via videotaped deposition was compared with in-court testimony (also presented via videotape), it was hypothesized that "jurors viewing the videotape deposition would perceive the prosecution witnesses and their testimonies more favorably, the defense witnesses and their testimonies less favorably, and give more guilty verdicts than jurors viewing the in court testimony" (p. 2). This study uncovered few effects of medium of presentation (live testimony versus videotaped deposition) on jurors' responses; nevertheless, the few differences that emerged tended to support the hypothesis that the use of a videotaped deposition would create a pro-prosecution bias. Jurors viewing the videotaped deposition indicated that they perceived the defendant as less accurate and less consistent, but more confident. Jurors viewing the videotaped deposition also indicated having more pro-prosecution feelings during several sections of the trial. Of interest, the pro-prosecution effects of the medium of presentation did not translate into an increase in guilty verdicts. In fact, verdicts revealed a somewhat pro-defense effect of the videotape deposition. The latter finding was confirmed by Ross, Hopkins, Sampson, and Lindsay (1993), who found that portrayal of a child's testimony via closed-circuit television rather than in open court in a simulated, videotaped trial tended to decrease the number of guilty verdicts. If jurors do not experience a negative bias toward the defendant as a result of the use of protective measures, then employment of these measures may be used with less controversy when children testify. Alternatively, if jurors are biased against the defendant by the use of closed-circuit technology, then perhaps these procedures should only be employed in extreme circumstances. Given the paucity of research to date, it is still an open question as to the effects of closed-circuit testimony on jurors' perceptions of the defendant and the child witness, and on jurors' willingness to reach a guilty verdict.

The Present Research

The goal of our research was to determine the effects of closed-circuit testimony on children's accuracy and jurors' perceptions of child witnesses. In the study, eighty-eight 6- and 8-year-olds individually participated in a play session with an unfamiliar male confederate. In this session, the confederate engaged each child in making a movie during which he guided the child through a set of activities. In the "defendant guilty" condition, the confederate had the child place stickers on exposed body parts (i.e., the child's arm, toes, and belly button). In the "defendant not guilty" condition, the confederate had the child place stickers on the child's clothing rather than on bare skin. Several weeks later, child subjects testified about the event at a downtown city courtroom. In the "regular trial" condition, children testified in a traditional courtroom setting; in the "closed-circuit" condition, children testified via one-way closed-circuit television. During courtroom questioning, attorneys asked children two free-recall questions (e.g., "Tell me everything you can remember about what happened when you made the movie."). A set of direct, cross, and redirect examination questions were asked as well; these questions were of three types, specific (e.g., "Where were you when you made the movie?"), misleading (e.g., "You had to take off some of your clothes to put the costume on, right?" when in fact children did not remove their clothes), and correctly leading (e.g., "And didn't Greg turn the TV and camera off before your mom or dad came back?" when in fact he did turn the equipment off). Mock jurors, recruited from the community in groups of 9 to 12 adults, viewed the court proceedings and made predeliberation ratings concerning the child witness and the defendant, deliberated on a verdict, and provided postdeliberation ratings. When alternate jurors are included in the count, a total of 1,201 jurors participated.

The study employed a more ecologically valid design than has been previously used in child witness research within an experimental paradigm. Child subjects testified about an event in which they actually participated. Child subjects were naive to the fact that they were in a study, and, for an approximately 30-minute period including while they testified, they believed that "a judge was holding a trial and wanted the child to testify about making the movie." This was accomplished after considerable ethical discussion, pilot testing, and refinement of the procedure over a 9-month period to ensure that adequate preparation of the children was accomplished so that the task was not too stressful for children within the age range tested. This pilot testing revealed the necessity of employing staff who could establish rapport quickly and well with children (e.g., graduate students in child clinical psychology, social workers who served as victim advocates in court) and of providing children with a tour of the courtroom and a chance to answer questions on the witness stand before being asked to testify, the opportunity to meet and have a friendly exchange with the prosecutor and judge before the trial, a chance to adjust to the courtroom and answer simple questions posed by the judge before the jury entered, and an emotionally supportive attitude maintained by the judge and attorneys toward the children at all times. The pilot testing also revealed the critical importance of the children's parents staying in the courtroom when the children testified, a privilege often denied actual child witnesses. Moreover, in the study when a child was asked to testify, if she or he exhibited distress either behaviorally or verbally (e.g., on standardized measures of state anxiety) or voiced a desire not to testify, the child was thanked and excused from the study. Although elimination of such children from the study may limit the generalizability of our findings, it should also be noted that children who are too frightened to testify in actual trials are also excluded from such trials.

For those children in our study who did take the stand, the atmosphere in the courtroom and the trial questioning approximated an actual trial, albeit a very benign one. Actors played the parts of judge, prosecutor, and defense attorney; their scripts were written in consultation with local attorneys, who modeled the roles for the actors. However, the questioning was never as harsh as it might be in some actual trials. Moreover, the defendant had been friendly and kind to the child; the fact that the children had not been hurt or threatened no doubt made the experience considerably less stressful than the experiences of actual child witnesses. After testifying, children were carefully debriefed, assured the trial was not real, and thanked by research staff, including the mock defendant.

Community-recruited mock jurors viewed each child's testimony live or on closed-circuit television in an actual courtroom setting. Each juror based his or her ratings and verdicts on perceptions of a unique child witness who testified about an experienced event using her or his own words.

Comparisons of regular courtroom testimony with closed-circuit testimony permit investigation of the effect of "testimony setting" on children's accuracy and jurors' perceptions of child witnesses. The findings of the study can be briefly summarized as follows.

CHILDREN'S TESTIMONY PERFORMANCE

As would be expected, older children recalled more correct information, $M = 25.22$, than younger children, $M = 12.93$. An unanticipated finding was that 8-year-olds, $M = 2.82$, recalled more incorrect information than 6-year-olds, $M = 1.07$, although similar reverse age effects have been reported elsewhere

(Goodman & Reed, 1986). Children's performance in answering the specific, misleading, and correctly leading questions combined revealed that 8-year-olds provided a higher proportion of correct information overall, $M = .78$, than 6-year-olds, $M = .69$. Likewise, the proportion of omission errors varied with age, with 8-year-olds making fewer omission errors, $M = .06$, than 6-year-olds, $M = .09$. Older children also made fewer commission errors, $M = .06$, than younger children, $M = .08$, with little consistent pattern of differences across testimony setting (closed-circuit versus regular trial condition). All of these effects were statistically significant. Finally, although 8-year-olds tended to make fewer noncommittal responses (e.g., "don't know"), $M = .09$, than 6-year-olds, $M = .13$, the difference was not significant.

In summary, when children's responses to specific, misleading, and correctly leading questions were combined, a relatively consistent set of findings emerged indicating that, overall, older children were generally more accurate witnesses than younger children regardless of trial condition, with the exception that older compared with younger children provided more incorrect responses in free recall. Younger children tended to make a greater proportion of commission errors than older children, but the pattern of commission errors was not consistently related to testimony setting.

Children's responses to misleading questioning provide an index of their suggestibility and are an important topic of debate concerning children's abilities as witnesses. We were thus interested in examining the children's responses to misleading questions specifically. As would be expected, 6-year-olds, $M = .56$, provided a lower proportion of correct responses to misleading questions than 8-year-olds, $M = .67$. Although 6-year-olds, $M = .12$, made more omission errors with these questions than 8-year-olds, $M = .08$, a more detailed analysis revealed that this age difference was evident mainly for children who testified in open court. For such children, 6-year-olds made significantly more omission errors, $M = .15$, than 8-year-olds, $M = .08$. In addition, the younger children made significantly more errors of omission in the regular trial condition than in the closed-circuit condition, $M = .10$. However, for children testifying in the closed-circuit setting, younger children did not make significantly more omission errors than older children, $M = .08$. Thus, compared with testifying via closed-circuit television, testifying in open court appeared to be problematic for the younger children because it was associated with an increase in omission errors to misleading questions.

Similarly, when the proportion of commission errors to the misleading questions was considered, adverse effects of testifying in open court were again detected. Specifically, when the defendant was guilty and the children testified in the open-court condition, younger children, $M = .21$, made significantly more commission errors than older children, $M = .11$. The age difference was not significant in the corresponding closed-circuit condition, $M = .15$. When the proportion of "don't know" responses to the misleading questions was analyzed, no significant effects emerged.

In summary, when responding to the misleading questions, older compared with younger children answered a higher proportion of questions correctly and made a lower proportion of omission errors. Of interest, younger children's errors with misleading questions were affected by trial condition. When testifying in regular trials (that is, in open court), younger children made significantly more commission and omission errors than older children. Younger children testifying in regular trials also made more errors of omission than their peers who testified in a closed-circuit television setting. Misleading questioning such as that occurring in a cross-examination has been found to be especially detrimental to the accuracy of young children's reports (Luss & Wells, 1992). In this case, young children who testified in open court were found to have more errors with misleading questions than older children and other children their age who testified from the more protective environment of the closed-circuit courtroom.

JURORS' RATINGS

In addition to examining the children's accuracy, we were also interested in the mock jurors' reactions to child witnesses who testified via closed-circuit television versus in open court. Would children be viewed as more or less credible witnesses when seen on a TV screen? In general, closed-circuit television was associated with more negative ratings of the child witnesses (see Table 11.1). Specifically, jurors rated children who testified via closed-circuit television as less believable, less accurate for both the prosecution and the defense attorney, less accurate in recalling the event, more likely to have made up the story, less able to testify based on fact rather than fantasy, less attractive, less intelligent, and less confident. Of interest, jurors also noted that children testifying in the closed-circuit condition were less stressed by testifying than children testifying in open court.

The children's age also influenced the mock jurors' ratings. Jurors were more likely to believe that the defendant was guilty when an older child testified. In general, jurors rated older children as more credible witnesses.

Table 11.1 Mock Jurors' Mean Predeliberation Ratings for Significant Main Effects of Trial Condition From Juror-Level Analyses of Variance (standard deviations in parentheses)

Variables	Regular	Closed Circuit
Child believable (1 = not believable; 6 = completely believable)	4.65 (1.19)	4.54 (1.29)
Accurate for prosecution (1 = extremely inaccurate; 6 = extremely accurate)	4.32 (1.19)	4.21 (1.31)
Accurate for defense attorney (1 = extremely inaccurate; 6 = extremely accurate)	4.37 (1.15)	4.27 (1.34)
Accurate in recalling the event (1 = extremely inaccurate; 6 = extremely accurate)	4.12 (1.19)	3.98 (1.25)
Likely child made up story (1 = extremely unlikely; 6 = extremely likely)	1.87 (1.15)	2.05 (1.39)
Testimony on fact not fantasy (1 = not at all able; 6 = completely able)	4.71 (1.12)	4.58 (1.23)
How attractive was child (1 = extremely unattractive; 6 = extremely attractive)	4.57 (1.00)	4.39 (0.99)
How intelligent was child (1 = extremely unintelligent; 6 = extremely intelligent)	4.55 (0.90)	4.45 (0.94)
How confident child seemed (1 = extremely unconfident; 6 = extremely confident)	4.46 (1.24)	4.34 (1.31)
How stressful testifying for child (1 = not at all; 6 = extremely)	3.60 (1.50)	3.37 (1.55)

Specifically, jurors perceived older children to be more accurate and believable, and less suggestible. Perceptions of children's emotional fragility were also affected by age. Jurors rated the trial as more stressful and less fair for younger than older witnesses (see Table 11.2).

As one would hope, jurors were significantly more confident of the defendant's guilt when jurors observed trials in which the defendant was in fact guilty, $M = .59$, versus when he was not guilty, $M = .23$, of the mock crime.

Table 11.2   Mock Jurors' Mean Predeliberation Ratings for Significant Main Effects of Child Age From Juror-Level Analyses of Variance (standard deviations in parentheses)

Variables	8-Year-Olds	6-Year-Olds
Guilt (0 = not guilty; 1 = guilty)	.45 (.50)	.35 (.48)
Certainty of guilt (1 = certain not guilty; 6 = guilty)	3.50 (1.99)	3.12 (1.84)
Certainty crime occurred (1 = certain not occurred; 6 = certain crime occurred)	3.77 (2.00)	3.42 (1.87)
Prosecutor proved case (0 = no; 1 = yes)	.44 (.50)	.38 (.48)
Believability (1 = not believable; 6 = completely believable)	4.79 (1.29)	4.35 (1.20)
Accuracy for prosecutor (1 = extremely inaccurate; 6 = extremely accurate)	4.49 (1.22)	3.98 (1.23)
Accuracy for defense (1 = extremely inaccurate; 6 = extremely accurate)	4.51 (1.17)	4.07 (1.17)
Accurately recalled event (1 = extremely inaccurate; 6 = extremely accurate)	4.28 (1.18)	3.75 (1.21)
Making up story (1 = extremely inaccurate; 6 = extremely accurate)	1.89 (1.25)	2.05 (1.21)
Child misunderstood (1 = extremely unlikely; 6 = extremely likely)	3.07 (1.63)	3.30 (1.50)
Influenced by prosecutor (1 = not at all influenced; 6 = extremely influenced)	2.66 (1.53)	2.88 (1.41)
Influenced by defense (1 = not at all influenced; 6 = extremely influenced)	2.33 (1.29)	2.69 (1.31)
Suggestibility (1 = not at all suggestible; 6 = extremely suggestible)	2.67 (1.50)	2.94 (1.39)
Honesty (1 = extremely dishonest; 6 = extremely honest)	5.20 (1.20)	4.96 (1.20)

continued

Table 11.2 Continued

Variables	8-Year-Olds	6-Year-Olds
Intelligence (1 = extremely unintelligent; 6 = extremely intelligent)	4.58 (.93)	4.41 (.91)
Differentiate fact/fantasy (1 = not at all able; 6 = completely able)	4.83 (1.14)	4.41 (1.17)
Consistency (1 = extremely inconsistent; 6 = extremely consistent)	4.71 (1.31)	4.08 (1.49)
Confidence (1 = extremely unconfident; 6 = extremely confident)	4.59 (1.25)	4.16 (1.27)
Fairness to child (1 = very unfair; 6 = very fair)	5.56 (.78)	5.41 (.93)
Stressful to child (1 = not at all stressful; 6 = extremely stressful)	3.39 (1.53)	3.63 (1.49)

However, whether or not the defendant was actually guilty interacted with age regarding mock jurors' votes to find the defendant guilty or not guilty. More specifically, although mock jurors were more likely to vote guilty when the defendant was guilty than when he was not guilty, mock jurors were more likely to vote guilty when an 8-year-old testified than when a 6-year-old testified, apparently indicating mock jurors' greater trust in older children's testimony. Of interest, when the defendant was guilty, children were seen as more suggestible, less able to differentiate fact from fantasy, and more influenced by the prosecutor than when the defendant was not guilty. A possible explanation for this pattern of findings is that the jurors were hesitant to believe the children's testimony when it was implicating an adult, even though the children's testimony still influenced the jurors' decisions.

However, regarding judgments of the children's suggestibility, jurors viewed 6-year-olds as significantly more suggestible than 8-year-olds in the not-guilty condition only. In addition, 8-year-olds were seen as more suggestible in guilty than in not-guilty trials, whereas judgments of 6-year-olds' suggestibility did not vary with guilt of the defendant. Thus jurors were the least likely to view children as suggestible when the children were older and testified in not-guilty trials. Regarding the children's actual performance as reported in the child analyses above, it is notable that the older children were indeed more accurate than younger children when answering misleading questions. Firm evidence does not exist to confirm that older children were more resistant to suggestion in the not-guilty trials than in the guilty trials.

In summary, when the defendant was guilty, jurors were more confident of his guilt and more likely to view the children as suggestible. It is encouraging that the defendant was more likely to be rated as guilty when that was indeed the case. Apparently the children provided jurors with information that was relevant to making accurate decisions. However, jurors were particularly concerned with children's suggestibility when the evidence indicated that the defendant was guilty. Thus, as perceptions of guilt increase, so may concerns about children's suggestibility.

CHILD-JUROR ANALYSES[1]

Former research indicated that jurors' perceptions of children's confidence and consistency would be positively related to jurors' perceptions of accuracy and believability. These trends were confirmed in the present study: Jurors' judgments of child confidence and accuracy ($r = .59, p < .001, n = 1,194$), child consistency and accuracy ($r = .62, p < .001, n = 1,192$), child confidence and believability ($r = .52, p < .001, n = 1,192$), and child consistency and believability ($r = .62, p < .001, n = 1,190$) were significantly related. Thus the often cited correlation between perceptions of confidence and consistency with accuracy and believability held true in the present study, confirming that jurors may use confidence and consistency as credibility cues when children testify. Of interest, jurors' ratings of confidence and consistency did not significantly correlate with any of the measures of children's actual accuracy, thus calling into question the usefulness of these cues.

We also examined whether jurors could discern the accuracy of children's testimony in the regular versus closed-circuit condition. Former studies indicate that jurors have considerable difficulty discerning the accuracy of children's testimony. If jurors can determine accuracy better when children testify via closed-circuit television, this finding would produce powerful support for use of closed-circuit technology. Alternately, if use of closed-circuit testimony interferes with jurors' abilities to discern accuracy (e.g., if it masks subtleties of the children's expression), then jurors may be less able to discriminate accurate from inaccurate testimony in the closed-circuit versus the regular trial condition.

Correlations between measures of children's accuracy overall and jurors' judgments of children's accuracy indicated little ability to accurately discern the children's testimony, and there was no indication that they could discern the children's accuracy better in the closed-circuit versus regular trial condition.

Finally, overall, jurors' ratings of the children's believability and the defendant's guilt were not significantly related to the children's actual accuracy (all $rs < .22$).

POSTDELIBERATION ANALYSES

So far, the results imply that jurors initially (that is, before they deliberate) view children's testimony with particular skepticism when children testify via closed-circuit television, when children are younger, and, at least in terms of suggestibility, when the defendant is guilty. However, the courts are more interested in postdeliberation than predeliberation judgments. It was thus of interest to examine votes of guilty versus not guilty after deliberation as well as ratings of certainty of guilt after deliberation. Jury-level analyses were performed on these dependent variables. Regarding votes of guilty versus not guilty, juries exposed to trials in which the defendant was not guilty were far less likely to vote guilty ($M = .09$) than juries exposed to trials in which the defendant was guilty ($M = .33$). The child's age was not related to guilt judgments and neither was whether the child testified in open court or via closed-circuit television. Thus, after deliberation, only guilt mattered.

Although it is encouraging that there were few false convictions of the defendant when he was innocent, it is somewhat disconcerting that, when he was guilty, he was infrequently convicted. Jurors apparently felt quite hesitant to convict based solely on the word of a child.

Conclusion and Caveats

The present study may have important implications for the use of closed-circuit technology when children testify. The protective atmosphere provided by the closed-circuit modality seemed most beneficial for young children, who were found to be less suggestible and who were rated as less stressed when not in the courtroom. However, the effects of testifying via closed-circuit television were not completely positive in regard to children's accuracy (e.g., for young children, the closed-circuit condition was also associated with more commission errors overall when the defendant was guilty). Despite this mixed pattern, the closed-circuit technology created consistent biases in the minds of the mock jurors against the child witnesses, indicating that a live witness will create a stronger case for the prosecution. From the viewpoint of the prosecution, closed-circuit testimony may be best left for more extreme circumstances, such as when children have been severely injured or threatened and refuse to testify unless they can do so via closed-circuit television. Ironically, defense attorneys who have been vocal in opposing use of closed-circuit television for children may find themselves advocating for it.

In contrast to the findings for child witnesses, the study did not uncover negative biases toward the defendant due to the employment of protective measures. Thus fears concerning the violation of the defendant's right to due process were not confirmed by the results of this program of research. Furthermore, opponents of protective measures have contended that use of these measures interferes with jurors' abilities to discern accurate from inaccurate testimony. Findings based on the present research do not support the notion that fact finders' discernment abilities are impaired by the use of closed-circuit technology. Instead, mock jurors had difficulty discerning the accuracy of children's testimony whether or not closed-circuit technology was employed.

However, considerable caution should be employed in applying our findings to actual cases or in using them as the basis for social policy. Although this research attempted to attain greater ecological validity than heretofore obtained in experiments on jurors' perceptions of children's testimony, it is not without its problems. Ethical constraints rightfully dampened the realistic nature of the study. Although the child witnesses testified in a fairly realistic setting, they were not nearly as stressed as they no doubt would have been in an actual trial. In addition, children in actual cases, such as those concerning child sexual abuse, may have been coached or told to keep a secret. Neither of these factors played a role in the present research.

Of course, the "crime" was clearly limited by ethical constraints as well; it lacked harmful and salacious components. The result on jurors' judgments of considering a noncriminal case is unknown. They may have been less willing to convict the defendant because the acts (exposing toes, upper arm, and belly button) were not at all heinous. It is difficult to speculate on how the relative innocuousness of the case affected jurors' perceptions of the child witness. Also, subject jurors knew that they were part of a research project and that the trial was not real. This knowledge may have affected their perceptions; if they believed they were making decisions that affected people's lives, their responses might have been different.

However, when the findings of the present study are considered in conjunction with those of several others (e.g., Davies & Noon, 1991; Ross et al., 1993), a relatively consistent picture begins to emerge. Testifying via closed-circuit television may be beneficial for some child witnesses, but it may also limit the impact of children's testimony on jurors' initial decisions. Fortunately, our results indicate that, after deliberations, the actual guilt of the defendant is the primary basis on which verdicts are reached. However, for better or for worse, jurors seem quite disinclined to convict a defendant based solely on a child's testimony.

When actual trials are studied and closed-circuit television is employed, researchers can gain valuable information about a number of important issues concerning the impact of closed-circuit testimony. However, when studies concern actual trials, it is difficult to evaluate the effects of closed-circuit technology on the accuracy of children's testimony or on the accuracy of jurors' decisions. This is so because the truth is not generally known. It is through mock-trial studies alone that issues such as these can be directly addressed.

Note

1. The large number of mock jurors included in the study resulted in considerable statistical power in juror-level analyses. Instead of using traditional alpha levels, a cutoff of .30 was employed for correlational analyses as an index of statistical significance.

12

Children's Testimony

Psychology on Trial

RHONA FLIN

In the last 10 years, the distress experienced by child victims testifying in British criminal courts has attracted significant media attention. Newspaper reports of distraught children in the witness box stimulated national concern over the suitability of our legal systems and procedures for dealing with children's evidence. The motives of the British press relate more to circulation figures than to legal reform; nevertheless, their unswerving interest in child sexual abuse trials publicly highlighted the deficiencies of the English and Scottish legal systems for dealing with child witnesses. Journalists' attention was first caught in July 1983 with a case involving two 8-year-old girls who were allegedly sexually assaulted by a man in a Lancashire public swimming pool. The trial would not normally have interested the national press but for the fact that the man was a leading actor from Britain's favorite soap opera *Coronation Street*, watched twice weekly by millions of viewers. The two little girls became very upset during their cross-examination and the accused, Peter Adamson, was found not guilty (although several years later he admitted in a newspaper article that he had committed the alleged acts). One journalist asked, "Do the ends of justice really require that a child of eight should be grilled to the point of tears in the intimidating surroundings of a packed courtroom?" (Dyer, 1983, p. 14; article first appeared in *The Times*, London, copyright © by C. Dyer).

Such cases raised the issue of whether the procedures for hearing and testing children's evidence could be reviewed in an attempt to devise a method of reducing stress for children testifying without jeopardizing the rights of the accused. Ten years later, video-link systems are slowly being introduced to English and Scottish courts. These permit children to give their evidence from outside the courtroom via closed-circuit television and should solve some of the problems for children giving evidence from the witness box (Davies, 1993; Flin, Kearney, & Murray, in press).

> Demand for an explanation follows the scrapping of a case after a vital 12 year old girl witness broke down while giving evidence. The girl was alleged to have been raped by a 46 year old offshore worker who faced seven charges alleging sexual offenses against young girls. The young witness was unable to continue giving evidence and recount details of the alleged assault when she broke down in tears in the courtroom. It was subsequently revealed that the trial was originally supposed to have taken place in Glasgow where closed circuit TV facilities to reduce the trauma for child witnesses were available. (Doult, 1992, p. 7; used with permission)

A second problem for the English courts (although not the Scottish) was that the rules governing children's evidence in England were based on a view of children's competence that seemed to be derived from an outmoded psychological perspective on child development. Thus children under the age of 8 years were not regarded as competent witnesses and for that reason their evidence would not be admitted in court. In the case of slightly older children, their evidence would have to be given unsworn, which meant that it would require corroboration. Given the private nature of sexual abuse offenses, this effectively prevented the prosecution of many cases of child sexual abuse in young children. The British press again began to focus on this nonsensical legal position: "At present the rules of criminal evidence read like a child molester's charter" (Spencer, 1987, p. 8; article first appeared in *The Times*, London, copyright © by J. Spencer).

The following cases are illustrative:

> A man charged with raping a five-year-old girl walked free from court yesterday without having to stand trial. The case [in Southampton] collapsed after a Judge

decided the alleged victim was too young to give evidence. . . . He then discharged without trial the accused man who, looking stunned, hurriedly left the court. ("Judge Frees," 1989, p. 7; reprinted by permission of *The Herald*, Glasgow)

At Winchester Crown Court [X] denied assaulting the girl, then aged six. . . . Judge Bracewell said that she was 'troubled by the tender age of the witness and needed time to consider the matter. She retired for 10 minutes before ruling: "This little girl is too young to be called as a witness in this case." . . . [X] was formally found not guilty and released. ("Girl Too Young," 1989, p. 2)

The law in England affecting children's evidence was revised in the Criminal Justice Acts of 1988 and 1991. In October 1992 the competency requirement was abolished to allow the admission of young children's evidence in criminal cases provided they are deemed competent by the judge (which had long been the position in Scotland). In both jurisdictions, there have also been major reforms of the procedures for presenting children's evidence to the court. This chapter reviews the contribution that psychology has made to the achievement of the reforms in relation to (a) competence and (b) stress, and then considers the latest psychological research that is attempting to identify optimal strategies for dealing with children's testimony.

Psychology Informs the Law? The Competence of the Child Witness

In England the traditional legal position on child witnesses was to treat their evidence with a considerable degree of caution and, as mentioned above, if a child was younger than 8 years of age, then the courts were unlikely to listen to her evidence at all. This view was predominant long before the advent of psychological research, but had the lawyers chosen to consult the writings of psychologists at the turn of the century, they would have found ample empirical evidence to support their view. As Goodman (1984a, p. 9) showed in her review of the first scientific studies of children's testimony: "Early studies tended to support some of the legal profession's stereotypes of children by claiming to show that children are 'the most dangerous of all witnesses' " (p. 9). Research from the first decades of developmental psychology might have led one to a similarly negative opinion on the reliability of young children's evidence. However, by the late 1970s there had been a systematic reappraisal of children's intellectual ability and the pioneering developmentalists' experiments were shown to have significantly underestimated children's competence to understand and retain information. Donaldson, Grieve, and Pratt (1983) commented: "Much of the research carried out in the first half of this century appears to have been curiously preoccupied with young children's incapacities" (p. 6). This is not surprising as the original aim had been to chart and explain age differences in intellectual performance rather than to identify the particular strengths of younger children's comprehension and memory.

By the early 1980s a handful of developmental psychologists in the United States and the United Kingdom had become interested in the problems arising from their adversarial legal systems' attitudes toward child witnesses. In the United States this movement was led by Gail Goodman, who began to develop an extensive program of research into children's testimony. In 1981 she coauthored an influential article dealing with the credibility of children's testimony published in *Psychology Today*, titled "Would You Believe a Child Witness?" (which won an award from the American Bar Association; Goodman & Michelli, 1981) and she subsequently edited the first volume of papers on children's testimony, which was published in the *Journal of Social Issues* (Goodman, 1984b).

In England the first psychological research into child witnesses was published 80 years ago (Pear & Wyatt, 1914), but modern developmentalists did not begin to study children's testimony until the late 1970s when Helen Dent published the findings from her doctoral thesis on children's eyewitness memory (Dent & Stephenson, 1979). The most influential British psychologist in the field of children's evidence has been Graham Davies, who in 1984 coauthored a review of children's suggestibility, which argued that children were not necessarily more suggestible than adults (Loftus & Davies, 1984). He also organized the first British psychological conference on children's evidence held in Oxford in 1986, called "The Child Witness: Do the Courts Abuse Children?" which attracted unprecedented media attention following a powerful press release announcing that psychologists believed that young children could be reliable witnesses and that their evidence should be treated seriously by the British courts (Davies & Drinkwater, 1988). At this time in England, the position was that the evidence of children who were too young to take the oath (usually under 14 years) had to be corroborated, although this was not the case for older children and adults. In response to growing demands for reform, the Home Secretary ordered a review of the psychological research on the reliability of children's evidence. The aim of the review was to discover whether the legal assumption that children's testimony is inherently too unreliable to form the sole basis for a conviction was justified on the basis of psychological research findings. It concluded that, despite the limitations of experimental studies and the lack of data from real witnesses,

> the general implication of the studies reviewed is that children need not be debarred from giving evidence simply on the basis of age. Their individual abilities and circumstances should be considered in deciding whether they would make competent and credible courtroom witnesses and whether they would sustain any psychological harm by so doing. (Hedderman, 1987, p. 34)

On the strength of this conclusion, the rule that there could be no conviction on the unsworn evidence of children was abolished in the Criminal Justice Act, which came into force in England in October 1988. (In Scotland the legal rules are different and there is a general corroboration rule that states that all evidence—whether from a child or an adult—has to be corroborated.)

In the late 1980s an accumulating body of psychological research data from both sides of the Atlantic provided lawyers and politicians pressing for further changes to the competency ruling with the ammunition they required, and the effective bar on younger children's evidence was lifted in 1992, although the clumsy drafting of the new legislation has left a number of undesirable loopholes (see Spencer & Flin, 1993). Many professionals from social work, psychiatry, pediatrics, the police, and the legal profession were also instrumental in the achievement of these legal reforms, but there was no doubt that psychologists had made a very significant contribution to the debate, and their research data argued with one voice that the competence of the child witness had been underestimated and that even young children had the right to be heard in the criminal justice system.

Children's Testimony: Psychological Research for the 1990s

To argue that the competence of child witnesses to provide valuable evidence had previously been underestimated in the English courts does not, however, mean that psychologists do not appreciate the special problems of obtaining and evaluating children's testimony. Recent research in Europe, North America, and Australia has been designed to develop our understanding of the strengths and weakness of children's evidence so as to improve the techniques used to interview child witnesses and to evaluate the quality of their testimony.

As in any other scientific domain, research tends to generate more questions than answers, and we know that the reliability of a given child's account of a particular incident is influenced by a host of cognitive, affective, and social factors. Nevertheless, an accumulating body of research data has helped to reveal the conditions that are likely to enhance or diminish the quality of a child's testimony in terms of reliability (Dent & Flin, 1992; Goodman & Bottoms, 1993), suggestibility (Ceci & Bruck, 1993a; Doris, 1991; Lindsay, Gonzales, & Eso, this volume), and honesty (Ceci, Leichtman, & Putnick, 1992). The present position is undeniably complex but the one finding that remains consistent is that the competence of the interviewer appears to be of as much relevance as the competence of the child. It is not only psychologists who are endeavoring to improve our knowledge of children's evidentiary abilities. British psychiatrists, faced with increasing numbers of child sexual abuse cases, have also been concerned with this issue, and they too have been developing new methods of interviewing child abuse victims since the mid-1980s (Bentovim, Elton, Hildebrand, Tranter, & Vizard, 1988; Jones, 1992).

The areas of investigation that now look set to dominate the 1990s appear to be as follows:

1. The study of interview techniques, particularly relating to the child's initial statements, has been undertaken. New British research projects are examining Fisher and Geiselman's cognitive interview technique (Memon & Bull, 1991; see Fisher & McCauley, this volume, for details of the method), videotaped interviews (Davies, 1993), and interviewer training techniques (Baxter, Warden, Hutcheson, & Telfer, in preparation). Ongoing studies such as those from the United States on the effects of repeated questioning (Poole & White, and Warren & Lane, this volume) and the use of anatomical dolls (Boat & Everson, 1993; DeLoache, this volume), from Australia on interviewing with toys as props and cues (Pipe, Gee, & Wilson, 1993), and from Germany on statement validity analysis (Steller & Boychuk, 1992) will provide soundly based practical recommendations for investigative and clinical practitioners. See Bull (this volume) for details of the new English guidelines for conducting videotaped interviews with child witnesses and a discussion of innovative interview techniques.

2. An emerging concern in the United Kingdom is the abuse of mentally and physically handicapped children and adults and the particular difficulties of obtaining their evidence (Dent, 1992; Westcott, 1991,

1994). Research in this difficult area may also improve our understanding of techniques suitable for interviewing normal children, particularly when they are reluctant to describe their experiences.

3. We need to know more about the testimonial competence of preschool
   children, and this is clearly an area in which basic developmental research has much to contribute (see, for example, Fivush & Shukat, this
   volume).

4. Recent attempts to enhance the quality of children's testimony by simple
   mnemonic training techniques look promising (Saywitz & Snyder, 1993).
   One fruitful development in this area might be to survey the techniques
   being adopted by prosecutors when preparing their witnesses for court.
   Wendy Harvey, a Canadian crown prosecutor, recently described a
   simple but obviously effective technique of using a blackboard with key
   headings to encourage child witnesses to report as fully as possible
   (Harvey, in press).

5. The developmental psychology literature on children's memory is very
   weak on certain issues that are pertinent to our understanding of
   testimonial competence, for example, the effects of long delays (Flin,
   Boon, Bull, & Knox, 1992; Goodman, Hirshman, Hepps, & Rudy, 1991;
   Plotnikoff & Woolfson, 1994); the effects of stress (a) at encoding
   (Baker-Ward et al. this volume; Goodman, in press; Ornstein, Gordon,
   & Larus, 1992) and (b) at retrieval (Goodman, Taub, et al. 1992; Saywitz
   & Nathanson, 1993; Saywitz, this volume); children's honesty (Haugaard &
   Repucci, 1992) and parental coaching (Tate, Warren, & Hess, 1992).
   These are topics that are notoriously awkward to study for ethical or
   logistical reasons but are crucial to a proper appreciation of the factors
   influencing the reliability of victim testimony in a typical sexual abuse
   prosecution.

6. An emerging concern in the United States is the question of "repressed
   memories" of abuse or other crimes. In these cases, adults apparently
   recall long forgotten memories from childhood, and the issue is whether
   such recollections are true or false. The American Psychological Association has established a working group to review and evaluate the
   literature on recovering childhood memories of childhood abuse. The
   topic of the recovery of repressed memories is controversial both within
   the association and as a public issue (see DeAngelis, 1993, p. 44).

If these areas of research are adequately supported and funded then there is good reason to predict that psychological research into children's competence will continue to inform the law during the 1990s as it has during the last decade. Psychologists must continually strive to synthesize the empirical findings from different laboratories to present a coherent voice to the legal consumers of our research output (see Matthews & Saywitz, 1992; McGough, 1994; Myers, 1992). This is not a plea to stifle scientific disagreement and debate, which are fundamental to the critical appraisal and development of our knowledge base. But academic disagreements are often based on differences that are more apparent than real, and, although intellectual disharmony is stimulating and important, we should also remember to publicize those issues where a significant consensus has been reached. One important mechanism in this process of synthesis is the opportunity for psychologists from basic and applied research as well as clinical practitioners to meet face-to-face in an international seminar such as the one this book is based on: The value of intensive meetings is illustrated by the results of the APA-supported meeting at Cornell in 1989 (Doris, 1991) and the 1992 NATO conference in Italy on children's testimony (Peters, in press). The second question to be considered in this chapter is the extent to which psychology has influenced legal thinking on the ability of child witnesses to cope with the demands of an adversarial trial.

Psychology Informs the Law? Child Witnesses in Court

In Scotland it has long been the practice to listen to children's evidence provided that the presiding judge believes the child to be competent. Child witnesses as young as 2 and 3 years of age have been admitted to give evidence in criminal trials. Their testimony is treated with due caution, but they are treated in law very much as adult witnesses are. In the 1980s professionals working with child victims in Scotland were therefore not as concerned with the issue of children's competence as their English neighbors, but they were worried about whether young children could in fact cope with the demands of performing as witnesses in a criminal trial. As the law began to change in England to allow the admission of younger children's testimony in the criminal courts, similar concerns were raised by professionals working with child victims regarding their treatment in the courtroom. Several notable trials folded in a blaze of publicity when children were so traumatized that they were unable to testify: For example, one English sexual abuse case collapsed when a 12-year-old boy hid in the lavatory of the Central Criminal Court in London, too frightened to give evidence. A conference titled "The Child: Victim of the Legal Process?" held in Edinburgh in September 1985 was well attended by the legal profession, although they were not entirely convinced of the need for change. Lord McCluskey, a senior Scottish judge, said in his address to the conference that "he could find no clear evidence that the child suffered unnecessary trauma and distress other than of a temporary nature and what one would normally expect of a witness before a court. His verdict on whether or not the child was a victim of the legal process was one of not proven" (Irvine & Dunning, 1985, p. 265).

Judicial indecision notwithstanding, in 1986 Graham Davies and I were awarded a research grant from the Scottish Home and Health Department to study child witnesses, both in court and using experimental techniques. The project was based in Aberdeen for 2 years (Flin, Davies, & Tarrant, 1988) and then in the much larger city of Glasgow for a further 2 years (Flin, Bull, Boon, & Knox, 1993). This was the first British study of child witnesses in court, although similar research was also being undertaken in the United States (Goodman, Taub, et al., 1992; Gray, 1993; Whitcomb et al., 1991). The aim of these research projects was to identify the sources of stress for child witnesses attending criminal courts to give evidence and to investigate whether attending criminal courts to give evidence had any long-term effects on the child's emotional well-being. Goodman, Taub, et al. (1992) found that, at 7 months after the initial testimony, the children who testified showed greater behavioral disturbance than the children who did not testify, especially if the testifiers took the stand several times, were deprived of maternal support, and lacked corroboration of their claims. Similarly, Whitcomb et al. (1991) concluded:

> Testifying, in itself, does not appear to produce significant changes in the child victims' mental health. However, measures of stressful testimony, which include testifying more than once and enduring long and/or harsh cross examination, do appear to have significant adverse effects. This finding was limited to children over the age of eight who were more likely than the younger children to experience more stressful testimony. (p. 139)

These investigations along with case reports, surveys of professionals working with child witnesses, and anecdotal evidence began to paint a fairly

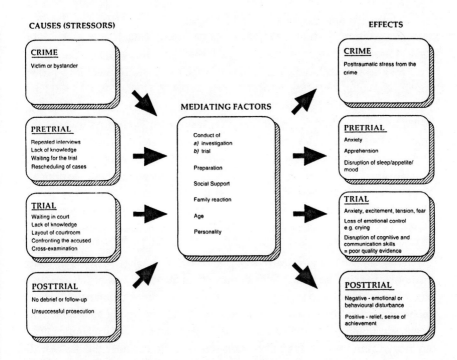

CAUSES (STRESSORS)

EFFECTS

MEDIATING FACTORS

Figure 12.1. Model of stress factors for child witnesses.
SOURCE: Spencer, J., & Flin, R. (1993). *The evidence of children: The law and the psychology* (2nd ed.). London: Blackstone. Reprinted by permission.

consistent picture of the causes and effects of stress for child witnesses. These are shown in the summary diagram (Figure 12.1) and are discussed in more detail in Spencer and Flin (1993).

There are a number of factors that appear to cause stress for children cited as bystanders or victim witnesses in criminal trials, but whether or not exposure to any of these stressors will produce a stress reaction depends on another set of variables that mediate between cause and effect; that is, they moderate the intensity of the stress effect resulting from exposure to the stressors. These mediating factors are of particular interest because some of them can be manipulated to reduce stress for child victims—for example, preparing children carefully for court, providing social support for the child during the prosecution process, and conducting the investigation and trial in a manner that is sensitive to the demands being placed on the child witness.

Psychologists have begun not only to develop techniques for pretrial preparation (Saywitz & Snyder, 1993; Sisterman-Keeney, Amacher, & Kastanakis,
1992) but also to demonstrate empirically that such interventions can have a
positive effect on children's ability to cope with giving testimony (Sas, Hurley,
Austin, & Wolfe, 1991; Sas, Hurley, Hatch, Malla, & Dick, 1993). In England
and Wales a special pack of three booklets has just been released (NSPCC,
1993) to prepare child witnesses for giving testimony. These are similar to the
Canadian and Australian materials that have been available for several years,
and they are long overdue for British children (Aldridge & Freshwater, 1993).

   In fairness, not all of the legal profession were unconcerned about the difficulties facing child witnesses who had to testify, particularly as victims of sexual
abuse. In 1986 the Lord Advocate referred the law governing the evidence of
children to the Scottish Law Commission. They published an important discussion paper in 1988 along with a research paper prepared by Kathleen Murray, a
psychologist from Glasgow University, who reported on "alternatives to in-court
testimony in criminal proceedings in the United States of America" based on a
study she had conducted in summer 1987. Following a consultation period, a final
report, *Report on the Evidence of Children and Other Potentially Vulnerable Witnesses*, was published in 1990. In England the government set up a Home Office
Advisory Committee with a rather narrower remit to consider the use of videotapes for children's evidence, and they produced a very radical report in
December 1989, which supported the admission of videotaped evidence. It is
interesting to note that, in recent Scottish, English, Irish, and Australian reports
on children's testimony, psychological research is referred to in support of the
legal arguments for reform.

Psychology Informs the Law? Legal Skepticism

   In this chapter, I have outlined the influence that psychological research has
had during the 1980s on the British criminal justice system's view of child
witnesses' competence and emotional frailties in the courtroom. Although
psychologists may believe that they have made a significant and valuable
contribution to legal debate and reform on these two issues, not all legal
scholars share this unequivocally positive appraisal. King and Piper (1990),
academic lawyers from Brunel University in London, have recently written a
book titled *How the Law Thinks About Children*. With reference to the work
of German theoretician Gunther Teubner (1989), they examine the legal

constructs of "the child" that are employed in a range of contexts surrounding the basic welfare/justice dichotomy such as child welfare, child offenders, children in divorce. In discussing the child as witness, they focus on the potential conflict between the two issues of competence and frailty that were reviewed above.

> The dilemma for the law is how to reconcile its own image of children as vulnerable, unformed, dependent creatures in need of protection with the necessity of extracting "reliable" information from child witnesses in order to convict an offender or protect the child from further abuse. The response of the law to this dilemma has been to seek solutions from discourses and social actors outside the law, to rush headlong, as Teubner would have it, into the epistemic trap. The results, as Teubner would have predicted, are conflict and confusion with the law sacrificing its own internal logic in order to accommodate concepts and procedures that are incompatible with its own discourse and processes for constructing truth.
>
> The problem that the law has faced has therefore been how to bring the evidence of young children before the court in a form that is likely to result in conviction and how, at the same time, to protect the child from the ill-effects of criminal procedures both outside and inside the courtroom which, according to some psychologists, have a more deleterious effect on the child than the abuse itself. Unable to solve such problems through its own internal communications, the law has turned to other discourses and to other institutions in its truth-constructing endeavours. . . .
>
> Enter social workers, forensic psychologists and child psychiatrists ready to assist the law by producing from behavioral science knowledge and procedures to solve these problems. (King & Piper, 1990, pp. 57-58)

King and Piper (1990) then describe three solutions that these professionals have provided: (1) The revised view of children as competent witnesses who can provide reliable evidence has resulted in the revision of several of the rules of evidence, as described earlier. They label this "reconstructing the image of children as witnesses." (2) Measures have been introduced to protect the child in court such as video links or the Israeli youth examiner system. (3) Another solution would be "improving the procedures and techniques employed by those engaged in helping children to disclose the fact that sexual abuse occurred by making them more resistant to attack by lawyers." The Great Ormond Street psychiatrists (Bentovim et al., 1988) are mentioned.

However, they do not regard the above as any kind of testament to the successful collaboration between law and the behavioral sciences; instead, they caution that in each of these three domains increasing attention to psychological research will lead the lawyers down a slippery slope.

The introduction of knowledge derived from scientific procedures to achieve forensic objectives will result firstly in the enslavement by law of the scientific concepts; and secondly, it will lead law deep into the epistemic trap through its increasing dependence on procedures external to law for the validation of knowledge. The consequence will be a loss for law of its epistemic authority over what constitutes truth for the purpose of criminal trials. (King & Piper, 1990, p. 59)

If this were not bad enough, they think there could be worse to come, warning that the protection of child witnesses in court may lead to the protection of other vulnerable witnesses, and, before we know it, the courts will be offering defendants protection from stress. "It is not hard to see how the erosion of a few pebbles could lead eventually to the crumbling of the whole cliff face" (p. 60).

Although this could be regarded as something of an alarmist perspective, these views need to be taken seriously by psychologists, as the developing role for forensic psychologists within the criminal justice system may be seen as territorially threatening in certain quarters of the legal profession. Davies and Westcott (this volume) discuss the same issue but from a rather more positive psychological perspective: empowerment or protection?

King and Piper's third area of concern, "the use of 'experts' from other disciplines, to carry out fact-finding investigation for the law," certainly has been justified in a number of cases heard in the English and Scottish courts, as the legal Inquiry reports of the Cleveland case (Butler-Sloss, 1988) and the Orkney case (Clyde, 1992) demonstrate (see Bissett-Johnson, 1993, for a thoughtful discussion). The potential conflict and contamination between therapeutic, diagnostic, and evidentiary interviewing is a significant problem but one that I hope is being addressed in the United Kingdom with the release of the new code for videotaped interviews (Home Office, 1992; see Bull, this volume) and the general acknowledgment of the need for improved training and assessment of interviewers.

Professional Consensus and Expert Witnesses: A Psychological Contradiction in Terms?

Had King and Piper been American lawyers, their fourth area of concern might have been the "hired gun" behavioral scientists who appear in North American courtrooms slugging it out as opposing expert witnesses. In the United Kingdom this problem has not occurred to the same degree because psychologists are rarely called to testify regarding the reliability of child witnesses in general or even the credibility of a particular child. The reasons for the reluctance of the British courts to use psychologists as expert witnesses are discussed at length in Spencer and Flin (1993). The only psychologists who do appear routinely in court are clinical or educational psychologists who will have been asked to report to the court on a specific issue. Perhaps for this reason the British research psychologists have to some extent presented a more united front to the legal profession than their North American counterparts. Possibly this is because the likelihood of them becoming entrenched or inextricably committed to a position they have been hired to publicly defend is somewhat reduced. There is, however, international concern regarding the methods of assessing the competence of expert witnesses providing psychological testimony. Those presenting expert psychological evidence should have qualifications and experience that would be endorsed by peer review. There would seem to be a sound argument for a national register of approved experts in a given field who are appointed by the court, as in the French inquisitorial system. These experts do not receive very high fees, but it is a recognized professional honor to be invited to join this select list. Such a system would reduce the risk of psychologists who are not highly regarded by their professional community achieving unwarranted attention in the courts, which is not good for psychology and is even worse for justice.

Conclusion

This chapter has reviewed the contribution that psychologists have made to our understanding of the strengths and weaknesses of children's testimony. Recent attempts to reform the law relating to children's evidence in the United Kingdom have paid unprecedented heed to the findings and opinions of research psychologists. The most influential psychological research has encompassed ecologically valid empirical investigations as well as court-based studies of child witnesses involved in the legal process. For empirical work to have any credibility with the legal profession, experimental designs must be founded not only on a proper understanding of developmental psychology but also on a clear appreciation of investigative and trial procedures (see, for example, Saywitz, this volume; Tobey & Goodman, et al., this volume).

It appears that this will be an arena for the 1990s in which experimental psychologists will be on trial. Can a promising start in the 1980s continue to inform legal reform in the present decade? Can better attempts be made to synthesize our basic and applied research findings to present a coherent and consistent psychological perspective? Can our profession monitor and maintain the quality of the psychologists operating in this sensitive domain?

Psychologists need to tackle these issues before the jury returns.

References

Ackerman, B. P. (1985). Children's retrieval deficit. In C. J. Brainerd & M. Pressley (Eds.), *Basic processes in memory development: Progress in cognitive development research* (pp. 1-46). New York: Springer-Verlag.

Aldridge, J., & Freshwater, K. (1993). The preparation of child witnesses. *Journal of Child Law, 5,* 25-27.

American Academy of Child and Adolescent Psychiatry (AACAP). (1985). *Guidelines for the clinical evaluation of child and adolescent sexual abuse: Sub-committee on Guidelines for Evaluation of Child Sexual Abuse.* Washington, DC: Author.

American Association for Protecting Children. (1988). *Highlights of official child neglect and abuse reporting 1986.* Denver, CO: American Humane Association.

American Professional Society on the Abuse of Children (APSAC). (1990). *Guidelines for psychosocial evaluation of suspected sexual abuse in young children: Task Force on the Psychosocial Evaluation of Suspected Sexual Abuse in Young Children.* Chicago: Author.

American Psychological Association. (1993). *Ethical principles and guidelines.* Washington, DC: Author.

Asher, S. (1976). Children's ability to appraise their own and other person's communication performance. *Developmental Psychology, 12,* 24-32.

August, R. L., & Forman, B. D. (1989). A comparison of sexually and nonsexually abused children's behavioral responses to anatomically correct dolls. *Child Psychiatry and Human Development, 20,* 39-47.

Baddeley, A. D. (1986). *Working memory.* Oxford: Oxford University Press.

Baker-Ward, L., Gordon, B. N., Ornstein, P. A., Larus, D., & Clubb, P. A. (1993). Young children's long-term retention of a pediatric examination. *Child Development, 64,* 1519-1533.

Baker-Ward, L., Hess, T. M., & Flannagan, D. A. (1990). The effects of involvement on children's memory for events. *Cognitive Development, 5,* 55-69.

Baker-Ward, L., Ornstein, F. A., & Gordon, P. A. (1993). A tale of two settings: Young children's memory in the laboratory and the field. In G. Davies & R. Logie (Eds.), *Memory in everyday life* (pp. 13-41). London: North Holland.

255

Bander, K. W., Fein, E., & Bishop, G. (1981). Evaluation of child-sexual-abuse programs. In S. M. Sgroi (Ed.), *Handbook of clinical interventions in child sexual abuse* (pp. 345-376). New York: Free Press.

Bartlett, F. C. (1932). *Remembering.* Cambridge: Cambridge University Press.

Batterman-Faunce, J. M., & Goodman, G. S. (1993). Effects of context on accuracy and suggestibility. In G. S. Goodman & B. L. Bottoms (Eds.), *Child victims, child witnesses: Understanding and improving testimony* (pp. 301-330). New York: Guilford.

Baxter, J. (1990). The suggestibility of child witnesses: A review. *Applied Cognitive Psychology, 4,* 393-407.

Baxter, J., Warden, D., Hutcheson, G., & Telfer, K. (in preparation). *Interviewing child witnesses: Skills and strategies for improving testimony.* (Final grant report R#000232968 to the Economic and Social Research Council, London)

Beitchman, J., Zucker, K., Hood, J., LaCosta, G., & Akman, D. (1991). A review of the short term effects of child abuse. *Child Abuse & Neglect, 15,* 537-556.

Bekerian, D. A., & Dennett, J. L. (1993). The cognitive interview technique: Reviving the issues. *Applied Cognitive Psychology, 7,* 275-298.

Belli, R. F., Windschitl, P. D., McCarthy, T. T., & Winfrey, S. E. (1992). Detecting memory impairment with a modified test procedure: Manipulating retention interval with centrally presented event items. *Journal of Experimental Psychology: Learning, Memory, and Cognition, 18,* 356-367.

Bentovim, A., Elton, A., Hildebrand, J., Tranter, M., & Vizard, E. (Eds.). (1988). *Sexual abuse within the family: Assessment and treatment.* Bristol, U.K.: John Wright.

Berliner, L., & Barbieri, M. K. (1984). Testimony of the child victim of sexual assault. *Journal of Social Issues, 40,* 125-137.

Birch, D. (1992, April). Children's evidence. *Criminal Law Review,* pp. 262-276.

Bissett-Johnson, A. (1993). Family violence: Investigating child abuse and learning from British mistakes. *Dalhousie Law Journal, 16,* 5-61.

Boat, B., & Everson, M. D. (1988a). Research issues in using anatomical dolls. *Annals of Sex Research, 1*(2), 191-204.

Boat, B. W., & Everson, M. D. (1988b). Use of anatomical dolls among professionals in sexual abuse evaluations. *Child Abuse & Neglect, 12,* 171-179.

Boat, B. W., & Everson, M. D. (1993). The use of anatomical dolls in sexual abuse evaluations: Current research and practice. In G. S. Goodman & B. L. Bottoms (Eds.), *Child victims, child witnesses: Understanding and improving testimony* (pp. 47-70). New York: Guilford.

Boggs, S., & Eyberg, S. (1990). Interview techniques and establishing rapport. In A. La Greca (Ed.), *Through the eyes of the child: Obtaining self-reports from children and adolescents* (pp. 85-108). Boston: Allyn & Bacon.

Boon, J., Davies, G., & Noon, E. (1992). Children in court. In R. Bayne & P. Nicholson (Eds.), *Counseling and psychology for health professionals* (pp. 209-220). London: Chapman & Hall.

Bower, G. H. (1967). A multicomponent theory of the memory trace. In K. W. Spence & J. T. Spence (Eds.), *The psychology of learning and motivation* (Vol. 1, pp. 299-325). New York: Academic Press.

Brainerd, C. J., & Ornstein, P. A. (1991). Children's memory for witnessed events: The developmental backdrop. In J. Doris (Ed.), *The suggestibility of children's recollections* (pp. 10-20). Washington, DC: American Psychological Association.

Brainerd, C. J., Reyna, V. F., Howe, M. L., & Kingma, J. (1990). The development of forgetting and reminiscence. *Monographs of the Society for Research in Child Development, 55*(3-4, Serial No. 222).

Brennan, M., & Brennan, R. (1988). *Strange language: Child victims under cross examination.* Riverina, Australia: Charles Stuart University.

Brennan, M., & Brennan, R. (1990). *Strange language* (3rd ed.). Wagga Wagga, Australia: Riverina Murray Institute of Higher Education.

Brigham, J., Vanverst, M., & Bothwell, R. (1986). Accuracy of children's eyewitness in a field setting. *Basic and Applied Social Psychology, 7,* 295-306.

Brown, A. (1976). The construction of temporal succession by the preoperational child. In A. Pick (Ed.), *Minnesota Symposium on Child Development* (Vol. 10, pp. 28-83). Minneapolis: University of Minnesota Press.

Bruck, M., Barr, R., Ceci, S. J., & Francouer, E. (1993). *I hardly cried when I got my shot! Influencing children's memories about a visit to their pediatrician.* Manuscript submitted for publication.

Bruner, J. (1987). Life as narrative. *Social Research, 54,* 11-32.

Bull, R. (1992). Obtaining evidence expertly: The reliability of interviews with child witnesses. *Expert Evidence: International Digest of Human Behavior Science and Law, 1,* 5-12.

Bull, R. (1994). Good practice for video recorded interviews with child witnesses for use in criminal proceedings. In G. Davies, S. Lloyd-Bostock, M. McMurran, & C. Wilson (Eds.), *Law and psychology.* Amsterdam: de Gruyter.

Bull, R., & Cullen, C. (1992). *Witnesses who may have mental handicaps.* (Document prepared for the Crown Office, Edinburgh)

Bull, R., & Cullen, C. (1993). Interviewing the mentally handicapped. *Policing, 9,* 88-100.

Burgess, A. W., & Holstrom, L. L. (1978). The child and family in the court process. In A. W. Burgess, A. N. Grota, L. L. Holstrom, & S. M. Sgroi (Eds.), *Sexual assault of children and adolescents* (pp. 205-230). Lexington, MA: Lexington.

Bussey, K., Lee, K., & Ross, C. (1991, April). Factors influencing children's lying and truthfulness. In M. DeSimone & M. Toglia (Chairs), *Lying and truthfulness among young children: Implications for their participation in legal proceedings.* Symposium presented at the Society for Research in Child Development, Seattle, WA.

Butler-Sloss, E. (1988). *Report of the inquiry into child abuse in Cleveland in 1987.* London: Her Majesty's Stationery Office.

Cahill, D., & Mingay, D. J. (1986). Leading questions and the police interview. *Policing, 2,* 212-224.

California Attorney General's Office. (1988). *California Child Victim Witness Judicial Advisory Committee: Final report.* Sacramento, CA: Office of the Attorney General.

Capelli, C. A., & Markman, E. M. (1982). Suggestions for training comprehension monitoring. *Topics in Learning & Learning Disabilities, 2*(1), 87-96.

Carris, M., Zaragoza, M., & Lane, S. (1992, May). *The role of visual imagery in source misattribution errors.* Paper presented at the annual meeting of the Midwestern Psychological Society, Chicago.

Cashmore, J. (1992). *The use of closed circuit television for child witnesses in the ACT.* Sydney: Australian Law Reform Commission.

Cassel, W. S. (1991). *Child eyewitness testimony: The search for truth and justice in the American way.* Unpublished master's thesis, Florida Atlantic University, Boca Raton.

Cassel, W. S., & Bjorklund, D. F. (in press). Developmental patterns of eyewitness memory and suggestibility: An ecologically based short-term longitudinal study. *Law and Human Behavior.*

Ceci, S., Bronfenbrenner, U., & Baker, J. (1988). Memory in context: The case of prospective remembering. In F. Weinert & M. Perlmutter (Eds.), *Universal changes and individual differences* (pp. 243-256). Hillsdale, NJ: Lawrence Erlbaum.

Ceci, S. J., & Bruck, M. (1993a). The suggestibility of the child witness: A historical review and synthesis. *Psychological Bulletin, 113,* 403-439.

Ceci, S. J., & Bruck, M. (1993b). Translating research into policy: The suggestibility of children. *SRCD Social Policy Report, 7*(3), 1-31.

Ceci, S., Leichtman, M., & Putnick, M. (Eds.). (1992). *Cognitive and social factors in early deception.* Hillsdale, NJ: Lawrence Erlbaum.

Ceci, S. J., Leichtman, M., & White, T. (in press). Interviewing preschoolers: Remembrance of things planted. In D. P. Peters (Ed.), *The child witness: Cognitive, social, and legal issues.* Deventer: Kluwer.

Ceci, S. J., Ross, D. F., & Toglia, M. P. (1987a). Age differences in suggestibility: Narrowing the uncertainties. In S. J. Ceci, M. P. Toglia, & D. F. Ross (Eds.), *Children's eyewitness memory* (pp. 79-91). New York: Springer-Verlag.

Ceci, S. J., Ross, D., & Toglia, M. (1987b). Age differences in suggestibility: Psycholegal implications. *Journal of Experimental Psychology: General, 117,* 38-49.

Ceci, S. J., Ross, D. F., & Toglia, M. P. (Eds.). (1989). *Perspectives on children's testimony.* New York: Springer-Verlag.

Ceci, S. J., Toglia, M. P., & Ross, D. F. (Eds.). (1987). *Children's eyewitness memory.* New York: Springer-Verlag.

Choi, S. (1991). Children's answers to yes-no questions: A developmental study in English, French, and Korean. *Developmental Psychology, 27,* 407-420.

Clare, I., & Gudjonsson, G. (1993). Interrogative suggestibility, confabulations, and acquiescence in people with mild learning disabilities (mental handicap): Implications for reliability during police interrogations. *British Journal of Clinical Psychology, 32,* 295-301.

Clubb, P. A., & Follmer, A. (1993, April). *Children's memory for a physical examination: Patterns of retention over a 12 week interval.* Poster presented at the biennial meeting of the Society for Research in Child Development, New Orleans, LA.

Clyde, J. (1992). *The report of the inquiry into the removal of children from Orkney in February 1991.* Edinburgh: Her Majesty's Stationery Office.

Cohn, D. S. (1991). Anatomical doll play of preschoolers referred for sexual abuse and those not referred. *Child Abuse & Neglect, 15,* 455-466.

Coles, W. (1990). Sexual abuse of persons with disabilities: A law enforcement perspective. *Developmental Disabilities Bulletin, 18,* 35-43.

Cooper, A. J. R., & Monk, A. (1976). Learning for recall and learning for recognition. In J. Brown (Ed.), *Recall and recognition* (pp. 131-156). New York: Wiley.

Cosgrove, J., & Patterson, C. (1978). Generalization of training for children's listening skills. *Child Development, 49,* 513-516.

Cox, M. V. (1991). *The child's point of view.* New York: Guilford.

Coy v. Iowa, 108 S.Ct. 2798, 101 L.Ed. 2d 857; 56 USLW 4931 (1988).

Craft, A. (1991). *NAPSAC in context: Newsletter of the National Association for the Protection from Sexual Abuse of Adults and Children with Learning Disabilities.* Nottingham: England.

Craig v. Maryland, 316 Md. 551 (1989).

Daehler, M. W., Lonardo, R., & Bukatko, D. (1979). Matching and equivalence judgments in very young children. *Child Development, 50,* 170-179.

Dahmen-Zimmer, K., & Loohs, S. (1992, September). *Is there truth in the eye of the beholder?* Paper presented at the Third European Law and Psychology Conference, Oxford.

Davies, G. (1991). Research on children's testimony: Implications for interviewing practice. In C. R. Hollin & K. Howells (Eds.), *Clinical approaches to sex offenders and their victims* (pp. 93-115). New York: Wiley.

Davies, G. (1993). *Videotaping children's evidence* (Grant Executive Survey). Leicester, U.K.: Leicester University.

Davies, G., & Drinkwater, J. (Eds.). (1988). *The child witness: Do the courts abuse children?* Leicester, U.K.: British Psychological Society.

Davies, G., & Noon, E. (1991). *An evaluation of the Live Link for child witnesses.* London: Home Office.

Davies, G., & Noon, E. (in press). The impact of CCTV on children's court testimony. In D. Peters (Ed.), *The child witness: Cognitive, social and legal issues.* Deventer: Kluwer.

Davies, G., & Thomson, D. (1988). *Memory in context: Context in memory.* New York: Wiley.

DeAngelis, T. (1993, November). APA panel is examining memories of child abuse. *APA Monitor,* p. 44.

Deffenbacher, K. A. (1980). Eyewitness accuracy and confidence. *Law and Human Behavior, 4,* 243-260.

DeLoache, J. S. (1986). Memory in very young children: Exploitation of cues to the location of a hidden object. *Cognitive Development, 1,* 123-137.

DeLoache, J. S. (1987). Rapid change in the symbolic functioning of very young children. *Science, 238,* 1556-1557.

DeLoache, J. S. (1990). Young children's understanding of models. In R. Fivush & J. Hudson (Eds.), *Knowing and remembering in young children* (pp. 94-126). New York: Cambridge University Press.

DeLoache, J. S. (1991). Symbolic functioning in very young children: Understanding of pictures and models. *Child Development, 62,* 736-752.

DeLoache, J. S. (1993, March). *What do young children understand about symbolic relations?* Paper presented at the meeting of the Society for Research in Child Development, New Orleans, LA.

DeLoache, J. S., & Burns, N. M. (1994). Early understanding of the representational function of pictures. *Cognition, 52,* 83-110.

DeLoache, J. S., & Marzolf, D. P. (in press). The use of dolls to interview young children: Issues of symbolic representation. *Journal of Experimental Child Psychology.*

DeLoache, J. S., Miller, K. F., Rosengren, K. S., & Bryant, N. (1993). Unpublished research.

Demorest, A., Meyer, C., Phelps, E., Gardner, H., & Winner, E. (1984). Words speak louder than actions: Understanding deliberately false remarks. *Child Development, 55,* 1527-1534.

Dent, H. (1977). Stress as a factor influencing person recognition in identification of parades. *Bulletin of the British Psychological Society, 30,* 339-340.

Dent, H. R. (1986). Experimental study of the effectiveness of different techniques of questioning mentally handicapped child witnesses. *British Journal of Clinical Psychology, 27,* 13-17.

Dent, H. (1991). Experimental studies of interviewing child witnesses. In J. Doris (Ed.), *The suggestibility of children's recollections* (pp. 138-146). New York: Springer-Verlag.

Dent, H. (1992). The effects of age and intelligence on eyewitnessing ability. In H. Dent & R. Flin (Eds.), *Children as witnesses* (pp. 1-13). Chichester, U.K.: Wiley.

Dent, H., & Flin, R. (Eds.). (1992). *Children as witnesses.* Chichester, U.K.: Wiley.

Dent, H. R., & Stephenson, G. M. (1979). An experimental study of the effectiveness of differential techniques of questioning child witnesses. *British Journal of Social and Clinical Psychology, 18,* 41-51.

Dezwirek-Sas, L. (1992). Empowering child witnesses for sexual abuse prosecution. In H. Dent & R. Flin (Eds.), *Children as witnesses* (pp. 181-200). Chichester, U.K.: Wiley.

Dezwirek-Sas, L., Hurley, P., Austin G., & Wolfe, D. (1991). *Reducing the system-induced trauma for child sexual abuse victims through court preparation, assessment and follow-up.* London, Canada: London Family Court Clinic.

Dickson, W. (1981). Referential communication activities in research and in the curriculum: A meta-analysis. In W. Dickson (Ed.), *Children's oral communication skills* (pp. 189-203). New York: Academic Press.

Dimitracopoulou, I. (1990). *Conversational competence and social development.* New York: Cambridge University Press.

Dollaghan, C., & Kaston, N. (1986). A comprehension monitoring program for language impaired children. *Journal of Speech and Hearing Disorders, 51,* 264-271.

Donaldson, M., Grieve, R., & Pratt, C. (Eds.). (1983). *Early childhood development and education.* Oxford: Blackwell.

Doris, J. (Ed.). (1991). *The suggestibility of children's recollections.* Washington, DC: American Psychological Association.

Doult, B. (1992, November 12). Law chief studies EE. *Aberdeen Evening Express,* p. 7.

Duggan, L. M., Aubrey, M., Doherty, E., Isquith, P., Levine, M., & Scheiner, J. (1989). The credibility of children as witnesses in a simulated child sex abuse trial. In S. J. Ceci, D. F. Ross, & M. Toglia (Eds.), *Perspectives on the child witness* (pp. 71-99). New York: Springer-Verlag.

Dunning, D., & Stern, L. B. (1992). Examining the generality of eyewitness hypermnesia: A close look at time delay and question type. *Applied Cognitive Psychology, 6,* 643-657.

Dyer, C. (1983, July 29). Ordeal by witness box. *The Times* (London), p. 14.

Dziech, B. W., & Schudson, C. B. (1991). *On trial: America's courts and their treatment of sexually abused children.* Boston: Beacon.

Engel, S. (1986, April). The role of mother-child interaction in autobiographical recall. In J. A. Hudson (Chair), *Learning to talk about the past.* Symposium conducted at the Southeastern Conference on Human Development, Nashville, TN.

Erdelyi, N. H., & Stein, J. B. (1981). Recognition hypermnesia: The growth of recognition memory (d') over time with repeated testing. *Cognition, 9,* 23-33.

Ervin-Tripp, S., & Michell-Kerman, C. (1977). *Child discourse.* New York: Academic Press.

Eugenio, P., Buckhout, R., Kostes, S., & Ellison, K. (1982). Hypermnesia in the eyewitness to a crime. *Bulletin of the Psychonomic Society, 19,* 83-86.

Everson, M., & Boat, B. (1990a). Are anatomical dolls too suggestive? *The Advisor: American Professional Society on the Abuse of Children, 3,* 6-14.

Everson, M. D., & Boat, B. W. (1990b). Sexualized doll play among young children: Implications for the use of anatomical dolls in sexual abuse evaluations. *Journal of the American Academy of Child and Adolescent Psychiatry, 29,* 736-742.

Fielding, N., & Conroy, S. (1992). Interviewing child victims: Police and social work investigations of child sexual abuse. *Sociology, 26,* 103-124.

Fisher, G. (1990). Interviewing mentally retarded children. In P. Barker (Ed.), *Clinical interviews with children and adolescents.* New York: Norton.

Fisher, R. P., & Chandler, C. C. (1991). Independence between recalling interevent relations and specific events. *Journal of Experimental Psychology: Learning, Memory, and Cognition, 17,* 722-733.

Fisher, R. P., & Cutler, B. L. (1992, September). *The relation between consistency and accuracy of eyewitness testimony.* Paper presented at the Third European Conference on Law and Psychology, Oxford, England.

Fisher, R. P., & Geiselman, R. E. (1992). *Memory-enhancing techniques for investigative interviewing: The cognitive interview.* Springfield, IL: Charles C Thomas.

Fisher, R. P., Geiselman, R. E., & Amador, M. (1989). Field test of the cognitive interview: Enhancing the recollection of actual victims and witnesses of crime. *Journal of Applied Psychology, 74,* 722-727.

Fisher, R. P., Geiselman, R. E., & Raymond, D. S. (1987). Critical analysis of police interviewing techniques. *Journal of Police Science and Administration, 15,* 177-185.

Fisher, R. P., Geiselman, R. E., Raymond, D. S., Jurkevich, L. M., & Warhaftig, M. L. (1987). Enhancing enhanced eyewitness memory: Refining the cognitive interview. *Journal of Police Science and Administration, 15,* 291-297.

Fisher, R. P., McCauley, M. R., & Geiselman, R. E. (1994). Improving eyewitness memory with the cognitive interview. In D. Ross, J. Read, & M. Toglia (Eds.), *Adult eyewitness testimony: Current trends and developments* (pp. 245-269). New York: Cambridge University Press.

Fisher, R. P., & Quigley, K. (1991). Applying cognitive theory in public health investigations: Enhancing food recall. In J. Tanur (Ed.), *Questions about questions* (pp. 154-169). New York: Russell Sage.

Fisher, R. P., Quigley, K., Brock, P., Chin, D., & Cutler, B. L. (1990, March). *The effectiveness of the cognitive interview in description and identification tasks.* Paper presented at the biennial meeting of the American Psychology and Law Society Meetings, Williamsburg, VA.

Fivush, R. (1988). The functions of event memory. In U. Neisser & E. Winograd (Eds.), *Remembering reconsidered: Traditional and ecological approaches to the study of memory* (pp. 277-282). New York: Cambridge University Press.

Fivush, R. (1993). Developmental perspectives on autobiographical recall. In G. Goodman & B. Bottoms (Eds.), *Child victims, child witnesses: Understanding and improving testimony* (pp. 1-24). New York: Guilford.

Fivush, R., Gray, J. T., & Fromhoff, F. A. (1987). Two year olds talk about the past. *Cognitive Development, 2,* 393-410.

Fivush, R., & Hamond, N. R. (1989). Time and again: Effects of repetition and retention interval on 2 year olds' event recall. *Journal of Experimental Child Psychology, 47,* 259-273.

Fivush, R., & Hamond, N. R. (1990). Autobiographical memory across the preschool years: Toward reconceptualizing childhood amnesia. In R. Fivush & J. A. Hudson (Eds.), *Knowing and remembering in young children* (pp. 223-248). New York: Cambridge University Press.

Fivush, R., Hamond, N. R., Harsch, N., Singer, N., & Wolf, A. (1991). Content and consistency in early autobiographical recall. *Discourse Processes, 14,* 373-388.

Fivush, R., Kuebli, J., & Clubb, P. A. (1992). The structure of events and event representations: A microdevelopmental analysis. *Child Development, 63,* 188-201.

Fivush, R., & Reese, E. (1992). The social construction of autobiographical memory. In M. A. Conway, D. C. Rubin, H. Spinnler, & W. Wagenaar (Eds.), *Theoretical perspectives on autobiographical memory* (pp. 115-132). London: Kluwer Academic.

Flavell, J. (1981). Cognitive monitoring. In W. Dickerson (Ed.), *Children's oral communication skills* (pp. 35-59). New York: Academic Press.

Flavell, J. H. (1985). *Cognitive development.* Englewood Cliffs, NJ: Prentice-Hall.

Flexser, A. J., & Tulving, E. (1978). Retrieval independence in recognition and recall. *Psychological Review, 85,* 153-172.

Flin, R. (1991). Commentary: A grand memory for forgetting. In J. Doris (Ed.), *The suggestibility of children's recollections* (pp. 21-23). Washington, DC: American Psychological Association.

Flin, R., Boon, J., Knox, A., & Bull, R. (1992). The effect of a five-month delay on children's and adults' eyewitness memory. *British Journal of Psychology, 83,* 323-336.

Flin, R., & Bull, R. (1990). Child witnesses in Scottish criminal prosecutions. In J. Spencer, G. Nicholson, R. Flin, & R. Bull (Eds.), *Children's evidence in legal proceedings* (pp. 193-200). Cambridge: Cambridge University Faculty of Law.

Flin, R. H., Bull, R., Boon, J., & Knox, A. (1990). *Child witnesses in Scottish criminal prosecutions* (Report to the Scottish Home and Health Department). Glasgow, Scotland: Glasgow College.

Flin, R., Bull, R., Boon, J., & Knox, A. (1992). Children in the witness box. In H. Dent & R. Flin (Eds.), *Children as witnesses* (pp. 167-179). Chichester, U.K.: Wiley.

Flin, R., Bull, R., Boon, J., & Knox, A. (1993). Child witnesses in Scottish criminal trials. *International Review of Victimology, 2,* 309-329.

Flin, R., Davies, G., & Tarrant, A. (1988). *The child witness.* Grant report to the Scottish Home and Health Department, Edinburgh.

Flin, R., Kearney, B., & Murray, K. (in press). Children's evidence in Scotland. In B. Bottoms & G. Goodman (Eds.), *International perspectives on child witnesses.* Thousand Oaks, CA: Sage.

Flin, R. H., Stevenson, Y., & Davies, G. (1989). Children's knowledge of court proceedings. *British Journal of Psychology, 80,* 285-297.

Folds, T. H., Footo, M., Guttentag, R. E., & Ornstein, P. A. (1990). When children mean to remember: Issues of context specificity, strategy effectiveness, and intentionality in the development of memory. In D. F. Bjorklund (Ed.), *Children's strategies* (pp. 67-91). Hillsdale, NJ: Lawrence Erlbaum.

Foley, M. A., & Johnson, M. K. (1985). Confusion between memories for performed and imagined actions. *Child Development, 56,* 1145-1155.

Foley, M. A., Johnson, M. K., & Raye, C. L. (1983). Age-related changes in confusion between memories for thoughts and memories for speech. *Child Development, 54,* 51-60.

Foley, M. A., Santini, C., & Sopasakis, M. (1989). Discriminating between memories: Evidence for children's spontaneous elaborations. *Journal of Experimental Child Psychology, 48,* 146-169.

Foos, P. W., & Fisher, R. P. (1988). Using tests as learning opportunities. *Journal of Educational Psychology, 80,* 179-183.

Ford, M., & Holmes, V. M. (1978). Planning units and syntax in sentence production. *Cognition, 6,* 35-53.

Friedman, W. (1982). *The developmental psychology of time.* New York: Academic Press.

Gallagher, T. (1981). Contingent query sequences within adult-child discourse. *Journal of Child Language, 8,* 51-62.

Garbarino, J., & Stott, F. (1991). *What children can tell us: Eliciting, interpreting, and evaluating information from children.* San Francisco: Jossey-Bass.

Garvey, C. (1977). The contingent query: A dependent act in conversation. In M. Lewis & L. Rosenblum (Eds.), *Interaction, conversation and the development of language* (pp. 63-93). New York: Wiley.

Geddie, L. (1993). *Children's memory for a pediatric examination as assessed through recognition measures.* Unpublished honor's thesis, University of North Carolina, Chapel Hill.

Geiselman, R. E., Fisher, R. P., Cohen, G., Holland, H., & Surtes, L. (1986). Eyewitness responses to leading and misleading questions under the cognitive interview. *Journal of Police Science and Administration, 14,* 31-39.

Geiselman, R. E., Fisher, R. P., MacKinnon, D. P., & Holland, H. L. (1985). Eyewitness memory enhancement in the police interview: Cognitive retrieval mnemonics versus hypnosis. *Journal of Applied Psychology, 70,* 401-412.

Geiselman, R. E., Fisher, R. P., MacKinnon, D. P., & Holland, H. L. (1986). Enhancement of eyewitness memory with the cognitive interview. *American Journal of Psychology, 99,* 385-401.

Geiselman, R. E., & Padilla, J. (1988). Interviewing child witnesses with the cognitive interview. *Journal of Police Science and Administration, 16,* 236-242.

Geiselman, R. E., Saywitz, K. J., & Bornstein, G. K. (1990). *Cognitive questioning techniques for child victims and witnesses of crime.* Unpublished manuscript, University of California, Los Angeles.

Gelman, R., Meck, E., & Merkin, S. (1986). Young children's numerical competence. *Cognitive Development, 1,* 1-29.

George, R. (1991). *A field and experimental evaluation of three methods of interviewing witnesses/ victims of crime.* Unpublished manuscript, Polytechnic of East London.

George, R., & Clifford, B. (1992, September). *A field comparison of the cognitive interview and conversation management.* Paper presented at the British Psychological Society Annual Conference, Bournemouth, U.K.

Gilbert v. Maryland, 110, Ct. Ap. 12 (1990).

Girl too young to testify in sex attacks. (1989, May 10). *Daily Telegraph,* p. 2.

Glaser D., & Collins, C. (1989). The response of young, non-sexually abused children to anatomically correct dolls. *Journal of Child Psychology and Psychiatry, 30,* 547-560.

Glidden, L., & Mar, H. (1978). Availability and access of information in the semantic memory of retarded and non-retarded adolescents. *Journal of Experimental Child Psychology, 25,* 33-40.

Globe Newspaper Co. v. Superior Court, 457 U.S. 596 (1982).

Gold, E., & Neisser, U. (1980). Recollections of kindergarten. *The Quarterly Newsletter of the Laboratory of Comparative Human Cognition, 2,* 77-80.

Goodman, G. S. (1984a). Children's testimony in historical perspective. *Journal of Social Issues, 40,* 9-31.

Goodman, G. S. (1984b). The child witness: An introduction. *Journal of Social Issues, 40,* 1-7.

Goodman, G. S. (1993, March). *Children's memory for stressful events: Theoretical and developmental considerations.* Paper presented at the meeting of the Society for Research in Child Development, New Orleans, LA.

Goodman, G. S. (in press). The reliability of children's testimony. In D. Peters (Ed.), *The child witness: Cognitive, social and legal issues.* Deventer: Kluwer.

Goodman, G. S., & Aman, C. (1990). Children's use of anatomically detailed dolls to recount an event. *Child Development, 61,* 1859-1871.

Goodman, G. S., & Bottoms, B. L. (Eds.). (1993). *Child victims, child witnesses: Understanding and improving testimony.* New York: Guilford.

Goodman, G. S., Bottoms, B., Herscovici, B. B., & Shaver, P. (1989). Determinants of the child victim's perceived credibility. In S. J. Ceci, D. F. Ross, & M. P. Toglia (Eds.), *Perspectives on children's testimony* (pp. 1-22). New York: Springer-Verlag.

Goodman, G. S., Bottoms, B., Schwartz-Kenney, B., & Rudy, L. (1991). Children's testimony about a stressful event: Improving children's reports. *Journal of Narrative and Life History, 7,* 69-99.

Goodman, G. S., Bulkley, J., Quas, J. A., & Shapiro, C. (in preparation). *Innovative techniques for child victims/witnesses: A survey of prosecutor's offices.*

Goodman, G. S., & Clarke-Stewart, A. (1991). Suggestibility in children's testimony: Implications for sexual abuse investigations. In J. Doris (Ed.), *The suggestibility of children's recollections* (pp. 92-105). Washington, DC: American Psychological Association.

Goodman, G. S., Golding, J., Helgeson, V., Haith, M. M., & Michelli, J. (1987). When a child takes the stand: Jurors' perceptions of children's eyewitness testimony. *Law and Human Behavior, 11,* 27-40.

Goodman, G. S., Hirshman, J., Hepps, D., & Rudy, L. (1991). Children's memories for stressful events. *Merrill-Palmer Quarterly, 37,* 109-158.

Goodman, G. S., Jones, D. P. H., Pyle, E. A., Prado-Estrada, L., Port, L. K., England, P., Mason, R., & Rudy, L. (1988). The emotional effects of criminal court testimony on child sexual assault victims: A preliminary report. In G. Davies & J. Drinkwater (Eds.), *The child witness: Do the courts abuse children?* (pp. 46-54). Leicester, U.K.: British Psychological Society.

Goodman, G. S., Levine, M., & Melton, G. B. (1992). The best evidence produces the best law. *Law and Human Behavior, 16,* 244-251.

Goodman, G. S., Levine, M., Melton, G. B., & Ogden, D. W. (1991). Child witnesses and the confrontation clause: The American Psychological Association brief in *Maryland v. Craig. Law and Human Behavior, 15*(1), 13-29.

Goodman, G. S., & Michelli, J. (1981, November). Would you believe a child witness? *Psychology Today,* pp. 82-95.

Goodman, G. S., & Reed, R. S. (1986). Age differences in eyewitness testimony. *Law and Human Behavior, 10,* 317-332.

Goodman, G. S., Rudy, L., Bottoms, B. L., & Aman, C. (1990). Children's concerns and memory: Issues of ecological validity in children's testimony. In R. Fivush & J. Hudson (Eds.), *Knowing and remembering in young children* (pp. 249-284). New York: Cambridge University Press.

Goodman, G. S., Taub, E. P., Jones, D. P. H., England, P., Port, L. K., Rudy, L., & Prado, L. (1992). Testifying in criminal court: Emotional effects on child sexual assault victims. *Monographs of the Society for Research on Child Development, 57*(5, Serial No. 229).

Gordon, B. N., & Follmer, A. (1994). Developmental issues in judging the credibility of children's testimony. *Journal of Clinical Child Psychology, 23,* 283-294.

Gordon, B. N., Ornstein, P. A., Nida, R. E., Follmer, A., Crenshaw, C., & Albert, G. (1993). Does the use of dolls facilitate children's memory of visits to the doctor? *Applied Cognitive Psychology, 7,* 459-474.

Gordon, B. N., Schroeder, C. S., Ornstein, P. A., & Baker-Ward, L. E. (in press). Clinical implications of research on memory development. In T. Ney (Ed.), *Child sexual abuse cases: Allegations, assessment and management.* New York: Brunner/Mazel.

Gordon, M. A. (1992). Recent Supreme Court rulings on child testimony in sexual abuse cases. *Journal of Child Sexual Abuse, 1,* 59-71.

Gray, E. (1993). *Unequal justice: The prosecution of child sexual abuse.* New York: Free Press.

Grice, H. (1975). Logic and conversation. In R. Cole & J. Morgan (Eds.), *Syntax and semantics: Speech acts.* New York: Academic Press.

Gudjonsson, G. (1992). *The psychology of interrogations, confessions and testimony.* Chichester, U.K.: Wiley.

Gudjonsson, G., & Gunn, J. (1982). The competence and reliability of a witness in a criminal court: A case report. *British Journal of Psychiatry, 141,* 624-627.

Hall, D. F., Loftus, E. F., & Tousignant, J. P. (1984). Postevent information and changes in recollection for a natural event. In G. L. Wells & E. F. Loftus (Eds.), *Eyewitness testimony: Psychological perspectives* (pp. 124-141). Cambridge: Cambridge University Press.

Hamond, N. R., & Fivush, R. (1990). *Memories of Mickey Mouse: Young children recount their trip to Disneyworld.* Manuscript submitted for publication.

Harsch, N., & Neisser, U. (1989, November). *Substantial and irreversible errors in flashbulb memories of the Challenger explosion.* Paper presented at the Psychonomic Society Meetings, Atlanta, GA.

Harvey, W. (in press). Preparing children for court. In D. Peters (Ed.), *The child witness: Cognitive, social and legal issues.* Deventer: Kluwer.

Hasher, L., & Griffin, M. (1978). Reconstructive and reproductive processes in memory. *Journal of Experimental Psychology, 4,* 318-330.

Haugaard, J., & Repucci, N. (1992). Children and the truth. In S. J. Ceci, M. Leichtman, & M. Putnick (Eds.), *Cognitive and social factors in early deception* (pp. 29-45). Hillsdale, NJ: Lawrence Erlbaum.

Hedderman, C. (1987). *Children's evidence: The need for corroboration* (Research and Planning Unit Paper 41). London: Home Office.

Hill, P., & Hill, S. (1987). Videotaping children's testimony: An empirical view. *Michigan Law Review, 85,* 809-833.

Home Office. (1989). *The use of video technology at trials of alleged child abusers.* London: Her Majesty's Stationery Office.

Home Office. (1992). *Memorandum of good practice on video recorded interviews with child witnesses for criminal proceedings.* London: Her Majesty's Stationery Office.

Howe, M. L. (1991). Misleading children's story recall: Forgetting and reminiscence of the facts. *Developmental Psychology, 27,* 746-762.

Howe, M. L., Kelland, A., Bryant-Brown, L., & Clark, S. L. (1992). Measuring the development of children's amnesia and hypermnesia. In M. L. Howe, C. J. Brainerd, & V. F. Reyna (Eds.), *Development of long-term retention* (pp. 56-102). New York: Springer-Verlag.

Howe, M. L., O'Sullivan, J. T., & Marche, T. A. (1992). Toward a theory of the development of long term retention. In M. L. Howe, C. J. Brainerd, & V. F. Reyna (Eds.), *Development of long-term retention* (pp. 245-255). New York: Springer-Verlag.

Hudson, J. A. (1986). Memories are made of this: General event knowledge and the development of autobiographic memory. In K. Nelson (Ed.), *Event knowledge: Structure and function in development* (pp. 97-118). Hillsdale, NJ: Lawrence Erlbaum.

Hudson, J. A. (1990a). The emergence of autobiographical mother-child conversation. In R. Fivush & J. Hudson (Eds.), *Knowing and remembering in young children* (pp. 166-196). New York: Cambridge University Press.

Hudson, J. A. (1990b). Constructive processing in children's event memory. *Developmental Psychology, 26,* 180-187.

Hudson, J. A., & Fivush, R. (1987). *As time goes by: Sixth graders remember a kindergarten experience* (Emory Cognition Project Report 13). Atlanta, GA: Emory University.

Hudson, J. A., & Fivush, R. (Eds.). (1990). *Knowing and remembering in young children.* New York: Cambridge University Press.

Hudson, J. A., Fivush, R., & Kuebli, J. (1992). Scripts and episodes: The development of event memory. *Applied Cognitive Psychology, 6,* 483-505.

Hudson, J. A., & Shapiro, L. (1991). Effects of task and topic on children's narratives. In A. McCabe & C. Peterson (Eds.), *New directions in developing narrative structure* (pp. 59-136). Hillsdale, NJ: Lawrence Erlbaum.

Ingram, D. (1976). *Phonological disability in children.* New York: Elsevier North-Holland.

Irish Law Reform Commission. (1989). *Consultation paper on child sexual abuse.* Dublin, Ireland: Law Reform Commission.

Irish Law Reform Commission. (1990). *Report on child sexual abuse.* Dublin, Ireland: Law Reform Commission.

Ironsmith, M., & Whitehurst, G. (1978). The development of listener abilities in communication: How children deal with ambiguous information. *Child Development, 49,* 348-352.

Irvine, R., & Dunning, N. (1985). The child and the criminal justice system. *Journal of the Law Society of Scotland, 30,* 246-266.

Irwin, J. (1982). *Pragmatics: The role in language development.* La Verne, CA: Fox Point.

Jacoby, L. L. (1991). A process dissociation framework: Separating automatic from intentional uses of memory. *Journal of Memory and Language, 30,* 513-541.

Jacoby, L. L., & Kelley, C. M. (1992). Unconscious influences of memory: Dissociations and automaticity. In D. Milner & M. Rugg (Eds.), *The neuropsychology of consciousness* (pp. 201-233). New York: Academic Press.

Jacoby, L. L., Lindsay, D. S., & Toth, J. P. (1992). Unconscious processes revealed: A question of control. *American Psychologist, 47,* 802-809.

Jacoby, L. L., Woloshyn, V., & Kelley, C. M. (1989). Becoming famous without being recognized: Unconscious influences of memory produced by dividing attention. *Journal of Experimental Psychology: General, 118,* 115-125.

Jampole, L., & Weber, M. K. (1987). An assessment of the behavior of sexually abused and non-sexually abused children with anatomically correct dolls. *Child Abuse & Neglect, 11,* 187-192.

Johnson, M. K., Hashtroudi, S., & Lindsay, D. S. (1993). Source monitoring. *Psychological Bulletin, 114,* 3-28.

Johnson, M. K., Kounios, J., & Reeder, J. A. (1992, November). *Time course studies of reality monitoring and recognition.* Paper presented at the 33rd annual meeting of Psychonomic Society, St. Louis, MO.

Jones, D. P. H. (1990). Child witnesses and victims in criminal court. *Child Abuse Review, 4,* 4-8.

Jones, D. (1992). *Interviewing the sexually abused child* (4th ed.). London: Gaskell.

Jones, D., & McQuiston, M. (1988). *Interviewing the sexually abused child*. Washington, DC: American Psychiatric Press.

Judge frees man accused of raping girl of five. (1989, May 19). *Glasgow Herald*, p. 7.

Kay, H. (1955). Learning and retaining verbal material. *British Journal of Psychology, 46*, 81-100.

Kendall-Tackett, K. A., & Watson, M. W. (1992). Use of anatomical dolls by Boston-area professionals. *Child Abuse & Neglect, 61*, 423-428.

King, M., & Piper, C. (1990). *How the law thinks about children*. Aldershot, Hants, U.K.: Gower.

Klajner-Diamond, H., Wehrspann, W., & Steinhauer, P. (1987). Assessing the credibility of young children's allegations of sexual abuse: Clinical issues. *Canadian Journal of Psychiatry, 32*, 610-614.

Kobasigawa, A. (1974). Utilization of retrieval cues by children in recall. *Child Development, 45*, 127-134.

Köhnken, G. (1990). The evaluation of statement credibility: Social judgement and expert diagnostic approaches. In J. Spencer, G. Nicholson, R. Flin, & R. Bull (Eds.), *Children's evidence in legal proceedings: An international perspective* (pp. 39-51). Cambridge: Cambridge University Faculty of Law.

Köhnken, G. (1992, September). *A meta-analysis on the effects of the cognitive interview*. Paper presented at the Third European Conference on Law and Psychology, Oxford.

Krafka, C., & Penrod, S. (1985). Reinstatement of context in a field experiment on eyewitness identification. *Journal of Personality and Social Psychology, 49*, 58-69.

Kurtz, B., & Borkowski, J. (1984). Children's metacognition: Exploring relations among knowledge, process and motivational variables. *Journal of Experimental Child Psychology, 43*, 129-148.

Labov, W. (1982). Speech actions and reaction in personal narrative. In D. Tannen (Ed.), *Analyzing discourse: Text and talk* (pp. 219-247). Washington, DC: Georgetown University Press.

Landis, J. R., & Koch, G. (1977). The measurement of observer agreement for categorical data. *Biometrics, 33*, 159-174.

Leibowitz, H. W., & Guzy, L. (1990, March). *Can the accuracy of eyewitness testimony be improved by the use of non-verbal techniques?* Paper presented at the American Psychology and Law Society Meetings, Williamsburg, VA.

Leippe, M. R., Brigham, J. C., Cousins, C., & Romanczyk, A. (1989). The opinions and practices of criminal attorneys regarding child eyewitnesses: A survey. In S. J. Ceci, D. F. Ross, & M. P. Toglia (Eds.), *Perspectives on children's testimony* (pp. 100-130). New York: Springer-Verlag.

Leippe, M. R., Manion, A. P., & Romanczyk, A. (1992). Eyewitness persuasion: How and how well do fact finders judge the accuracy of adults' and children's memory reports? *Journal of Personality and Social Psychology, 63*, 181-197.

Leippe, M. R., Manion, A. P., & Romanczyk, A. (1993). Discernability or discrimination? Understanding jurors' reactions to accurate and inaccurate child and adult eyewitnesses. In G. S. Goodman & B. Bottoms (Eds.), *Child victims, child witnesses: Understanding and improving testimony* (pp. 169-202). New York: Guilford.

Leippe, M. R., & Romanczyk, A. (1987). Children on the witness stand: A communication/persuasion analysis of jurors' reactions to child witnesses. In S. J. Ceci, M. P. Toglia, & D. F. Ross (Eds.), *Children's eyewitness memory* (pp. 155-177). New York: Springer-Verlag.

Leippe, M. R., & Romanczyk, A. (1989). Reactions to child (versus adult) eyewitnesses: Influence of juror's preconceptions and witness behavior. *Law and Human Behavior, 13*, 103-132.

Leventhal, J. M., Hamilton, J., Rekedal, S., Tebano Micci, A., & Eyster, C. (1989). Anatomically correct dolls used in interviews of young children suspected of having been sexually abused. *Pediatrics, 84*, 900-906.

Libai, D. (1969). The protection of the child victim of a sexual offense in the criminal justice system. *Wayne Law Review, 15*, 977-1032.

Lindberg, M. A. (1980). Is knowledge base development a necessary and sufficient condition for memory development? *Journal of Experimental Child Psychology, 30,* 401-410.

Lindsay, D. S. (1990). Misleading suggestions can impair eyewitnesses' ability to remember event details. *Journal of Experimental Psychology: Learning, Memory, and Cognition, 16,* 1077-1083.

Lindsay, D. S. (1994). Memory source monitoring and eyewitness testimony. In D. F. Ross, D. J. Read, & M. P. Toglia (Eds.), *Adult eyewitness testimony: Current trends and developments.* New York: Cambridge University Press.

Lindsay, D. S., & Jacoby, L. L. (1994). Stroop process dissociations: The relationship between facilitation and interference. *Journal of Experimental Psychology: Human Perception and Performance, 20,* 219-234.

Lindsay, D. S., & Johnson, M. K. (1987). Reality monitoring and suggestibility: Children's ability to discriminate among memories from different sources. In S. J. Ceci, M. P. Toglia, & D. F. Ross (Eds.), *Children's eyewitness memory* (pp. 92-121). New York: Springer-Verlag.

Lindsay, D. S., & Johnson, M. K. (1989a). The eyewitness suggestibility effect and memory for source. *Memory & Cognition, 17,* 349-358.

Lindsay, D. S., & Johnson, M. K. (1989b). The reversed eyewitness suggestibility effect. *Bulletin of the Psychonomic Society, 27,* 111-113.

Lindsay, D. S., Johnson, M. K., & Kwon, P. (1991). Developmental changes in memory source monitoring. *Journal of Experimental Child Psychology, 52,* 297-318.

Lipton, J. P. (1977). On the psychology of eyewitness testimony. *Journal of Applied Psychology, 62,* 90-95.

List, J. (1986). Age and schematic differences in the reliability of eyewitness testimony. *Developmental Psychology, 22,* 50-57.

Lodico, M., Ghatala, E., Levin, J., Pressley, M., & Bell, J. (1983). The effects of strategy-monitoring on children's selection of effective memory strategies. *Journal of Experimental Psychology, 35,* 263-277.

Loftus, E. F. (1979). *Eyewitness testimony.* Cambridge, MA: Harvard University Press.

Loftus, E., & Davies, G. (1984). Distortions in the memory of children. *Journal of Social Issues, 40,* 51-67.

Loftus, E. F., Miller, D. G., & Burns, H. J. (1978). Semantic integration of verbal information into a visual memory. *Journal of Experimental Psychology: Human Learning and Memory, 4,* 19-31.

Luss, C. A., & Wells, G. L. (1992). The perceived credibility of child eyewitnesses. In H. Dent & R. Flin (Eds.), *Children as witnesses* (pp. 73-92). Chichester, U.K.: Wiley.

Maan, C. (1991). Assessment of sexually abused children with anatomically detailed dolls: A critical review. *Behavioral Sciences and the Law, 9,* 43-51.

MacFarlane, K. (1985). Diagnostic evaluations and the use of videotapes in child sexual abuse cases. *University of Miami Law Review, 40,* 135-165.

Madigan, S. (1976). Reminiscence and item recovery in free recall. *Memory & Cognition, 4,* 233-236.

Malpass, R. S., & Devine, P. G. (1981). Guided memory in eyewitness identification. *Journal of Applied Psychology, 66,* 343-350.

Mandler, J. (1990). Recall and its verbal expression. In R. Fivush & J. Hudson (Eds.), *Knowing and remembering in young children* (pp. 317-330). New York: Cambridge University Press.

Marin, B. V., Holmes, D. L., Guth, M., & Kovac, P. (1979). The potential of children as eyewitnesses. *Law and Human Behavior, 3,* 295-305.

Markman, E. (1977). Realizing that you don't understand: A preliminary investigation. *Child Development, 48,* 986-992.

Markman, E. (1979). Realizing that you don't understand: Elementary school children's awareness of inconsistencies. *Child Development, 50,* 643-655.

Maryland v. Craig, 110 S.Ct. 3157; 47 Cr.L. 2258 U.S. Sup.Ct. (1990).

Matthews, E., & Saywitz, K. (1992). Child victim witness manual. *California Center for Judicial Education and Research Journal, 12,* 5-81.

McCauley, M., & Fisher, R. (1992, March). *Improving children's recall of action with the cognitive interview.* Paper presented at the meeting of the American Psychology and Law Society, San Diego, CA.

McCloskey, M., Wible, C. G., & Cohen, N. J. (1988). Is there a special flashbulb memory mechanism? *Journal of Experimental Psychology: General, 117,* 171-181.

McCloskey, M., & Zaragoza, M. (1985). Misleading postevent information and memory for events: Arguments and evidence against memory impairment hypotheses. *Journal of Experimental Psychology: General, 114,* 1-16.

McGarrigle, J., & Donaldson, M. (1974). Conservation accidents. *Cognition, 3,* 341-350.

McGough, L. (1994). *Fragile voices: The child witness in American courts.* New Haven, CT: Yale University Press.

McGurk, H., & Glachan, M. (1988). Children's conversation with adults. *Children and Society, 2,* 20-34.

Melton, G. B. (1984). Child witnesses and the first amendment: A psycholegal dilemma. *Journal of Social Issues, 40,* 109-123.

Melton, G. B., & Limber, S. (1989). Psychologists' involvement in cases of child maltreatment. *American Psychologist, 44,* 1225-1233.

Melton, G., Limber, S., Jacobs, J., & Oberlander, L. (1992). *Preparing sexually abused children for testimony: Children's perceptions of the legal process* (Final report to the National Center on Child Abuse & Neglect, Grant No. 90-CA-1274). Lincoln: University of Nebraska–Lincoln.

Memon, A., & Bull, R. (1991). The cognitive interview: Its origins, empirical support, evaluation and practical implications. *Journal of Community and Applied Psychology, 1,* 291-307.

Memon, A., Cronin, O., Eaves, R., & Bull, R. (1992, September). *An empirical test of the mnemonic component of the cognitive interview: Can they explain the apparent memory enhancing effects of the CI?* Paper presented at the Third European Law and Psychology Conference, Oxford.

Memon, A., & Köhnken, G. (1992). Helping witnesses to remember more: The cognitive interview. *Expert Evidence, 1,* 39-48.

Middleton, D., & Edwards, D. (Eds.). (1990). *Collective remembering.* London: Sage.

Miller, P., & Sperry, L. (1988). Early talk about the past: The origins of conversational stories of personal experiences. *Journal of Child Language, 15,* 292-315.

Montoya, J. (1992). On truth and shielding in child abuse trials. *Hastings Law Review, 43,* 1259-1319.

Morgan, J., & Plotnikoff, J. (1990). Children as victims of crime: Procedure at court. In J. R. Spencer, G. Nicholson, R. Flin, & R. Bull (Eds.), *Children's evidence in legal proceedings: An international perspective* (pp. 189-192). Cambridge: Cambridge University Faculty of Law.

Morgan, J., & Williams, J. (1992). Child witnesses and the legal process. *Journal of Social Welfare and Family Law, 1,* 484-496.

Morgan, J., & Zedner, L. (1992). *Child victims: Crime, impact and criminal justice.* Oxford: Clarendon.

Moston, S. (1987). The suggestibility of children in interview studies. *Child Language, 7,* 67-78.

Moston, S. (1989). *Social support and the quality of children's eyewitness testimony.* Unpublished doctoral thesis, University of Kent.

Moston, S. (1990). How children interpret and respond to questions: Situational sources of suggestibility in eyewitness interviews. *Social Behaviour, 5,* 155-167.

Moston, S., & Engelberg, T. (1992). The effects of social support on children's eyewitness testimony. *Applied Cognitive Psychology, 6,* 61-75.

Murray, K. (1988). *Research paper on evidence from children: Alternatives to in-court testimony in criminal proceedings in the United States of America.* Edinburgh: Scottish Law Commission.

Myers, J. (1987). *Child witness law and practice.* New York: Wiley.

Myers, J. (1992). *Legal issues in child abuse and neglect.* Newbury Park, CA: Sage.

Neisser, U. (1962). Cultural and cognitive discontinuity. In T. E. Gladwin & W. Sturtevant (Eds.), *Anthropology and human behavior* (pp. 54-71). Washington, DC: Anthropological Society of Washington.

Neisser, U., Winograd, E., Bergman, E. T., Schrieber, C. A., Palmer, S. E., & Weldon, M. S. (1994). *Remembering the earthquake: Direct experience vs. hearing the news.* Manuscript submitted for publication.

Nelson, K. (1986). *Event knowledge: Structure and function in development.* Hillsdale, NJ: Lawrence Erlbaum.

Nelson, K. (1988). The ontogeny of memory for real events. In U. Neisser & E. Winograd (Eds.), *Remembering reconsidered: Traditional and ecological approaches to the study of memory* (pp. 244-277). New York: Cambridge University Press.

Nelson, K. (1990). Remembering, forgetting, and childhood amnesia. In R. Fivush & J. A. Hudson (Eds.), *Knowing and remembering in young children* (pp. 301-316). New York: Cambridge University Press.

Nelson, K. (1992). Emergence of autobiographical memory at age 4. *Human Development, 35,* 172-177.

Nelson, K., & Hudson, J. (1988). Scripts and memory: Functional relationships in development. In F. Weinert & M. Perlmutter (Eds.), *Memory development: Universal changes and individual differences* (pp. 221-242). Hillsdale, NJ: Lawrence Erlbaum.

Newhoff, N., & Launer, P. (1984). Input as interaction: Shall we dance? In R. Naremore (Ed.), *Language science: Recent advances* (pp. 37-65). San Diego, CA: College Hill.

Nigro, G. N., Buckley, M. A., Hill, D. E., & Nelson, J. (1989). When juries "hear" children testify: Effects of eyewitness age and speech style on jurors' perceptions of testimony. In S. J. Ceci, D. F. Ross, & M. P. Toglia (Eds.), *Perspectives on the child witness* (pp. 37-56). New York: Springer-Verlag.

NSPCC. (1993). *The child witness pack.* (Available from the National Society for the Prevention of Cruelty to Children, Headley Library, 67 Saffron Hill, London EC1N 8RS)

Oates, R. (1990). Children as witnesses. *Australian Law Journal, 64,* 129-134.

Ornstein, P. A., Baker-Ward, L., Gordon, B. N., & Merritt, K. A. (1993, March). *Children's memory for medical procedures.* Paper presented at the meeting of the Society for Research in Child Development, New Orleans, LA.

Ornstein, P. A., Baker-Ward, L. E., & Naus, M. J. (1988). The development of mnemonic skill. In F. E. Weinert & M. Perlmutter (Eds.), *Memory development: Universal changes and individual differences* (pp. 31-50). Hillsdale, NJ: Lawrence Erlbaum.

Ornstein, P. A., Gordon, B. N., & Baker-Ward, L. (1992). Children's memory for salient events: Implications for testimony. In M. Howe, C. Brainerd, & V. Reyna (Eds.), *Development of long-term retention* (pp. 135-158). New York: Springer-Verlag.

Ornstein, P., Gordon, B. N., & Larus, D. (1992). Children's memory for a personally experienced event: Implications for testimony. *Applied Cognitive Psychology, 6,* 49-60.

Ornstein, P. A., Larus, D., & Clubb, P. A. (1991). Understanding children's testimony: Implications of research on the development of memory. In R. Vasta (Ed.), *Annals of child development* (Vol. 8, pp. 145-176). London: Jessica Kingsley.

Paivio, A. (1971). *Imagery and verbal processes.* New York: Holt, Rinehart & Winston.

Paris, S. (1988). Motivated remembering. In F. Weinert & M. Perlmutter (Eds.), *Memory development: Universal changes and individual differences* (pp. 221-242). Hillsdale, NJ: Lawrence Erlbaum.

Parnell, M., & Amerman, J. (1983). Answers to Wh- questions: Research and application. In T. Gallagher & C. Prutting (Eds.), *Pragmatic assessment and intervention issues in language* (pp. 129-150). San Diego, CA: College Hill.

Patterson, C., Massad, C., & Cosgrove, J. (1978). Children's referential communication: Components of plans for effective listening. *Developmental Psychology, 14,* 401-406.

Payne, D. G. (1987). Hypermnesia and reminiscence in recall: A historical and empirical review. *Psychological Bulletin, 101,* 5-27.

Payne, D. G., Hembrooke, H. A., & Anastasi, J. S. (1993). Hypermnesia in free recall and cued recall. *Memory & Cognition, 21,* 48-62.

Pear, T., & Wyatt, S. (1914). The testimony of normal and mentally defective children. *Journal of Psychology, 3,* 388-419.

Perry, N. W. (1992). When children take the stand: Permissible innovations in the US courts. *Expert Evidence, 1,* 54-59.

Perry, N. W., & Wrightsman, L. (1991). *The child witness: Legal issues and dilemmas.* Newbury Park, CA: Sage.

Peters, D. (1990, March). Confrontational stress and children's testimony: Some experimental findings. In S. Ceci (Chair), *Do children lie? Narrowing the uncertainties.* Symposium conducted at the meeting of the American Psychology and Law Society, Williamsburg, VA.

Peters, D. (1991). The influence of arousal and stress on the child witness. In J. Doris (Ed.), *The suggestibility of children's recollections* (pp. 60-76). Washington, DC: American Psychological Association.

Peters, D. (Ed.). (in press). *The child witness: Cognitive, social and legal issues.* Deventer: Kluwer.

Peterson, C., & McCabe, A. (1983). *Developmental psycholinguistics: Three ways of looking at a child's narrative.* New York: Plenum.

Piaget, J. (1928). *Judgment and reasoning of the child.* London: Kegan-Paul.

Piaget, J. (1954). *The construction of reality in the child.* New York: Ballantine.

Pigot, T. (Judge). (1989). *Report on the advisory group on video evidence.* London: Home Office.

Pigott, M., & Brigham, J. C. (1985). Relationship between accuracy of prior description and facial recognition. *Journal of Applied Psychology, 70,* 547-555.

Pillemer, D., & White, S. H. (1989). Childhood events recalled by children and adults. In H. W. Reese (Ed.), *Advances in child development and behavior* (Vol. 22). New York: Academic Press.

Pipe, M. E. (1992, May). *Recalling events one and two years later: Cues, props and reminiscence.* Paper presented at NATO ASI, The Child Witness in Context, Italy.

Pipe, M. E., Gee, S., & Wilson, J. (1993). Cues, props and context: Do they facilitate children's event reports? In G. S. Goodman & B. Bottoms (Eds.), *Child victims, child witnesses: Understanding and improving testimony* (pp. 25-45). New York: Guilford.

Pipe, M. E., & Goodman, G. S. (1991). Elements of secrecy: Implications for children's testimony. *Behavioral Science and the Law, 9,* 33-41.

Pipe, M. E., & Wilson, J. (1994). Cues and secrets: Influences on children's event reports. *Developmental Psychology, 30,* 515-525.

Plotnikoff, J. (1990). Support and preparation of the child witness: Whose responsibility? *Journal of Law & Practice, 1,* 21-30.

Plotnikoff, J., & Woolfson, R. (1994, March 24). Victims of time. *Community Care,* pp. 12-13.

Poole, D. A., & Lindsay, D. S. (1994, March). *Interviewing preschoolers: Effects of nonsuggestive techniques, parental coaching, and leading questions on reports of nonexperienced events.* Paper presented at the American Psychology and Law Society Meeting, Santa Fe, NM.

Poole, D. A., & White, L. T. (1991). Effects of question repetition on the eyewitness testimony of children and adults. *Developmental Psychology, 27,* 975-986.

Poole, D. A., & White, L. T. (1993). Two years later: Effects of question repetition and retention interval on the eyewitness testimony of children and adults. *Developmental Psychology, 29,* 844-853.

Pratt, C. (1990). On asking children—and adults—bizarre questions. *First Language, 10,* 167-175.

Pressley, M., Borkowski, J. G., & Johnson, C. J. (1987). The development of good strategy use: Imagery and related mnemonic strategies. In M. McDaniel & M. Pressley (Eds.), *Imagery and related mnemonic processes* (pp. 274-297). New York: Springer-Verlag.

Pressley, M., Forrest-Pressley, D., & Elliott-Faust, D. (1988). What is strategy instructional enrichment and how to study it: Illustrations from research on children's prose memory and comprehension. In F. Weinert & M. Perlmutter (Eds.), *Memory development: Universal changes and individual differences* (pp. 101-130). Hillsdale, NJ: Lawrence Erlbaum.

Pressley, M., Ross, K., Levin, J., & Ghatala, E. (1984). The role of strategy utility knowledge in children's strategy decision making. *Journal of Experimental Child Psychology, 38,* 491-504.

Price, D., & Goodman, G. (1990). Visiting the wizard: Children's memory for a recurring event. *Child Development, 61,* 664-680.

R. v. Smellie, 14 Cr. App. R. 128 (1919).

R. v. X, Y, Z, 91 Cr. App. R. 36 (1990).

RAND. (1975). *The criminal investigative process* (Vols. 1-3, RAND Corporation Technical Report R-1777-DOJ). Santa Monica, CA: Author.

Raskin, D., & Esplin, P. (1991). Statement validity assessment: Interview procedures and context analysis of children's statements of sexual abuse. *Behavioural Assessment, 13,* 265-291.

Raye, C. L., Johnson, M. K., & Taylor, T. H. (1980). Is there something special about memory for internally-generated information? *Memory & Cognition, 8,* 141-148.

Reese, E., Haden, C., & Fivush, R. (1993). Mother-child conversations about the past: Relations of style and memory over time. *Cognitive Development, 8,* 403-430.

Reich, P. (1986). *Language development.* Englewood Cliffs, NJ: Prentice-Hall.

Revelle, G., Wellman, H., & Karabenik, J. (1985). Comprehension monitoring in preschool children. *Child Development, 5,* 654-663.

Richardson, J. T. (1985). The effects of retention tests upon memory: An historical review and an experimental analysis. *Educational Psychology, 5,* 85-114.

Robinson, J. (1992). First experience memories: Contexts and functions in personal histories. In M. A. Conway, D. C. Rubin, H. Spinnler, & W. Wagenaar (Eds.), *Theoretical perspectives on autobiographical memory* (pp. 223-240). London: Kluwer Academic.

Roediger, H. L., & Thorpe, L. A. (1978). The role of recall time in producing hypermnesia. *Memory & Cognition, 6,* 296-305.

Roediger, H. L., Wheeler, M. A., & Rajaram, S. (1993). Remembering, knowing and reconstructing the past. In D. L. Medin (Ed.), *The psychology of learning and motivation: Advances in research and theory* (Vol. 30, pp. 97-134). New York: Academic Press.

Rogoff, B., & Mistry, J. (1990). The context of children's remembering. In R. Fivush & J. A. Hudson (Eds.), *Knowing and remembering in young children* (pp. 197-222). New York: Cambridge University Press.

Ross, D. F., Dunning, D., Toglia, M. P., & Ceci, S. J. (1989). Age stereotypes, communication modality and mock jurors' perceptions of the child witness. In S. J. Ceci, D. F. Ross, & M. P. Toglia (Eds.), *Perspectives on the child witness* (pp. 37-56). New York: Springer-Verlag.

Ross, D., Hopkins, S., Sampson, E., & Lindsay, R. (1993, March). *The impact of protective shields and videotaped testimony on jurors' decision making in trials of child sexual abuse.* Paper presented at the meeting of the Society for Research in Child Development, New Orleans, LA.

Ross, D. F., Miller, B. S., & Moran, P. B. (1987). The child in the eyes of the jury: Assessing mock jurors' perceptions of the child witness. In S. J. Ceci, M. P. Toglia, & D. F. Ross (Eds.), *Children's eyewitness memory* (pp. 142-154). New York: Springer-Verlag.

Rovee-Collier, C., & Shyi, C. W. G. (1992). A functional and cognitive analysis of infant long-term retention. In M. L. Howe, C. J. Brainerd, & V. F. Reyna (Eds.), *Development of long-term retention* (pp. 3-55). New York: Springer-Verlag.

Rudy, L., & Goodman, G. S. (1991). Effects of participation on children's reports: Implications for children's testimony. *Developmental Psychology, 27*, 527-538.

Runyan, D., Everson, M., Edelsohn, G., Hunter, W., & Coulter, M. (1988). Impact of legal intervention on sexually abused children. *Journal of Pediatrics, 113*, 647-653.

Ryan, S., Hegion, A., & Flavell, J. (1970). Nonverbal mnemonic mediation in preschool children. *Child Development, 41*, 539-550.

Sanders, G. S. (1986). *The usefulness of eyewitness research from the perspective of police investigators.* Unpublished manuscript, State University of New York, Albany.

Sanders, G. S., & Warnick, D. (1980). Some conditions maximizing eyewitness accuracy: A learning/memory analogy. *Journal of Criminal Justice, 8*, 395-403.

Sas, L. (1991). *Reducing the system-induced trauma for child sexual abuse victims through court preparation, assessment and followup* (Final Report for Project #4555-1-125). London, Canada: Health and Welfare, Canada, National Welfare Grants Division.

Sas, L., Hurley, P., Austin, G., & Wolfe, D. (1991). *Reducing the system-induced trauma for child sexual abuse victims through court preparation, assessment and follow-up.* London, Canada: London Family Court Clinic.

Sas, L., Hurley, P., Hatch, A., Malla, S., & Dick, T. (1993). *Three years after the verdict: A longitudinal study of the social and psychological adjustment of child witnesses referred to the Child Witness Project.* London, Canada: London Family Court Clinic.

Saywitz, K. J. (1989). Children's conception of the legal system: Court is a place to play basketball. In S. J. Ceci, D. F. Ross, & M. P. Toglia (Eds.), *Perspectives on children's testimony* (pp. 131-157). New York: Springer-Verlag.

Saywitz, K., Geiselman, R. E., & Bornstein, G. (1992). Effects of cognitive interviewing and practice on children's recall performance. *Journal of Applied Psychology, 77*(5), 744-756.

Saywitz, K., Goodman, G., Nicholas, E., & Moan, S. (1991). Children's memories of physical examinations that involve genital touch: Implications for reports of sexual abuse. *Journal of Consulting and Clinical Psychology, 59*(5), 682-691.

Saywitz, K., Jaenicke, C., & Comparo, L. (1990). Children's knowledge of legal terminology. *Law and Human Behavior, 14*(6), 523-535.

Saywitz, K., & Moan-Hardie, S. (1994). Reducing the potential for distortion of childhood memories. *Consciousness and Cognition, 3*, 257-293.

Saywitz, K., & Nathanson, R. (1992, August). Effects of environment on children's testimony and perceived stress. In B. Bottoms & M. Levine (Chairs), *The actual and perceived competency of child witnesses.* Symposium conducted at the 100th annual convention of the American Psychological Association, Washington, DC.

Saywitz, K., & Nathanson, R. (1993). Children's testimony and their perceptions of stress in and out of the courtroom. *International Journal of Child Abuse & Neglect, 17*, 613-622.

Saywitz, K., Nathanson, R., Snyder, L., & Lamphear, V. (1993). *Preparing children for the investigative and judicial process: Improving communication, memory, and emotional resiliency* (Final Report to National Center on Child Abuse and Neglect, Grant No. 90-CA-1179). Los Angeles: University of California.

Saywitz, K., & Snyder, L. (1991, April). *Preparing child witnesses: The efficacy of comprehension monitoring training.* Paper presented at the biennial meeting of the Society for Research on Child Development, Seattle, WA.

Saywitz, K., & Snyder, L. (1993). Improving children's testimony with preparation. In G. S. Goodman & B. Bottoms (Eds.), *Child victims, child witnesses: Understanding and improving testimony* (pp. 117-146). New York: Guilford.

Saywitz, K., Snyder, L., & Lamphear, V. (1990, August). *Preparing child witnesses: The efficacy of memory strategy training.* Paper presented at the 98th Annual Convention of the American Psychological Association, Boston.

Schactel, E. G. (1982). On memory and childhood amnesia. In U. Neisser (Ed.), *Memory observed* (pp. 189-200). San Francisco: Freeman.

Schooler, J. W., & Engstler-Schooler, T. Y. (1990). Verbal overshadowing of visual memories: Some things are better left unsaid. *Cognitive Psychology, 22*, 36-71.

Schooler, J. W., Foster, R. A., & Loftus, E. F. (1988). Some deleterious consequences of the act of recollection. *Memory & Cognition, 16*, 243-251.

Scottish Law Commission. (1988). *The evidence of children and other potentially vulnerable witnesses* (Discussion paper 75). Edinburgh: Author.

Scottish Law Commission. (1990). *Report on the evidence of children and other potentially vulnerable witnesses* (SLC No. 125). Edinburgh: Author.

Scrivner, E., & Safer, M. A. (1988). Eyewitnesses show hypermnesia for details about a violent event. *Journal of Applied Psychology, 73*, 371-377.

Selman, R., & Byrne, D. (1974). A structural-developmental analysis of role-taking in middle childhood. *Child Development, 45*, 803-806.

Shatz, M., & Gelman, R. (1973). The development of communication skills: Modifications in the speech of young children as a function of listener. *Monographs of the Society for Research in Child Development, 38*(5, Serial No. 152).

Sheingold, K., & Tenney, Y. J. (1982). Memory for a salient childhood event. In U. Neisser (Ed.), *Memory observed* (pp. 201-212). San Francisco: Freeman.

Short, E., & Ryan, E. (1984). Metacognitive differences between skilled and less skilled readers: Remediating deficits through story grammar and attribution training. *Journal of Educational Psychology, 76*, 225-235.

Shuy, R. (1986). Language and the law. *Annual Review of Applied Linguistics, 7*, 50-63.

Siegal, M. (1991). *Knowing children: Experiments in conversation and cognition.* London: Lawrence Erlbaum.

Siegal, M., Waters, L. J., & Dinwiddy, L. S. (1988). Misleading children: Causal attributions for inconsistency under repeated questioning. *Journal of Experimental Child Psychology, 45*, 438-456.

Sigel, I. E. (1953). Developmental trends in the abstraction ability of children. *Child Development, 24*, 131-144.

Sigel, I. E., Anderson, L. M., & Shapiro, H. (1966). Categorization behavior of lower and middle class Negro preschool children: Differences in dealing with representation of familiar objects. *Journal of Negro Education, 35*, 218-229.

Sigelman, C., Budd, E., Spanhel, C., & Schoenrock, C. (1981). Asking questions of retarded persons: A comparison of yes-no and either-or formats. *Applied Research in Mental Retardation, 5*, 347-357.

Singer, J., & Flavell, J. (1981). Development of knowledge about communication: Children's evaluations of explicitly ambiguous messages. *Child Development, 52*, 1211-1215.

Singer, D., & Revenson, T. (1978). *How a child thinks.* New York: Plume.

Sisterman Keeney, K., Amacher, E., & Kastanakis, J. (1992). The court prep group: A vital part of the court process. In H. Dent & R. Flin (Eds.), *Children as witnesses.* Chichester, U.K.: Wiley.

Sivan, A. B., Schor, D. P., Koeppl, G. K., & Noble, L. D. (1988). Interaction of normal children with anatomical dolls. *Child Abuse & Neglect, 12*, 295-304.

274   MEMORY AND TESTIMONY IN THE CHILD WITNESS

Slamecka, N. J., & Katsaiti, L. T. (1988). Normal forgetting of verbal lists as a function of prior testing. *Journal of Experimental Psychology: Learning, Memory, and Cognition, 14,* 716-727.

Spence, D. P. (1988). Passive remembering. In U. Neisser & E. Winograd (Eds.), *Remembering reconsidered: Traditional and ecological approaches to the study of memory* (pp. 311-325). New York: Cambridge University Press.

Spencer, J. (1987, October 3). Child abuse: The first steps to justice. *The Times* (London), p. 8.

Spencer, J., & Flin, R. (1990). *The evidence of children: The law and the psychology.* London: Blackstone.

Spencer, J., & Flin, R. (1993). *The evidence of children: The law and the psychology* (2nd ed.). London: Blackstone.

Spencer, J., Nicholson, G., Flin, R., & Bull, R. (1990). *Children's evidence in legal proceedings: An international perspective.* Cambridge: Cambridge University Faculty of Law.

Stein, N., & Glenn, C. (1978). *The role of temporal organization in story comprehension* (Tech. Rep. No. 71). Urbana: University of Illinois, Center for Study of Reading.

Steller, M., & Boychuk, T. (1992). Children as witnesses in sexual abuse cases: Investigative interview and assessment techniques. In H. Dent & R. Flin (Eds.), *Children as witnesses* (pp. 47-71). Chichester, U.K.: Wiley.

Steller, M., & Köhnken, G. (1989). Criteria-based statement analysis. In D. Raskin (Ed.), *Psychological methods in criminal investigation and evidence* (pp. 217-245). New York: Springer.

Stone, W., & Lemanek, K. (1990). Developmental issues in children's self-reports. In A. La Greca (Ed.), *Through the eyes of the child: Obtaining self-reports from children and adolescents* (pp. 18-56). Boston: Allyn & Bacon.

Swim, J., Borgida, E., & McCoy, K. (1992). *Videotaped versus in-court witness testimony: Is protecting the child witness jeopardizing due process?* Manuscript submitted for publication.

Tanenbaum, R. R. (1991). *The effects of memory strategies and repeated testing on eyewitness recall for high and low arousal events.* Unpublished doctoral dissertation, State University of New York, Binghamton.

Tate, C., Warren, A., & Hess, T. (1992). Adults' liability for children's "lie-ability": Can adults coach children to lie successfully? In S. J. Ceci, M. Leichtman, & M. Putnick (Eds.), *Cognitive and social factors in early deception* (pp. 69-87). Hillsdale, NJ: Lawrence Erlbaum.

Tedesco, J., & Schnell, S. (1987). Children's reaction to sex abuse: Investigation and litigation. *Child Abuse & Neglect, 11,* 267-272.

Terr, L. C. (1988). What happens to early memory of trauma? A study of twenty children under age five at the time of documented traumatic events. *Journal of the American Academy of Child and Adolescent Psychiatry, 27,* 96-104.

Teubner, G. (1989). How the law thinks: Towards a constructivist epistemology of law. *Law and Society Review, 23,* 727-756.

Tobey, A., & Goodman, G. (1992). Children's eyewitness memory: Effects of participation and forensic content. *Child Abuse & Neglect, 16,* 779-796.

Tobin, K. (1987). The role of wait time in higher cognitive level learning. *Review of Educational Research, 57,* 69-95.

Todd, C., & Perlmutter, M. (1980). Reality recalled by preschool children. In M. Perlmutter (Ed.), *New directions for child development: Vol. 10. Children's memory* (pp. 69-86). San Francisco: Jossey-Bass.

Toglia, M. P., Ross, D. F., Ceci, S. J., & Hembrooke, H. (1992). The suggestibility of children's memory: A social-psychological and cognitive interpretation. In M. L. Howe, C. J. Brainerd, & V. F. Reyna (Eds.), *Development of long-term retention* (pp. 217-241). New York: Springer-Verlag.

Tousignant, J. P., Hall, D., & Loftus, E. F. (1986). Discrepancy detection and vulnerability to misleading postevent information. *Memory & Cognition, 14,* 329-338.

Tucker, A., Mertin, P., & Luszcz, M. (1990). The effect of a repeated interview on young children's eyewitness testimony. *Australian and New Zealand Journal of Criminology, 23,* 117-124.

Tulving, E., & Thomson, D. M. (1973). Encoding specificity and retrieval processes in episodic memory. *Psychological Review, 80,* 352-373.

Turk, V., & Brown, H. (1992). Sexual abuse and adults with learning disabilities. *Mental Handicap, 20,* 56-58.

Underwager, R., & Wakefield, H. (1990). *The real world of child interrogations.* Springfield, IL: Charles C Thomas.

Underwager, R., & Wakefield, H. (1992). Poor psychology produces poor law. *Law and Human Behavior, 16,* 233-243.

Undeutsch, V. (1982). Statement reality analysis. In A. Trankell (Ed.), *Reconstructing the past* (pp. 27-56). Deventer: Kluwer.

van Hekken, S. M. J., & Roelofsen, W. (1982). More questions than answers: A study of question-answer sequences in a naturalistic setting. *Journal of Child Language, 9,* 445-460.

Verdonik, F. (1988). Reconsidering the context of remembering: The need for a social description of memory processes and their development. In F. Weinert & M. Perlmutter (Eds.), *Memory development: Universal changes and individual differences* (pp. 257-270). Hillsdale, NJ: Lawrence Erlbaum.

Vizard, E. (1991). Interviewing children suspected of being sexually abused: A review of theory and practice. In C. R. Hollin & K. Howells (Eds.), *Clinical approaches to sex offenders and their victims* (pp. 117-148). Chichester, U.K.: Wiley.

Wagenaar, W. A., & Groeneweg, J. (1990). The memory of concentration camp survivors. *Applied Cognitive Psychology, 4,* 77-87.

Walker, A. G. (1993). Questioning young children in court. *Law and Human Behavior, 17*(1), 59-81.

Warren, A., Hulse-Trotter, K., & Tubbs, E. C. (1991). Inducing resistance to suggestibility in children. *Law and Human Behavior, 15,* 273-285.

Warren-Leubecker, A. (1991). Commentary: Development of event memories or event reports? In J. Doris (Ed.), *The suggestibility of children's recollections* (pp. 24-26). Washington, DC: American Psychological Association.

Warren-Leubecker, A., Tate, C., Hinton, I., & Ozbek, I. (1989). What do children know about the legal system and when do they know it? First steps down a less traveled path in child witness research. In S. J. Ceci, D. F. Ross, & M. P. Toglia (Eds.), *Perspectives on children's testimony* (pp. 158-183). New York: Springer-Verlag.

Wattam, C. (1992). *Making a case in child protection.* London: Longman.

Wehrspann, W. H., Steinhauer, P. D., & Klajner-Diamond, H. (1987). Criteria and methodology for assessing credibility of sexual abuse allegation. *Canadian Journal of Psychiatry, 32,* 615-623.

Wells, G. L. (1985). Verbal descriptions of faces from memory: Are they diagnostic of identification accuracy? *Journal of Applied Psychology, 70,* 619-626.

Wells, G. L., & Murray, D. M. (1984). Eyewitness confidence. In G. L. Wells & E. F. Loftus (Eds.), *Eyewitness testimony: Psychological perspectives* (pp. 155-170). New York: Cambridge University Press.

Wells, G. L., & Turtle, J. W. (1987). Eyewitness testimony research: Current knowledge and emergent controversies. *Forensic Psychology, 19,* 363-388.

Wells, G. L., Turtle, J. W., & Luss, C. A. E. (1989). The perceived credibility of child eyewitnesses: What happens when they use their own words? In S. J. Ceci, D. F. Ross, & M. P. Toglia (Eds.), *Perspectives on the child witness* (pp. 23-46). New York: Springer-Verlag.

Westcott, H. (1991). The abuse of disabled children: A review of the literature. *Child: Care, Health and Development, 17,* 243-258.

Westcott, H. (1992a). The cognitive interview: A useful tool for social workers? *British Journal of Social Work, 22,* 519-533.

Westcott, H. (1992b, May). *The disabled child witness.* Paper presented at NATO ASI, The Child Witness in Context, Italy.

Westcott, H. (1994). The *Memorandum of Good Practice* and children with disabilities. *Journal of Law and Practice, 3,* 21-32.

Westcott, H., Davies, G., & Clifford, B. (1989). The use of anatomical dolls in child witness interviews. *Adoption and Fostering, 13,* 6-14.

Westcott, H., Davies, G., & Clifford, B. (1991). The credibility of child witnesses seen on closed-circuit television. *Adoption and Fostering, 15,* 14-19.

USA ✱ Whitcomb, D. (1992). *When the victim is a child* (2nd ed.). Washington, DC: National Institute of Justice.

Whitcomb, D., Runyan, D., et al. (1991). *Child victim as witness: Research and development programme.* (Grant Report 87-MC-CX-0026 to U.S. Department of Justice)

USA ✱ Whitcomb, D., Shapiro, E. R., & Stellwagen, L. D. (1985). *When the victim is a child: Issues for judges and prosecutors.* Washington, DC: National Institute of Justice.

White, S. (1990). *The investigatory interview with suspected victims of child sexual abuse.* Boston: Allyn & Bacon.

White, S., Strom, G., Santilli, G., & Halpin, B. (1986). Interviewing young children with anatomically correct dolls. *Child Abuse & Neglect, 10,* 519-529.

Wickens, D. D. (1970). Encoding categories of words: An empirical approach to meaning. *Psychological Review, 77,* 1-15.

Wilkinson, A. C., & Koestler, R. (1983). Repeated recall: A new model and tests of its generality from childhood to old age. *Journal of Experimental Psychology: General, 112,* 423-451.

Wilson, C. E. (1989). Criminal procedure—presumed guilty: The use of videotaped and closed circuit televised testimony in child sex abuse prosecutions and the defendant's right to confrontation—*Coy v. Iowa. Campbell Law Review, 11,* 381-396.

Wilson, J., & Pipe, M. E. (1989). The effects of cues on young children's recall of real events. *New Zealand Journal of Psychology, 18,* 65-70.

Winer, G. A. (1980). Class-inclusion reasoning in children: A review of the empirical literature. *Child Development, 51,* 309-328.

Winer, G. A., Rasnake, K., & Smith, D. A. (1987). Language versus logic: Responses to misleading classificatory questions. *Journal of Psycholinguistic Research, 16,* 311-327.

Winograd, E., & Neisser, U. (1992). *Affect and accuracy in recall.* New York: Cambridge University Press.

Wrightsman, L. (1991). *Psychology and the legal system* (2nd ed.). Pacific Grove, CA: Brooks/Cole.

Yarmey, A. D., & Jones, H. P. T. (1983). Is the psychology of eyewitness identification a matter of common sense? In S. M. A. Lloyd-Bostock & B. R. Clifford (Eds.), *Evaluating witness testimony: Recent psychological research and new perspectives* (pp. 13-40). Chichester, U.K.: Wiley.

Yates, A., & Terr, L. (1988). Anatomically correct dolls: Should they be used as a basis for expert testimony? *Journal of the American Academy of Child and Adolescent Psychiatry, 27,* 254-257.

Yuille, J. (1988). The systematic assessment of children's testimony. *Canadian Psychology, 29,* 247-262.

Zaragoza, M. S. (1987). Memory, suggestibility, and eyewitness testimony in children and adults. In S. J. Ceci, M. P. Toglia, & D. F. Ross (Eds.), *Children's eyewitness memory* (pp. 53-78). New York: Springer-Verlag.

Zaragoza, M. S. (1991). Preschool children's susceptibility to memory impairment. In J. Doris (Ed.), *The suggestibility of children's recollections: Implications for eyewitness testimony* (pp. 27-39). Washington, DC: American Psychological Association.

Zaragoza, M. S., Dahlgren, D., & Muench, J. (1992). The role of memory impairment in children's suggestibility. In M. L. Howe, C. J. Brainerd, & V. F. Reyna (Eds.), *Development of long-term retention* (pp. 184-216). New York: Springer-Verlag.

Zaragoza, M. S., & Koshmider, J. W., III. (1989). Misled subjects may know more than their performance implies. *Journal of Experimental Psychology: Learning, Memory, and Cognition, 15,* 246-255.

Zaragoza, M. S., & Lane, S. (1991, November). *The role of attentional resources in suggestibility and source monitoring.* Paper presented at the annual meeting of the Psychonomic Society, San Francisco.

Zaragoza, M. S., & Lane, S. (1994). Source misattributions and the suggestibility of eyewitness memory. *Journal of Experimental Psychology: Learning, Memory, and Cognition, 20,* 934-945.

Index

Accuracy:
actual vs. perceived, 224, 226; age-related differences, 236; assessment of, 72-77, 81-84; closed-circuit television vs. open-court, 231-232; cognitive interview, 147, 148, 149, 152, 154, 155-156, 157; comprehension monitoring training improves, 125; doll use and, 174-175; effect of long delays, 26-27; effects of timing and type of questioning on, 44-60; fluency and, 226; free recall, 28-29, 55, 192; impact of environment on, 137; in children, 6, 12, 184; in use of dolls, 164; jurors' perceptions of witness's, 220-223, 226-227, 232-236; mentally-retarded persons', 192; multiple interviews, 26-27; reminiscence, 33-34; retention interval, 33-34; school-aged children, 12; specific questions, 192; suggestibility and, 12, 32; timing of initial interview, 56; using narrative elaboration, 130; within-session repetition, 37-38, 41; witness motivation, 32

Acquiescence:
authority figures, 59; due to misunderstanding of intent, 118-119; in mentally-retarded persons, 190; inability to remember, 30, 131, 184, 186; inappropriate questions and, 33; resistance strategy training, 130-131; specific questions, 185; strength of memory and acquiescence to, 41; within-session repetition, 35-36, 39-40; see also Suggestive questions

Across-session repetition. See Multiple interviews

Activities, in preschoolers' recall, 9

Adamson, Peter, 240-241

Adults, effect of delays on recall, 26-27

Age:
content of recall and, 8; memory performance and, 72-74; source monitoring ability, 58, 91-92

Age of child:
credibility and, 225, 232; use of dolls and, 161-162

Albert, G., 167, 174, 178

Amacher, E., 203, 204, 250

Aman, C., 19, 162, 164, 166-167, 173, 174, 176-177, 178, 187

American Academy of Child and Adolescent Psychiatry (AACAP), 114

American Association for Protecting Children, 217

American Bar Association, 243

American Professional Society on the Abuse of Children (APSAC), 114, 181

American Psychological Association, 246, 247

About the Editors

Yossef S. Ben-Porath is Assistant Professor of Psychology at Kent State University. His research interests involve assessment and forensic psychology. He has published books on the MMPI-2 and MMPI-A and is coeditor of a forthcoming Sage publication on forensic applications of the MMPI-2.

John R. Graham, Professor and Chair of Psychology at Kent State University, is a world-renowned authority on the Minnesota Multiphasic Personality Instrument (MMPI). He is the author of the internationally acclaimed book, *MMPI-2: Assessing Personality and Psychopathology.*

Gordon C. N. Hall is Associate Professor of Psychology at Kent State University. His research interests are in sexual aggression and in ethnic minority issues. He recently edited *Sexual Aggression: Issues in Etiology, Assessment, and Treatment.* He is President of the Society for the Psychological Study of Ethnic Minority Issues, Division 45 of the American Psychological Association.

Richard Hirschman is Professor of Psychology and former Director of Clinical Training in the Department of Psychology at Kent State University. His training is in clinical and community psychology and psychophysiology, and he has published numerous articles in these areas. Currently his primary research is in sexual aggression.

Maria S. Zaragoza is Associate Professor of Psychology at Kent State University. Since 1985 she has been a major contributor to research on the suggestibility of eyewitness memory in both children and adults, as evidenced by her publication in edited volumes and leading journals in the field. Her research on suggestibility is funded by grants from the National Institute of Mental Health.

About the Contributors

Jennifer K. Ackil is a graduate student in the Department of Psychology at Kent State University.

Lynne Baker-Ward is Associate Professor of Psychology at North Carolina State University in Raleigh. A graduate of Wake Forest University and Emory University, she received her doctorate in developmental psychology from the University of North Carolina at Chapel Hill. She has long-standing interests in early memory development and in applied developmental psychology, which intersect in her current work on children's testimony. For several years, she has collaborated with colleagues at the University of North Carolina at Chapel Hill in research examining young children's abilities to remember and report a variety of medical experiences. This endeavor, described as the Children's Memory Project, involves a number of ongoing investigations designed to better understand children's reports of salient personal experiences.

Jennifer M. Batterman-Faunce obtained her Ph.D. in clinical psychology at the State University of New York at Buffalo in 1994. That year, she also completed an internship in child and adolescent psychology at Strong Memorial Hospital in Rochester, New York. She is currently Assistant Professor of Psychiatry (Psychology) at the State University of New York at Buffalo School of Medicine and Biomedical Sciences and Staff Psychologist on the Adolescent

Inpatient Psychiatry Unit at Erie County Medical Center. She has coauthored several book chapters on children's eyewitness testimony.

Ray Bull is Head of the Department of Psychology at the University of Portsmouth in England. Currently he holds (or coholds) research grants from the Police Research Group of the Home Office and from the Economic and Social Research Council. Notable books are *The Psychology of Person Identification* (with Brian Clifford) and *The Social Psychology of Facial Appearance* (with Nichola Rumsey). He regularly acts as an "expert witness" in criminal cases involving witnessing. He is a member of a number of international and national committees and is currently (1992-1995) Chair of the Association of Heads of University Psychology Departments.

Karen L. Chambers is a graduate student in the Department of Psychology at Kent State University.

Patricia A. Clubb received her undergraduate degree from Emory University and is currently completing her doctorate in developmental psychology at the University of North Carolina at Chapel Hill. A specialist in memory development, she has for several years examined the relation between young children's prior knowledge and their subsequent reports of personally experienced events. Her dissertation research addresses the ways in which interviewers can best elicit accurate and complete reports from young children.

Graham Davies is Professor and Head of the Department of Psychology at the University of Leicester, England. His main research interests lie in the area of eyewitness testimony in both children and adults, on which he has published extensively. Among his coauthored books are *Perceiving and Remembering Faces* (1981), *Identification Evidence: A Psychological Evaluation* (1982), *Memory in Context* (1988), and *Child Witnesses: Do the Courts Abuse Children?* (1988) and his latest book *Memory in Everyday Life*. He was responsible for the evaluation of the Livelink scheme for child witnesses for the British Home Office and is currently engaging in a similar evaluation of the scheme to permit children's videotaped interviews to be admitted as evidence in criminal cases. He is a Fellow of the British Psychological Society and a Chartered Forensic Psychologist.

Judy S. DeLoache is Professor of Psychology at the University of Illinois. She is a developmental psychologist whose main area of research interest involves early cognitive development, especially the origins and early development of symbolization. She is a Fellow of the American Psychological Association and the American Psychological Society.

Karen Eso is a graduate student at the University of Victoria, British Columbia, Canada, where she is working on her master's thesis. She is interested in the intersection between clinical and cognitive child psychology (e.g., cognitive studies of children diagnosed with attention deficit disorder).

Ronald P. Fisher is currently Professor of Psychology at Florida International University. His theoretical research interests in memory retrieval overlap with applied research interests in developing more effective techniques to interview victims and witnesses of crime. He is one of the codevelopers of the cognitive interview technique, which is described in a recent book, *Memory-Enhancing Techniques for Investigative Interviewing: The Cognitive Interview*. His combination of theoretical/applied interests is reflected in his serving as a consulting editor for *Memory & Cognition* and conducting training programs for police investigators.

Robyn Fivush is Associate Professor of Psychology and Associated Faculty in Women's Studies at Emory University. She has published numerous journal articles and book chapters examining preschoolers' memories for both recurring and novel events. Her research addresses the accuracy and retention of early autobiographical memories, the social context in which autobiographical memory develops, and gender differences in autobiographical memory. She has coedited a book with Judith Hudson, *Knowing and Remembering in Young Children*, and has a forthcoming book coedited with Ulric Neisser, *The Remembering Self: Accuracy and Construction in the Life Narrative*. She has also written a book with Susan Golombok, *Gender Development*.

Rhona Flin is Professor of Applied Psychology at the Robert Gordon University, Aberdeen. She has been carrying out research on child witnesses in Scotland for 10 years and is particularly interested in children's ability to give evidence in criminal trials. She is coauthor (with John Spencer) of *The Evidence of Children* (1993) and coeditor (with Helen Dent) of *Children as Witnesses* (1992).

Andrea Follmer, a graduate of Dartmouth College, is currently a doctoral student in developmental psychology at the University of North Carolina at Chapel Hill. She is involved in ongoing research examining the effects of alternative protocols on children's reports of events. In addition to her interests in memory development, she is concerned with methodological issues related to the study of development. She currently serves as Laboratory Manager for the Children's Memory Project.

Valerie Gonzales is a graduate student at the University of Victoria, British Columbia, Canada, where she is completing her doctoral work. Her research focuses on children's cognitive development, with a particular emphasis on age-related changes in performance on indirect (implicit) and direct (explicit) tests of memory.

Gail S. Goodman is Professor of Psychology at the University of California, Davis, and author of numerous scientific articles and chapters on children's eyewitness memory. She is a Fellow of the American Psychological Association and has served as President of its Division of Child, Youth, and Family Services. Her research, funded by federal grants, has been influential in U.S. Supreme Court decisions concerning children's testimony. In 1992 she received the Research Career Achievement Award from the American Professional Society on the Abuse of Children. She obtained her Ph.D. in developmental psychology from the University of California, Los Angeles, in 1977.

Betty N. Gordon is Associate Professor of Psychology at the University of North Carolina at Chapel Hill. She received her undergraduate degree from the University of Rochester and her Ph.D. in developmental and clinical child psychology from the University of Washington. As a clinical child psychologist, she has worked extensively with sexually abused children and has often served as an expert witness in legal proceedings. With her colleague Carolyn Schroeder, she is the author of the 1991 volume *Assessment and Treatment of Childhood Problems: A Clinician's Guide.* Her current research examines event memory in children with developmental disabilities. She is a coinvestigator with the Children's Memory Project.

Peggy Lane received her M.A. in psychology from the University of Tennessee in Chattanooga in 1993. Her research focus is memory development across the life span. She currently serves as an Instructor at the University of Tennessee at Chattanooga. She served as a member of the Student Editorial Board for *Law and Human Behavior*.

Sean M. Lane is a graduate student in the Department of Psychology at Kent State University.

D. Stephen Lindsay is Associate Professor of Psychology at the University of Victoria in British Columbia, Canada. He earned his Ph.D. in cognitive psychology at Princeton University in 1987. His research explores the cognitive processes by which mental events of various kinds (e.g., thoughts, images, feelings) are attributed to particular sources (e.g., memory, thinking, perception). A major component of his research program concerns age-related changes in children's ability to identify the sources of current mental experiences (e.g., discriminating between memories of past fantasies and memories of past actual events). In the context of eyewitness memory, his work has focused on theories of how and why misled witnesses sometimes come to believe that they actually witnessed things that were merely suggested to them.

Michelle R. McCauley is currently a graduate student in the applied psychology Ph.D. program at Florida International University.

Holly K. Orcutt is a doctoral student in psychology at the State University of New York at Buffalo. Her research interests include children's eyewitness testimony, the impact of child sexual abuse, and risky sexual behavior among adolescents. She received her undergraduate degree in psychology from the University of Illinois, Urbana-Champaign.

Peter A. Ornstein is Professor of Psychology and Director of the Developmental Psychology Program at the University of North Carolina at Chapel Hill. He was educated at Harpur College, Queens College, and the University of Wisconsin, where he received his doctorate in experimental psychology. An expert on the development of memory, he edited the volume *Memory Development in Children* in 1978. He recently served as Associate Editor of *Developmental Psychology*. His current research examines children's long-term retention of personally experienced events, and he has published extensively in this area. He is the principal investigator with the Children's Memory Project and has received research support from the National Institute of Mental Health for this work.

Debra Ann Poole received her B.A. in psychology from the University of Connecticut and her M.A. and Ph.D. degrees in developmental psychology from the University of Iowa. She is currently Associate Professor of Psychology at Central Michigan University. She is especially interested in the relationships between basic research and social policy. Her research on question repetition was funded by a grant from the National Institute of Mental Health.

Toby Sachsenmaier received her Ph.D. in clinical psychology at the State University of New York at Buffalo in 1992. She currently works as a clinical psychologist in the Buffalo area.

Karen J. Saywitz (Ph.D.) is Assistant Professor on the faculty of the School of Medicine, Department of Psychiatry, University of California, Los Angeles. She is Director of Child and Adolescent Psychology at the Harbor-UCLA Medical Center. She is the author of numerous articles regarding the capabilities, limitations, and needs of child witnesses. In her research on interviewing children and preparing them for court, she develops and tests innovative interventions to enhance children's memory performance, communicative competence, emotional resilience, and resistance to suggestive questions. Also, she is on the faculty of the National Judicial College, where she teaches principles of child development for judicial application. She coauthored an amicus curiae brief for the U.S. Supreme Court and a bench guide for California judges. Her articles have been cited by more than 40 appellate courts.

Jennifer R. Shukat was an undergraduate at Emory University, where she graduated with highest honors. She is currently a graduate student at Temple University.

Ann E. Tobey obtained her undergraduate degree at the University of Alaska, Fairbanks, in 1988 and her Ph.D. in clinical psychology at the State University of New York at Buffalo in 1994. Her dissertation, titled *Fact-Finders' Perceptions of Child Witnesses: Effects of Closed-Circuit Testimony,* received the American Psychological Association Division 41/American Psychology-Law Society Dissertation Award in the 1993 competition. She recently completed a Clinical Fellowship in Psychology at the Harvard Medical School and a Predoctoral Clinical Internship at the Massachusetts Mental Health Center. Currently, she is a Clinical Fellow in Psychology at the Harvard Medical School and a

Postdoctoral Fellow in the Children and Law Division of the Law and Psychiatry Service at Massachusetts General Hospital.

Amye R. Warren (Ph.D.) is currently Professor of Psychology at the University of Tennessee in Chattanooga. She received her Ph.D. in general experimental psychology in 1984 from the Georgia Institute of Technology. Her expertise and research interests are in the areas of memory and language development. She has published articles and chapters on reducing suggestibility in child witnesses, the language of adults who interview child witnesses, language development in social contexts, and memory for emotional events. She also serves on the editorial board of *Law and Human Behavior*.

Helen Westcott is Research Officer with the National Society for the Prevention of Cruelty to Children (NSPCC) in London. She previously worked on the *Child Witness Project* at the Polytechnic of East London and has an enduring interest in children's evidence. Her current research is examining best practice in child-centered interviewing as well as the language professionals use with child witnesses. She has recently completed projects investigating the abuse of children who are disabled as well as children's perspectives on social casework.

Lawrence T. White is Associate Professor and Chair of Psychology at Beloit College in Wisconsin. He received his Ph.D. in social psychology from the University of California at Santa Cruz in 1984. His research interests include the questioning of child witnesses and capital penalty trials. He has published articles in *Law and Human Behavior, Behavioral Science and the Law, Developmental Psychology,* and the *Journal of Applied Social Psychology*. He also consults with attorneys and has testified as an expert witness in numerous criminal trials.

Printed in the United Kingdom
by Lightning Source UK Ltd.
9374700001B